Why Statu

To Sally
Queen of Cheltenham SitP
with best wishes

from Chris

Why Statues Weep

The Best of *The Skeptic*

edited by
Wendy M. Grossman
and
Christopher C. French

THE **P**
PHILOSOPHY
PRESS

First published in the UK by The Philosophy Press in 2010

ISBN 978-0-9537611-2-8

Typeset by Domex
Cover design by Paul Cooper

The Philosophy Press Ltd
Dunstan House
14 as St Cross Street
London EC1N 8XA, UK
Tel +44 (0)20 7841 1959
Fax +44 (0)20 7242 1474

Email: info@philosophypress.co.uk
Website: www.philosophypress.co.uk/books

A catalogue record of this book is available from the British Library

This book was printed in the UK by MPG Books Group. The paper used is FSC certified.

Mixed Sources
Product group from well-managed forests and other controlled sources
www.fsc.org Cert no. SA-COC-1565
© 1996 Forest Stewardship Council

Contents

Foreword by Simon Hoggart   vii
Introduction by Wendy M. Grossman   x
A Note on Sources   xiv
Skeptical Stats   xv

1 THERE MUST BE SOMETHING IN IT (Wendy M. Grossman)   1
   Seeing is Believing? (Susan Blackmore)   2
   Psychic Con-Men (Richard Wiseman and Emma Greening)   7
   In Search of Monsters? (Charles Paxton)   10
   Millennium (Kevin McClure)   15

2 FAVOURITE POPULAR MYTHS (Wendy M. Grossman)   18
   Nostradamus Said What? (David Hambling)   19
   Myths of Secret Powers (Andrew Brice)   21
   The Ten-Percent Solution (Barry Beyerstein)   24
   The Mary Celeste Revisited (Alan Hunt)   30
   Behind the Red Planet (Paul Chambers)   34

3 WHAT EVER HAPPENED TO ... ? (Wendy M. Grossman)   41
   The Summer of '91 (Martin Hempstead)   42
   Explaining the Shroud: Steve Donnelly Interviews Joe Nickell   46
   What Hath Carlos Wrought? (Robert McGrath)   51
   Rendlesham: Britain's Roswell (David Clarke)   54
   Foreign Objects: Testing an Alien Implant (Susan Blackmore
       and David T. Patton)   62

4 BEYOND A JOKE (Wendy M. Grossman)   66
   Miracle Cures: Only Believe (John Diamond)   67
   Sprite 1 (Donald Rooum)   70
   What's Wrong with Alternative Medicine? (Thurstan Brewin)   71
   Motivated Distortion of Personal Memory for Trauma
       (Mark Pendergrast)   78
   The Mosaic of Memory (Chris French)   82

5 FAKING IT (Wendy M. Grossman)   87
   Muddying the Waters (David Langford)   88
   Knock: Some New Evidence (David Berman)   92
   A Case of Spirits (Chris Willis)   98
   Sprite 2 (Donald Rooum)   100

The Amazing Dummy Pill (Edzard Ernst)   101
Radio Ga-Ga (Tony Youens)   105

6   SCIENCE AND ANTI-SCIENCE (Wendy M. Grossman)   114
Death and the Microtubules (Susan Blackmore)   115
A Look at Probability and Coincidence (Chip Denman)   119
Abduction Theory (Nick Rose)   125
Sprite 3 (Donald Rooum)   128

7   SKEPTICS SPEAK (Wendy M. Grossman)   129
Proper Criticism (Ray Hyman)   130
A Panoply of Paranormal Piffle: Stephen Fry (Steve Donnelly)   135
Women are NOT from Gullibull (Lucy Sherriff)   141
Paul Daniels (Michael Hutchinson)   143

8   STATE OF THE ART (Wendy M. Grossman)   147
Perpetuum Mobile: The Perpetual Search for Perpetual
    Motion (Anthony Garrett)   148
Women and the New Age (Lucy Fisher)   155
An Anaesthesiologist Examines the Pam Reynolds
    Story (Gerald Woerlee)   162
Why Have UFOs Changed Speed over the Years?
    (Martin S. Kottmeyer)   171
Magicians, Mediums and Psychics (David Alexander)   177

9   DO YOU BELIEVE IN MIRACLES? (Wendy M. Grossman)   180
Something to Shout About: The Documentation of a Miracle?
    (Dr Peter May)   181
Scourge of the Godmen: B. Premanand (Lewis Jones)   187
The Trouble with Psychics (Richard Wiseman)   190

Index of Contributors   193
Index of subjects and sources   194

Foreword

Perfectly intelligent, thoughtful people often have two reactions to accounts of the paranormal. They either say, 'Well, there must be something in it ... I can't think of any other explanation', or they ask why it matters. Isn't it all a bit of fun?

And it can be tricky for the average skeptic. 'I went to a spiritualist, and she knew that my uncle had died recently, and that when I was a teenager I broke my leg so I couldn't go skiing! I bet you can't explain that!'

And we – or most of us – are raised to be polite, so we don't say what we should, which is, 'Oh, come on, did she really know your uncle had just died, or did she say "I see death, I see grief ..." And she knew you broke your leg, did she? Or did she say that she detected a broken bone in your past, and that had led to disappointment?' What kid doesn't break one limb or another and find they miss some kind of treat?

Or you could ask what she got wrong. Like the way she kept saying that she saw a Kevin in your life, and you couldn't think of anyone called Kevin except that lad who sometimes works Saturdays in the greengrocers. Or the time she said she saw romantic bliss, and you thought no, you weren't getting on well with your partner. You didn't remember that bit, did you?

But on the whole we don't say that. And even when we do nobody thanks us for it. I wrote an article years ago in which I analysed a TV performance by the late Doris Stokes, who claimed to hear messages from the dead. At one point she guessed that a youth who'd died had suffered a heart attack. Told that he was actually killed in a motorcycle crash, she smoothly declared that he had had a heart attack just before the accident. Then, discussing a little boy who had died in hospital, she thought he was still alive. And her interlocutor was not his mother, but his aunt. When I pointed this out in the article, the aunt wrote an angry letter pointing out that she had got his hair colour right, and that Mrs Stokes's words had been a great comfort to the family.

I'm sure they were. No wonder, since as well as using cold-reading techniques Mrs Stokes often simply fed back to the families information she had already got from them. People would phone her and get her husband. They would pour out their troubles to him, he would promise them free tickets for her next appearance in their area, and she would present the information back to them as if it had been provided by spirit voices.

Few in her audience ever said, 'Excuse me, I told your husband all that a few weeks ago!' People were in great distress. They were desperate to hear something that implied that their loved ones were happy in the afterlife. The fact that they were being spoon-fed lies, fictions, and evasions didn't matter to them. Like all of us, they preferred to clutch at hope rather than drown in despair.

So why does it matter? Perhaps we shouldn't mind. Mysteries are great fun. It's much more beguiling to think that space aliens travel across the cosmos for hundreds of our earth-years and, on arriving in Britain, decide to trample the crops in artistic circles before starting back on the long journey home. Far more interesting than putting it down to local pranksters. We all want some kind of assurance that the things that go wrong in our lives are not our fault. What better than to blame the heavens? You get fired. A partner leaves you. Someone close tells you exactly what they think of you. How soothing to learn that it has nothing to do with your failings!

'Mars in the ascendant prefigures difficulties at work ... Geminis are liable to have romantic problems ... Scorpios are startled by close friends ...' Again, many people just say that astrology is a bit of fun, but plenty of people attach great weight to it. (Nancy Reagan did, and made sure that her husband, the president, took key decisions at 'propitious' times, including signing bills at midnight.)

Some decades ago, the sub-editor on the *Daily Mirror* in Manchester had the job of writing the daily astrology forecast. Once, bored out of his mind with writing nonsense about 'romance beckons' and 'financial worries may be settled', he wrote 'all the sorrows of yesteryear are as nothing compared to what will befall you today'. The switchboard was jammed, and the star-reader was fired.

And, as it happens, all astrologers disagree. If it were a serious science, as they so often claim, you might imagine that they would all roughly take the same view, just as real scientists are able to agree on the boiling point of water. One year's end I found myself in a radio studio with Shelley von Strunckel, who divines the stars for the *Sunday Times* and London's *Evening Standard*. We got into a heated argument. She promised to send me a copy of her prognostications for the previous year, just to show how right she had been. She had highlighted her best prediction, which was: 'President Clinton will continue to skate on thin ice.' American president faces problems! Is that the best the stars can come up with? You might as well write: 'Persons will die in road traffic accidents', or 'Celebrities will say dumb things'.

And real scientists build on their work. People who believe in telepathy have a few very inconclusive experiments which are pored over time and again. And nothing has come of them. But real scientists detect, say, radio waves and out of that comes radar, safe air travel, TV, mobile phones, microwave ovens, and the internet. Pseudoscience is permanently stuck in the past, trying to find significance in the meaningless.

I would love it if there were a monster in Loch Ness. Wouldn't that be fun? But there ain't – if there were we'd have heard by now. And why wasn't it spotted for hundreds of years before a London surgeon put a cardboard neck and head on a water bottle he floated into the lake? (In these days, Photoshop means that all pictures are even less reliable than in the past.)

And a few more mysteries about the mysteries. How is it that Nostradamus's predictions always turn out to be about events that are already past, and are no use at predicting the future? Why do people prefer to believe that Roswell was about space aliens who travelled here in a tiny, fragile craft not unlike the detector balloon sent up by the US military? The great sage William of Ockham said that when trying to work something out, there was no need to multiply entities. By this he meant if there is an explanation in the nature we know, we shouldn't invent one out of thin air. If we know that conjurers can do amazing things, such as bending cutlery and reading minds, why imagine that it's being done by mysterious, unknown powers? Why suppose that rain is the angels crying when we know that it is condensed water vapour? William's guideline is known as 'Ockham's razor' and it should be included on the Swiss army knife.

I return to the question: does it matter? Isn't it simply amusing? I don't think so. We are, in the modern age, surrounded by lies, exaggeration, misleading nonsense, and spin. We are bombarded by politicians, TV programmes, advertisers, PR persons, people who want to sell us insurance, double-glazing, penis enlargement, and who wish to persuade us that we can earn millions by cooperating with the widow of a corrupt West African plutocrat. Vance Packard, in a seminal book, called some of these manipulators *The Hidden Persuaders*. They are not hidden any more. They are all around us. We are surrounded by what broadcasters call 'noise': the crackling, hissing, constant background din of untruths and semi-truths. We don't need any more. We don't need people trying to persuade us that space aliens are running our lives, or that the stars can foretell what is going to happen to us, or that the world was created in six days so that dinosaurs walked with men because the Bible implies it.

Now, perhaps more than ever before, the plain, unvarnished truth is important for our survival. We need to know what is really happening, or at least to get as close to reality as we can. This book will help us all to get there.

Simon Hoggart

Introduction

In May 1987, the Irish press was filled with stories about the weeping statue in a north Dublin suburban home. A website documenting the story[1] now says there were others in Cork and the south of Dublin around the same time. In fact, the site comments, the 1980s generally were a good time for weeping Rosa Mystica statues, which were found not only in Ireland but in Belgium, Sri Lanka, the US, and Italy.

I was living in Dublin at the time, and *The Skeptic* was a few months old. The stories seemed dramatic and mysterious. Weeping statues!

By then *The Skeptic* had some subscribers, who had begun sending in newspaper clippings. (This may seem quaint to younger readers, but at the time the Web hadn't been invented, few outside universities had email, and mine wasn't one that did.) One of these was a snipped letter to the *Daily Telegraph* written by someone in the plaster trade. He explained the phenomenon thusly: the plaster that statues are made of retains some water, and so plaster that statues are sealed with a plastic coating. If you poke holes in the coating, water will ooze out. If you poke those holes at the eyes, the statue will seem to weep.

I loved this for many reasons. For one thing, it seemed to me to prove that *The Skeptic* was worth doing to try to help make sure stuff like this didn't get lost. For another, the explanation had the same elements that appealed to me so much about the decades' worth of murder mysteries I'd read: an apparently impossible situation and a plausible and natural explanation. For a third, you could test this explanation's validity for yourself by buying a few cheap plaster statues and poking holes in them and seeing what happened.

That last is the key element of what good skeptics do, or should. Contrary to what most people, particularly in the UK, seem to think, skepticism isn't about saying no to everything all the time. Instead, it means inquiry. What is the evidence for a particular claim? How can it be tested?

If it can't be tested – if, in other words, the claim is what philosopher of science Karl Popper called an 'unfalsifiable hypothesis' – there's nothing for a skeptic to do, really. You are free to believe that a small, invisible, unmeasurable pink cloud occupies a permanent spot in the sky like a geostationary satellite and directs all human affairs, and if you do skeptics are unlikely to try to interfere because we're talking about a matter of faith, for which there are no tests. But if you start claiming that the pink cloud is coming down to Earth at night and making crop circles, *that* is a physical effect that can be examined, and a hypothesis can be formed about the cause and then tested.

---

[1] Full details of references and sources can be found on *The Skeptic's* website at www.skeptic.org.uk. See p. xiv for further details.

However, that doesn't tell you anything about how *The Skeptic* was founded, except that I am the kind of person who is excited by unexpected, natural explanations. That personality trait made me receptive in late 1986, when Mark Plummer, then the executive director of the US-based Committee for Scientific Investigation of Claims of the Paranormal (now the Committee for Skeptical Inquiry, or CSI), said to me, 'Do you think you could start a newsletter over there?' I was living in Dublin, where I knew hardly anyone, and I had been reading the committee's own publication, *Skeptical Inquirer*, for more than five years after running across first a live lecture/demonstration by magician and debunker James Randi and then a copy of *Science: Good, Bad, and Bogus* by Martin Gardner.

Starting a newsletter didn't really seem like much, but you never knew. And sometimes things work in non-obvious ways. If you ask people now, 22 years later, what *The Skeptic* has changed, you won't necessarily get an encouraging response. After all, the alternative 'medicine' market is booming in defiance of any scientific research; books, magazines, and TV shows promoting paranormal claims continue to proliferate; and the average person you meet at a party still always knows their star sign. On the other hand, there seem to be a lot more skeptics – and a lot more visible skeptics – all over the landscape, and when you're a founder that seems like a result.

In 1986, I remember practically throwing things at the television when, in a daytime discussion of spiritualism, the only opposition to a medium's claims was a Church of England minister who said that any spirit contacted by such a means was evil. Why wasn't there a skeptic to question whether there were any spirits to begin with?

That doesn't happen now (and not just because I don't watch daytime television). Within a couple of years of *The Skeptic*'s founding, you wouldn't see a TV show promoting paranormal claims without a skeptical viewpoint. That is, of course, still not an entirely satisfying state of affairs, because so often what happens is you're the token skeptic and the show is really about paranormal claimants and the wonders they perform. Skeptics who can be proactive and set the agenda are few and far between; a few years later along came Richard Wiseman, who is doing just that.

It feels, anyway, as though there are a lot more skeptics and skepticism around in 2009 than there were in 1987. How much of a role *The Skeptic* has played in that can be debated by others.

What has definitely become noticeable since 1987 – especially in the process of reviewing and selecting among 21 years' worth of *Skeptic* articles and writing the introductions for this volume – is that that there are fashions in belief as there are in everything else. Certainly there are perennials that just don't die – astrology being the most obvious case. UFOs continue to baffle sky-watchers, and today's 'alternative' medicine is a panoply of remedies that have been around for 150 years and more. Ghosts, numerology, dowsing, graphology: all still with us. Still others – physical spirit manifestations, spirit photography – die off because technology has overtaken them. But others are just short-lived fads. Who now talks about biorhythms or crop circles, both much in the public consciousness in *The Skeptic*'s early years?

Crop circles had the rare distinction of being a native phenomenon. No one suggested a pink cloud was causing them, but there were some other theories that seemed just as unlikely: currents in the Earth's magnetic field (Colin Andrews), UFOs, whirlwinds (Terence Meaden). Watching the evolution of these theories as new phenomena made them even more unlikely was instructive. Terence Meaden, for example, had to adapt his whirlwind idea after the discovery in about 1990 of crop circle formations that featured rectangular elements; the whirlwinds, he said, were intelligent plasma vortices. It was a fine example of a phenomenon that was to become rather familiar: the theory that is stretched mercilessly by adherents unable to accept that new developments had invalidated it.

Many, if not most, of the new and trendy beliefs in the UK over the past 21 years came from elsewhere, usually the US (although see also feng shui). I will say that British skeptics often seem to me to overestimate the common sense of the British public as contrasted with the gullibility of Americans. In the early 1990s, for example, I was told categorically that British folks would never believe in alien abductions, then an emerging belief in the US. 'We're too sensible', I was told. By five years later you were seeing abductees talk about their terrifying experiences on daytime talk shows here, too. To be followed, a few years later, by believers in angels.

Similarly, about four years ago, when I tried to write a piece about the growth of creationism in the UK, the received wisdom held that creationism would never gain ground here – British people understood more about science, and anyway evangelical Christianity didn't have much of a hold. Cut to February 2009 and here is the headline on page 15 of the *Daily Telegraph*: 'Half of UK population "believe in creationism"'.

But creationism is a perfect example of what a very small number of passionate skeptics can achieve. One of the reasons so many people thought that Britain was somehow insulated from creationism was that the subject made some noise in the late 1980s and then seemed to die off. What they didn't know was that it didn't die by itself; instead, the disappearance of creationism from the national consciousness was the result of a thought-out, diligent and persistent attack by Michael Howgate, who founded a little (two-member) organization he called APE, or the Association for the Protection of Evolution. Howgate made a point of going along to creationist meetings and doing his best to ask awkward questions, point out errors of fact, correct quotations taken out of context and embarrass the speakers until they stopped holding public meetings.

These days, the internet has made it easy for like-minded people to find each other, but for much of *The Skeptic*'s lifetime so far it took a printed publication.

Skepticism is a hard sell, to both supporters and outsiders. In the UK, people seem to see the word as negative and closed-minded instead of open-minded and inquiring. Skeptics are generally used to feeling – and being – isolated. And much of skepticism is not media-friendly: there is no story in saying that astrology is just a 2,000-year-old first attempt at understanding astronomy, or that the apparent success rate of 'alternative' therapies is generally due to a poor understanding of the principle that 'the plural of anecdote is not data'.

In 1996, Wayne Spencer and Tony Youens got together and put a notice in *The Skeptic* looking for like-minded people to start a membership organization. Their group, the Association for Skeptical Enquiry (ASKE) was founded in 1997, and represents Britain as a member of the European skeptical umbrella organization ECSO. Similarly, the monthly meeting 'Skeptics in the Pub' was founded in my living room while stuffing magazines into envelopes one day in 1999, when Scott Campbell, new in London from Australia, said, 'I was thinking of starting a pub meet.' My sole contribution was to say, 'Sounds great. Go for it.' Skeptics in the Pub is now ten years old, attracts standing-room-only crowds every month, and is being copied around the country.

The thing I am actually proudest of in fact is not my own contribution in starting *The Skeptic*. What I am proud of is that it has attracted so many persistent supporters who have worked far harder to keep it alive and make it prosper than I ever did myself: Chris French and his Goldsmiths students; Hilary Evans, who has contributed both illustrations from the Mary Evans Picture Library and his own writing for so many years; cartoonists Donald Rooum and Ted Pearce; Toby Howard and Steve Donnelly, who edited the magazine for eight years and did the brutally hard work of growing the subscriber base; Peter O'Hara, my partner in getting the magazine out when it was photocopied and posted by hand; Michael Hutchinson; and the many, many contributors of articles and other features to the magazine who are too numerous to list. It is not a great thing to start a newsletter. But it is a great thing 20 years later to see it still alive and not dependent on you for its survival. That is really the key, because for something to have real, long-term impact it must be a community effort.

As it turns out, like many phenomena, weeping statues can have more than one explanation – and more than one manifestation. Since then (and before) there have been many stories about statues weeping blood and oil, and, conversely, drinking milk. Soak a sponge in scented or coloured oil or water and stuff it in the empty head cavity of a plaster statue and poke a pair of those ever-useful holes, and the statue will weep oil or 'blood'. A number of skeptics have by now built even cleverer models, because, really, what good is it being a skeptic in 2009 if you can't improve on a medieval miracle?

Wendy M. Grossman
London, May 2009

A Note on Sources

Many of the articles included here have a long list of references and sources that appeared alongside them when they were originally published in *The Skeptic*. These footnotes do not appear in the book; instead we have placed them on *The Skeptic*'s website, at www.skeptic.org.uk. Since a good percentage of the references are web addresses, putting them online instead of printing them serves two purposes: (1) it's easier to click on an address than to painstakingly type it in; (2) they can be easily updated when pages move or are withdrawn, and added to when newly published research dictates.

Skeptical Stats

We started running Skeptical Stats, a feature loosely copied from Harper's, in 1998. Anyone can subscribe to the emailed digest, which includes Skeptical Stats, the news pages (Hits and Misses), and Skeptics in the Pub announcements, by signing up at http://www.skeptic.org.uk/newsnetworks/digest

1. Number of properties the National Trust advertises as having ghosts: **72**
2. Percentage of the nuclear matter in today's universe that is *not* hydrogen or helium: **less than 2**
3. Educated estimate of the number of slaves, worldwide, in 2002: **27,000,000**
4. Percentage of all people who have ever lived that are alive today: **10**
5. Number of small metal egg-shaped objects Uri Geller claims were given to him by John Lennon, who was given it by aliens: **1**
6. Number of dominoes knocked over after a sparrow inadvertently flew into a world record 'domino toppling' attempt: **23,000** (The sparrow was subsequently cornered and shot by an angry competitor)
7. Percentage of UK students who say they believe in creationism and intelligent design: **30**
8. Percentage of UK students who say they believe evolutionary theory is true: **56**
9. Number of people in Britain phoning psychic lines every month: **75,000**
10. Number of extra Planet Earths it would take to support every person in the world at present US levels of consumption with existing technology: **4**
11. Percentage by which human DNA differs from that of chimpanzees and bonobos: **1.6**
12. Amount by which global water availability is expected to drop over the next 20 years: **a third**
13. Price of sending a message to the dead via the website Afterlife Telegrams via terminally ill volunteers: **$5 a word** (five-word minimum)
14. Number of messengers the site currently has available: **1**
15. Number of black rhinos in Africa a century ago: **1 million**
16. Number now, due to the demand for rhino horn in Chinese medicine: **2,500**
17. Percentage of conclusions drawn in papers published in scientific journals that are arguably false: approximately **50**
18. Estimated number of people in Britain who claim to have psychic abilities: **150,000**

19. Proportion of the world's wildlife which has been lost since 1970: **approximately 27 percent**
20. Likelihood that God exists, according to calculations carried out by Dr Stephen Unwin, author of *The Probability of God*: **67 percent**
21. Average number of scientific questions out of 12 answered correctly by tabloid readers: **4.13**
22. Average number of scientific questions out of 12 answered correctly by broadsheet readers: **5.78**
23. Height of a statue of St Anthony of Padua, patron saint of lost and stolen items, that disappeared from a Peterborough church in July 2005: **2 feet**
24. Number of previous driving licence suspensions or revocations Michael Wiley, a one-legged, armless man, had prior to evading Florida police in a 100 mph car chase in the spring of 2007: **18**
25. Cost of a James Randi doll on which to perform voodoo experiments: **$24**

1

There Must Be Something in It

There must be something in it. There's no smoke without fire. Isn't that what people always say? The implication: who are you, you puny little skeptic, to call millions of people wrong?

True story. In 1993 I appeared on a show on Anglia Television called *Anglia Live*. The programme featured about 200 people in a live audience; the authors of a new book about their interactions with ghosts (the usual story – see Nick Rose and Susan Blackmore on sleep paralysis later in this book); and me, the token skeptic. There was also a telephone poll frequently trailed during the show: do you believe in ghosts? At the end of the show they presented the results. No less than 86 percent of the callers said yes. 'What', demanded the show's host, 'do you say to that?'

'That people who believe in ghosts are more likely to pick up the telephone,' I said promptly. And then all the 199 other people in the studio *yelled* at me.

Were they right? Of course not. Winning the popular vote isn't scientific proof. It isn't even evidence. They may have liked the stories they'd just heard, but as the mathematician Matt Blaze is fond of saying, the plural of anecdote is not data.

The problem for skeptics is that it's very much easier to make a claim than to disprove one. Two hundred people can say they've seen ghosts and it sounds impressive. A dedicated skeptic with a large amount of available time could investigate each case and find a natural explanation. But that still does not prove that there has never been a ghost, only that these cases were not instances of one.

The topics in this section are all examinations of why popularity doesn't count.

And there can, too, be smoke without fire. I lived in Ireland with a solid fuel central heating system and a clogged chimney, so I know.

Seeing is Believing?
Susan Blackmore

*It helps to understand the mechanics of belief: why something improbable can seem plausible under the right circumstances – and why beliefs are sometimes immutable no matter what logic or facts you throw at the holder. Are psychic experiences illusions? And if so, why are they so persuasive? Providing this analysis is **Susan Blackmore**, a freelance writer, lecturer, broadcaster and a visiting lecturer at the University of the West of England, Bristol. Since completing a PhD in parapsychology at the University of Surrey in 1980, her research interests have grown to include memes, evolutionary theory, consciousness and meditation; her books include **The Meme Machine** and **Consciousness**. Appeared in V.6.*

There have been lots of surveys of psychic experiences and beliefs in Europe and the USA and according to these about half the population believes in paranormal phenomena of one kind or another. The main reason people give is their own psychic experiences – and belief is highly correlated with having such psychic experiences. So why are psychic experiences so common?

I think we should not look on psychic experiences as some kind of mental aberration or mistake people make, but as a natural consequence of the way our minds work. They are a kind of illusion that naturally occurs when we try to make sense of a complicated and unpredictable world.

I am here defining psychic experiences as any experience which is interpreted by the experient as psychic or paranormal. I am not making any stipulation about whether anything paranormal does or does not happen. If the person interprets it as paranormal then I call it a psychic experience. The issue of whether paranormal events ever do occur is quite a different question and one I am not going to tackle.

The comparison I want to make is with visual illusions. In both visual illusions and psychic experiences the experience is real but the origin lies in internal processes, not peculiarities in the observable world. Both arise from cognitive strategies or heuristics which are usually appropriate but under certain circumstances give the wrong answer. For example, visual illusions may occur when depth is seen inappropriately, as in the famous 'railway lines' illusion (Figure 1). The top line looks longer because the brain automatically interprets the lines receding into the distance. You cannot make this illusion go away by looking hard at it, intellectually arguing with yourself or screwing up your eyes (you can reduce it a bit by turning the page around). Similarly, psychic experiences may occur when it is inappropriately assumed that a cause is operating or an explanation is required when actually it isn't. Like visual illusions, these experiences cannot be argued away and they do not

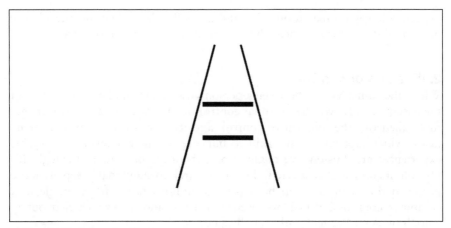

Figure 1 The 'railway lines' illusion

occur because you are stupid. Rather the reverse: they occur because the brain is doing its job of trying to make sense of the world.

I have divided these kinds of illusions up into five types.

1. Illusions of connection

Experiences of telepathy, clairvoyance, and precognition imply a coincidence which is 'too good to be just chance' (such as dreams which come true). Some people just shrug and assume it was a chance coincidence, but others find the coincidence too compelling and look for a causal explanation. If none can be found they may start looking for one and, if they cannot find one, end up invoking extra-sensory perception (ESP). Two types of error may be made here: treating connected events as chance, or treating chance events as connected. Of course in the real world both inevitably occur. It is only the latter that produce ESP experiences. From this I predicted that people who more frequently look for explanations for chance coincidences (that is, underestimate their probability) are more likely to have psychic experiences.

Although much is known about the heuristics people use to make probability judgements and the factors which affect them, there has been little research relating these to the paranormal. At Bristol University (Blackmore and Troscianko, *British Journal of Psychology*, 1985, 459–68) we found that sheep (believers) performed worse than goats (disbelievers) on various probability tasks. For example, in a coin-tossing computer game subjects guessed how many hits they would be likely to get by chance when ten were expected. Sheep estimated only 7.9 and goats 9.6. We called this the 'chance baseline shift' and it was clear that sheep suffered from it more than goats.

2. Illusions of control

Where the coincidence is between a person's own action and an external event the assumed cause will be personal control or PK. Psychologist Ellen Langer first called this the 'illusion of control' and it is known to appear in many tasks which appear to be skilled but are actually chance. If psychic experiences are illusions we might expect them to come about through this illusion of control. As expected, there is research to show that sheep are more prone to this than goats in both psi and non-psi tasks, for example in a computer coin-tossing task we used at Bristol, and in tests carried out in Zurich by Peter Brugger and his colleagues.

3. Illusions of pattern and randomness

All sensory processes involve extracting pattern from noise. Again, two kinds of error can occur; failing to detect patterns which are there and seeing patterns which are not. An example of the latter is shown in Figure 2 – most people will see patterns or forms in the figure which is simply a randomly meandering line. People may also search for a cause for patterns which are not really there, and, finding none, turn to the paranormal. I predicted that people who make this kind of error are more likely to have psychic experiences and believe in the paranormal.

Figure 2 People often see patterns where there are none, such as in this randomly meandering line

One way of investigating this is by what is called 'subjective random number generation', or SRG. When asked to generate a string of random numbers people typically avoid repetitions of the same digit (Wagenaar, *Psychological Bulletin*, 1972, 65–72). This is related to the 'Gambler's Fallacy': for example, imagining a string of reds must be followed by black. ESP experiments are often equivalent to SRG and have been shown to have the same bias.

Brugger, Landis and Regard *(British Journal of Psychology,* 1990, 455–68) showed that sheep were more likely than goats to avoid repetitions in this kind of task. Indeed, they found this effect in several types of task. On the other hand, Troscianko and I at Bristol failed to find this in our early experiments. I therefore carried out further experiments in 1992 with a student, Katherine Galaud. We compared SRG for different numbers of choices, predicting that repetition avoidance and sheep-goat differences would be greater for lower probabilities. This we did not find, and nor did we confirm Brugger's finding. So we are planning further experiments to explore this.

4. Illusions of form

A large part of perception entails recognizing objects or forms in complicated stimuli. This too can entail two types of error: seeing things that are not there and failing to see things that are. Again, you cannot avoid making errors: shift your criterion one way and you will make more of one type; shift it the other and you will make more of the other. You can never be accurate all the time.

The relevance to the paranormal is that those people who are more likely to see forms when none are present are possibly also those who see apparitions or ghosts, or who seek paranormal explanations when none are required.

In another experiment, with another student, Catherine Walker, we tested this idea. And we also tested the idea of differences in accuracy versus criterion. Sheep might simply be less cautious in saying they see forms than goats with the same accuracy for distinguishing them, or they may actually make more errors.

We gave 50 subjects a Belief in the Paranormal Scale and an object identification task in which they were very briefly shown a whole series of pictures ranging from barely identifiable blobs to clear outline shapes of leaves, a bird, a fish, and an axe. After each presentation, subjects were asked whether they could see any shape or not and, if they could, what shape it was. We predicted that sheep would report seeing forms earlier in the series than goats (that is, their criteria would be lower) but would not be more accurate in identifying the forms. This is just what we found. Their scores on the belief scale were correlated with the number of forms they said they saw but not with the number of correct identifications. Although other interpretations are certainly possible (and need investigating) these findings fit the idea that paranormal belief is encouraged in those who more often see form in ambiguity.

5. Illusions of memory
Selective memory may make coincidences appear to occur more often than they do – a factor in reporting psychic experiences that was pointed out as long ago as 1886 by Gurney, Myers, and Podmore in their classic study of 'Phantasms of the Living'. It is now known that meaningfully related events are selectively recalled and people misremember their previous predictions to conform with what actually happened. If psychic experiences can sometimes be illusions of memory then we would expect that sheep would be more prone to such effects than goats. This has not, to my knowledge, been tested yet and is something I hope to explore in further research.

Some conclusions
These five illusions may be the basis for many spontaneous psychic experiences and, because they are so common, may generate belief in the paranormal. The tendency for sheep to show these effects more than goats is at least suggestive evidence that this is so. Of course, it must be remembered that this has no bearing on psi experiments with adequate target randomization and hence on the laboratory evidence for psi. The findings simply suggest that we should expect to find a high incidence of psychic experiences and widespread belief in the paranormal whether or not psychic phenomena occur.

I think one of the exciting prospects for skeptical inquiry into the paranormal is going to be gaining a greater understanding of how these experiences come about – and to do this we can leave on one side the thorny issue of whether genuinely paranormal events ever do occur.

Psychic Con-men
Richard Wiseman and Emma Greening

One reason paranormal events seem to occur is that psychics work to convince us that they do. Skeptics arguing with psychics often have a problem: the psychics come across as nice people genuinely interested in helping their distressed clients. How true is that perception? **Richard Wiseman** *heads the Perrott-Warrick Research Unit at the University of Hertfordshire.* **Emma Greening**, *a psychologist at the University of Hertfordshire, had recently joined the unit. Together they set out to investigate what visiting London psychics is really like. Appeared in X.5-6.*

A few months ago we were approached by Carlton Television's *The Investigators* programme and asked whether we could help make an investigative documentary about exploitative 'psychics'. The project sounded interesting and we agreed to be involved. After several meetings with the programme makers we decided to help set up an undercover 'sting' operation. Basically, we would send two actresses to several alleged psychics. Each actress would say that she had recently experienced a great deal of bad luck in her life (including, for example, family bereavements, problems at work, and with boyfriends) and was eager for some 'psychic' help. The psychics would be unaware that these problems were completely fictitious and, perhaps more importantly, that the actresses were fitted with hidden cameras which filmed each of the consultations.

We chose five London-based psychics from adverts in various newspapers (for example, *Eastern Eye*, *Ms London*), focusing on those that claimed to be able to remove curses. We thought that one or two might try to exploit their seemingly vulnerable clients – however, nothing had prepared us for what we were about to encounter.

First up was Psychic A, who operates from a cosmetics and hair products shop in Hackney. The actress claimed that she had just split up with her boyfriend. Psychic A assured her that he could help and went on to recommend that the actress buy some white underwear and return in a couple of days for a herbal bath. This would 'loosen her up' and bring her boyfriend back to her. The cost of this 'treatment' would be £450. After the consultation, the actress remarked that she had felt very unsettled by the implicitly sexual nature of certain comments made by Psychic A.

The same actress then visited Psychic B in Camberwell. This time, the actress claimed that she had always had a difficult relationship with her sister, and that matters had recently been made worse by the death of their mother. Psychic B informed the actress that her sister was jealous of her, was trying to drive her boyfriend away, and 'doesn't care how far she goes to destroy your future'. Psychic B had a solution to this problem. If her client burnt five candles, at £150 each, then her sister 'will in the end give you the things that belong to you and let you lead your own life ...' Psychic B also stressed that her client must not tell anybody about the consultation, noting, 'Because if you do say something about it then the work that we will have to do is just going to be for no reason, it's just going to collapse in front of us, and you will not have anyone else to help you through this.'

Our actress next consulted with Psychic C in Ilford. He told his client that her bad luck was due to her planets being misaligned, that only he could realign them. However, when he had finished his work her spell of misfortune would end and that '... your purpose of coming here will be fulfilled. You will have future children, and be able to meet your mother, your health is not good, that will be okay. Your future will be okay.' Psychic C then informed his client that this service would cost her £630.

Our second actress was first sent to Psychic D and asked to say that she had been experiencing a great many problems with both her boyfriend and sister. Psychic D said that she should be able to get her boyfriend back because, 'He is destined in your life lines, which means he was supposed to be with you all the time.' She then went on to talk about the problem of the sister, noting, 'She wants your life to be empty and desolate. She wants your life to be worth nothing. Your hopes and dreams must be shattered, for you to be like a beggar on the street ...' Psychic D then told her client the bad news: her sister had been to a 'spiritual worker' (that is, another psychic) and had a curse put on her. Next came the good news: Psychic D thought that she might be able to lift this curse by lighting various candles, and that this would cost around £900.

Finally, we sent our second actress to see Psychic E, and asked her to tell him the story of her errant boyfriend. Psychic E said that the boyfriend could be brought back by using a number of different creams and lotions. These were available for £450.

Although the psychics operated from different locations, there were a number of common themes running through their consultations. First, none of them offered any form of mainstream counselling, or even suggested that their obviously distressed client (during three of the consultations the actresses feigned tears) seek out professional help. Second, several of the psychics were eager to convince their client that her run of bad luck was due to a curse that had been put on her by a seemingly close friend or family member. Third, many of them tried to distance the client from any possible social support, often asking her not to mention the consultation to friends or family. Fourth, and perhaps most worrying of all, each and every psychic suggested that they alone could solve the client's problem, and asked between £450 and £900 for their services.

For many people, the adverts in newspapers and magazines appear to offer quick and easy solutions to their personal problems. However, the psychics that we investigated only exploited the vulnerable and offered services that were more likely to confound, than to assist, clients' difficulties. We were appalled at the way in which all five 'psychics' were prepared to act in such an unethical way and appeared to be more concerned with emptying wallets than giving comfort to apparently distressed people. One could perhaps argue that such behaviour might be excusable if these people really are psychic. However, our project inadvertently resulted in some data strongly suggesting that this is not the case. Not one of the five 'psychics' was able to use their 'supernatural' powers to detect that their clients were actresses, or that they were being secretly filmed for a television programme that intended to expose their shoddy behaviour!

In Search of Monsters?
Charles Paxton

*Everyone loves monsters: King Kong, the dinosaurs in **Jurassic Park** ... even the allegedly non-fictional Loch Ness monster has an affectionate nickname. But what do you call someone who studies monsters and how seriously can you study them? Cryptozoology, sometimes compared to UFOlogy, is typically defined as the study of hidden animals: that is, animals unknown to science (cryptids). **Charles Paxton**, a fisheries ecologist/statistician at the University of St Andrews, debates whether writing a book on sea monsters in his spare time makes him a cryptozoologist. Appeared XV.3.*

There is an important distinction between cryptozoology and, for example, UFOlogy. The basic assumption underlying cryptozoology is neither irrational nor improbable: the list of the world's fauna is not complete. Discoveries of new animals are still being made – and these new animals are not just microbes or insects; they can be ever so slightly larger things like whales (described in 1991 and 1995), giant stingrays (1990), and sharks (1981). Therefore, the probability of the imminent discovery of further large animals, especially in the marine environment, is not minuscule; given a number of (potentially dubious) caveats and extrapolations about human knowledge it may even be calculable.

Unknown species are being seen by zoologically qualified observers. For example, scientists on whale surveys in the eastern Pacific have observed a beaked whale (*Mesoplodon* species B) which differs from the existing known species and may represent an unknown species of whale; or it could be a living specimen of the little-known beaked whale *Mesoplodon bahamondi*, which was only described in 1995. So cryptozoology does have an empirical footing firmer than most other fringe topics based upon eyewitness testimony. Unlike the potential existence of homoeopathic remedies, ghosts, or astrological influences on mankind, the existence of unknown animals does not undermine or even tweak the fundamentals of physics, chemistry, or biology.

In my experience, most cryptozoologists do not believe and never have believed that cryptids are supernatural in origin. They are open to the idea of observer error and misidentification, although they probably have a higher view of observer accuracy than the average reader of *The Skeptic*. There is a fringe which believes in supernatural origins of Bigfoot, Nessie, and the Great Sea Serpent, but these individuals are avoided by mainstream cryptozoologists and increasingly they give their subject its own title, the delightful neologism 'para-cryptozoology'.

Cryptozoology may use eyewitness testimony, but this is not by any means its sole source of data. Several cryptozoologists have argued that any deductive technique that could be used to predict the existence of animals would be cryptozoological. The French cryptozoologist Michel Raynal presents the prediction and subsequent discovery of the Madagascan subspecies of the moth *Xanthopan morgani* as a triumph of the cryptozoological method. In 1862, Charles Darwin predicted in *On the Various Contrivances by which British and Foreign Orchids are Fertilised by Insects* the existence of a long-tongued moth in Madagascar. Something had to be availing itself of the nectaries of the orchid *Angraecum sesquipedale* because otherwise there would have been no fertilization and the plant would have become extinct. The nectaries were 28.6 cm long, with only the lower 3.6 cm filled with nectar. Later authors speculated that the mystery moth would have affinities with the mainland African *X. morgani*, as this group of moths was characterized by long tongues. In 1903, forty-one years after the original prediction, the subspecies *praedicta* was found in Madagascar. If such a prediction is cryptozoological, then this would cover all cases where the existence of a new zoological species may have been inferred prior to the discovery of actual physical remains.

If cryptozoology were based solely on studies such as these it would have a high claim as a scientific subdiscipline of zoology, or, at the very least, if not strictly scientific in the experimental sense, to be at least scientific in the sense of the rigorous systematic collection of data. The problem with this argument is that the people who actually discovered the moth published their work as zoology and might, if they were anything like most present-day zoologists I know, have run a mile rather than describe themselves as cryptozoologists. This case of course occurred before Bernard Heuvelmans had coined the term 'cryptozoology', and before 1988, when Heuvelmans added that cryptozoology is 'the scientific study of hidden animals, that is, of still unknown animal forms about which only testimonial and circumstantial evidence is available, or material evidence considered insufficient by some'.

A more pertinent example would be the recent observations of another unknown species of beaked whale from the eastern Pacific. This species had been seen at least as far back as 1983 and referred to in the marine mammal scientific literature as *Mesoplodon* species A. Separately, there was physical evidence of a new species of whale in the form of various body parts that had appeared in the Peru region since 1976. Finally, in 1991, Julio Reyes and his colleagues described a new species of toothed whale, *Mesoplodon peruvianus*. Only recently has *M. peruvianus* become well enough known for Robert Pitman and his co-workers to argue convincingly that *M. peruvianus* actually is *Mesoplodon* species A. However, none of those involved in this story have, as far as I am aware, described themselves as cryptozoologists.

Furthermore, by Heuvelmans's extended definition of cryptozoology outlined above, any extension of the geographical range of any recognized animal could be considered cryptozoological. Thus, even more conventional zoologists would find themselves described as cryptozoologists. There would be no distinction between the predictive zoology of discovery and cryptozoology.

The trouble is that the formal definition of cryptozoology (and its extension above) doesn't accurately describe what most self-styled cryptozoologists actually study. The few journals and magazines of cryptozoology are not crammed full of discoveries of just any old new species of beetle or even (my own personal favourites) fish. Only news of new species of slightly odd or large animals seems to make it. Giant geckos get in, new species of small lizard do not. An out-of-place mammal might get a mention – kangaroos in Scotland for example – and any news of certain known animals (for example, the giant squid *Architeuthis* sp.) will almost certainly be reported on, although not others – cattle or dogs for example.

Of course, much of cryptozoology concerns evaluation of evidence prior to the discovery stage. Some cryptozoologists go out and actively hunt for Bigfoots, Nessies, and the Mokele-Mbembes (allegedly, a large reptilian inhabitant of the swamps of central Africa). The more bookish sort peruse ancient tomes, artefacts, or even buildings for evidence of unknown animals known to the ancients. Some analyze travellers' tales and the traditions of indigenous peoples. Most commonly of all, there are those who seek to collate, interpret, and analyse testimonial evidence from observers who have claimed to have seen, and sometimes filmed, monstrous creatures as yet unknown to science.

So, does any definition link those that claim the all-inclusive scientific basis of cryptozoology and the sometimes more unsystematic collectors of information? In my view, there is one definition of cryptozoology that does take in this wide church and does reflect the interests of the cryptozoologists. It relies on looking at not only what cryptozoologists do but also what attracts their attention.

The animals have to be weird (like the coelacanth *Latimeria* sp.), perhaps on a once-prolific but now pruned branch of the tree of life, or they have to be odd for their type (like giant squid). So perhaps cryptozoology is the study of weird (misshapen, ugly?), little-known but potentially exciting (and often big for their type) animals. This isn't a great definition, but it is accurate. Of course there is a shorthand for this: cryptozoology is the study of *monsters*.

Just as some skeptics would take delight in my definition, some cryptozoologists would be horrified. Both groups would feel that such a subject of study is perhaps improper and intellectually dubious. I disagree; I don't use the word 'monster' pejoratively at all. The validity of cryptozoology rests on its methods, not on its subject of enquiry. How rigorous is cryptozoology? This varies.

Clearly cryptozoologists collect a lot of data from a variety of different sources, but it is often not systematic nor is it normally collected in the light of an hypothesis, and hence it may not constitute 'scientific study'. This is not necessarily a problem. Data unsystematically collected can still be amenable to scientific scrutiny by other workers, and the journals of cryptozoology do contain a little quantitative analysis of photographic and testimonial evidence. For example, the 1987 edition of *Cryptozoology*, the irregularly appearing but peer-reviewed journal of the International Society of Cryptozoology, contained a quantitative analysis of the famous Wilson Nessie photograph (although admittedly the analysis was subsequently criticized by British skeptic Steuart Campbell and the photo itself has been subsequently revealed as a hoax).

Of course, sometimes cryptozoologists collect data sloppily or, more commonly, interpret their data without any critical evaluation or any consideration of Ockham's razor. What this normally means is that the unassignable, be it sightings or sounds or even, I suppose, smells, can be taken as evidence for unknown species rather than simply incomplete information.

However, what the very best cryptozoologists do very well is dig up and evaluate very obscure information from very obscure sources. This could include newspaper reports from the far corners of the world or obscure references in ancient travel books. In this way, cryptozoology has more in common with history than zoology. The Canadian (crypto)zoologist Ben Roesch has compared it to natural history. It also has some similarity to an historical science like palaeontology. Odd specimens/accounts/artefacts turn up that have to be interpreted in context and are often subject to re-evaluation. Cryptozoology, as actually done by the most methodically rigorous cryptozoologists, is an intellectually valid and exciting area of study. But often there is little quantification and data are not always interpreted in the most parsimonious manner. A cryptozoologist will pay lip service to the idea that alternative simpler hypotheses should be considered when evaluating eyewitness claims of encounters with unknown animals, but will not always accept them. For example, in his epic book on sea serpents Heuvelmans gave the following quotation concerning a strange animal washed up on the Norwegian coast:

Anno 1744 one Dogfind Korsbeck catched [sic], *in the parish of Sundelvems on Sundmoer, a monstrous fish, which many people saw at his house. Its head was almost like that of a cat; it had four paws, and about the body was a hard shell like a lobster's: it purred like a cat, and when they put a stick at it, it would snap at it. The peasants looked upon it as a Trold, or ominous fish, and were afraid to keep it; and consequently, a few hours later, they threw it into the sea again.*

Heuvelmans seemed puzzled by this account and speculated that it may have been a (presumably juvenile) giant marine otter, but it seems to me, rather obviously, to have been a turtle.

Another problem that cryptozoology has is that many of the assumptions of its data acquisition have not been put to rigorous test. Is there any reason to believe the ancients would have known about species that are still living but unknown to us today? Are secondary sources for eyewitness testimony reliable? In primary accounts, are observers accurately recollecting an anomalous (to them) animal? How good are people at recognizing whether an animal is unknown to science? Are cryptids only seen under certain conditions? Is it possible to predict when and where unknown animals may be seen? It is these sorts of questions on which the validity of cryptozoology as a method rests.

Cryptozoology isn't a science, but that doesn't make it an invalid form of study. History is not a science but it is still a rigorous form of intellectual endeavour. Nor does the fact that cryptozoology is not currently a science mean it won't be in the future. Cryptozoology is slowly becoming self-critical. *Cryptozoology* was full of criticisms of published studies. Other recent articles have even criticized the conclusions of Heuvelmans, the 'Father of Cryptozoology', himself. A new generation of (crypto)zoologists is suggesting that more attention be paid to pertinent psychological and palaeontological literature. People lie. Hoaxes happen. Eyewitness testimony is often flawed. Large, unknown predators don't generally exist where there is no food to support them. Sixty-five-million-year-old fossil species really are unlikely to be alive today.

Skeptical criticism can only be a good thing for any discipline, including cryptozoology. With a few notable exceptions, there has seldom been a sustained look at monster accounts by skeptics; easier targets seem to be preferred. The plausible (but not necessarily probable) nature of many of the claims of cryptozoology means that a dismissive, dry, skeptical approach simply will not work. More than any other fringe subject, there really is the chance of some startling discoveries and some of these may well be anticipated by cryptozoologists. In the future there will be monsters ...

Millennium
Kevin McClure

People don't exactly love an apocalypse – but those who predict them often do so with copious detail that barely conceals their relish. The pending arrival of the year 2000 was the cue for many to predict TEOTWAWKI – The End of the World As We Know It – and we're not just talking about the elaborate survivalist fantasies of the extreme fringe regarding the Y2K computer problem and financial 'gurus' who predicted a total market collapse (yet were curiously optimistic throughout 2008). But, said Kevin McClure, *civil servant and author of* **The Fortean Times Book of the Millennium**, *predictions of the end of the world have a long history. Appeared in X.5–6.*

Should you want a job for life – or longer, if you can face the concept – you could commit yourself to reporting on apocalyptic, end-of-the-world beliefs. Of all the varieties of conviction of the occurrence of irrational, extraordinary events, caused by non-human agencies able to intervene irrevocably in the affairs of our race, this is the Magic Porridge Pot. Or maybe the Enormous Turnip. Something immense and indefatigable, anyway.

I've been fascinated by this material for years, and first started collecting the literature in the aftermath of the Russian invasion of Afghanistan, when I published a couple of speculative issues of the *End Times Bulletin*. It won only a limited audience, but brought together the early strands of the Survivalist movement, which has developed into the Militias, early New Age material, including UFO landings in England to carry off the chosen, and more traditional biblical interpretations. It didn't matter much that few people bought it; I ceased publishing because as the crisis passed so, too, did the sense of panic and divine mission that was helping fill the pages.

Asked in 1996 to write *The Fortean Times Book of the Millennium*, I returned eagerly to the fray. I had become a more skeptical writer and researcher than I was fifteen years before, but hopefully a more compassionate one, too, so long as people aren't exploiting and damaging each other. I'd anticipated that the nature and motivations in the millennial field hadn't changed much since 1981–2, but I was wrong. The prospect of a year that has three noughts on the end brought some strange and greedy people out of the woodwork. And some dilemmas for the concerned skeptic, too.

Of course, I found some easy targets. Foremost among these is Nostradamus, whose history has already been dealt with fairly and capably by James Randi. I couldn't avoid concluding that however good or bad a prophet he may have been, Nostradamus had a remarkable mind, and a high level of commitment as a plague doctor, and I think that Randi has little argument with that viewpoint. What Randi wasn't, perhaps, aware of, is the extent of the money-grubbing dishonesty of those who feign interpretation of the obscure French quatrains to produce snappy references to current events.

Even bestselling authors Peter Lorie and V. J. Hewitt have knowingly produced gems like the following:

> *Diana Spencer will become a queen who joins her pensive king in reviving a fleeting monarchy ... Beginning in 1992 and ending in 1993, the coronation of King Charles and the Olympic Games will be followed by a great earthquake, triggered off by a shifting in the San Andreas fault ... A mass evacuation begins from cities and towns before the earthquake. The State Governor organises the exodus to the border where it stays outside the ring, the shadow, the zone ... San Diego ... disappears beneath the sea ...Hollywood film studios collapse ... America burns 1993–1996.*

The important point to remember is that it is abundantly clear that Nostradamus neither wrote those words nor intended his own to be understood in that way. Such prophecies – and their ignominious failure – are the responsibility of Lorie and Hewitt alone. Many others have done the same, or worse, and continue to do so. We shouldn't aim for a long-dead target.

I'm conscious that most skeptics don't mess with mainstream religions, but the Book of Revelation dominates apocalyptic belief, and I couldn't avoid taking a position. Simply, I look at the shadowy, and maybe substantially unreal, St John of Patmos like any other person who claims to have experienced visions. I've never supported the view that skepticism should ring-fence 'respectable' religions, and this most influential of books of the Bible adopts so much earlier material, is put together so awkwardly, contains such vivid, graceless, and cruel imagery, so many threats and so little love, that it seems scarcely Christian. And scarcely credible, too.

Yet it has close parallels with the output of so many other individuals who have their own visionary experience and then amalgamate its content with that of other and earlier visions, thus validating and supporting their own, making themselves part of what is probably an entirely subjective tradition. It was little more than luck and the support of a few powerful individuals at the right moment that took Revelation into the main biblical canon. I find it quite daunting to realize what that chance inclusion has led to, what potential it has provided for more charismatic believers to control and terrify others. What would Jim Jones, David Koresh, Hal Lindsey, and a thousand others have done without it?

Some individuals came out quite well. I rather like Mother Shipton, who never spoke or wrote a single word of the prophecies attributed to her but seems to have been a general good egg, a woman of wisdom in a time when it was difficult to be respected for that, something of a herbalist, and a caring mother in difficult circumstances. William Miller, of the Millerite movement, worried terribly about publicizing his interpretation of the Book of Daniel. Maybe he realized how easy it is to gain followers, and how seldom they retain the power of independent thought. Whoever thought up the Prophecies of St Malachy may have known an uncanny thing or two, as did the Virgin Mary who appeared to two young children at La Salette and gave surprisingly well-vindicated messages about forthcoming crop blights and an epidemic that afflicted young children in the surrounding area. Skeptical I may be, but there are occasional prophecies, recorded before the events they foretell, that seem to have worked. I can't pretend that they didn't.

2

Favourite popular myths

Probably the most popular myth we could include here is astrology, the idea that movements of distant planets and stars influence human personalities and behaviour. *The Skeptic* has indeed covered astrology many times – and also other old favourites such as graphology, numerology, and reflexology. Here, however, the selection is a bit more broad and eclectic. We see why the belief that we only use 10 percent of our brains defies logic, and find out about the appearance of faces and canals on Mars and the disappearance of the sailors aboard the *Mary Celeste*. But first ... heard the one about Nostradamus predicting 9/11?

Nostradamus Said What?
David Hambling

For any major event there will always be people who can find it was predicted in the writings of sixteenth-century French 'seer' Nostradamus, and 9/11 was no exception. Writer **David Hambling**, *who specializes in scientific and military topics for publications including the* **Guardian**, *analysed the quatrains. Appeared XIV.4.*

Did Nostradamus foresee the attack on the World Trade Center, and does he predict terrible events to come? According to an email doing the rounds in September 2001, the sixteenth-century astrologer and cookery writer warns us:

> *In the year of the new century and nine months,*
> *From the sky will come a great King of Terror...*
> *The sky will burn at forty-five degrees.*
> *Fire approaches the great new city...*
>
> *In the city of York there will be a great collapse,*
> *2 twin brothers torn apart by chaos*
> *while the fortress falls the great leader will succumb*
> *third big war will begin when the big city is burning*

This would be quite amazing if it were accurate. In fact, the lines have been cobbled together from different sources and changed to fit the situation. The main body of Nostradamus's predictions are the *Centuries*, each of which contains one hundred four-line verses.

From *Century* 10, there is the famous quatrain 72:

> *The year 1999, seventh month,*
> *From the sky will come a great King of Terror:*

So we're a couple of years late on that one.

From *Century* 6, quatrain 97:

> *At forty-five degrees the sky will burn,*
> *Fire to approach the great new city:*

Except that New York is at 41 degrees latitude, not 45 degrees. Forty-five degrees would be more like Montreal, or, as it happens, Belgrade.

The next three lines are not Nostradamus at all. They come from Neil Marshall, a Canadian student who used them as an illustration of a vague prediction that could be interpreted many ways. His actual words were somewhat different:

> *In the city of GOD there will be a great THUNDER*
> *Two brothers torn apart by chaos*
> *While the fortress ENDURES the great leader*
> *will succumb*

(My emphasis on the changed words)

The final line, about the third big war, appears to be a complete fabrication. This kind of forgery is all quite unnecessary. With so many hundreds of quatrains to choose from, all written in cryptic ambiguities, you can always find something to fit the case with a little creative interpretation. *Century 2*, quatrain 83:

> *The Great Trade of a great Lyons changed,*
> *The most part turns to early ruin*
> *Prey to the soldiers swept away by pillage:*
> *Smoke through the mountains.*

The Great Trade' is the World Trade Center; 'a great Lyons' is New York (like Lyons it is not the capital but a major banking centre), and the 'mountains' are the skyscrapers of Manhattan. How amazingly accurate ... I may have creatively translated 'fog' as 'smoke' and left out the reference to Switzerland, but how many people are likely to notice that? Or that the quatrain was previously regarded as an uncannily accurate prediction of the siege of Lyons in 1795?

Myths of Secret Powers
Andrew Brice

Martial arts look really cool on film – and what about those mental powers that let expert practitioners break a pile of bricks with a single swipe of the hand? **Andrew Brice,** *a software engineer with a black belt in ju-jitsu, considers whether there are really mysterious energies that can be unlocked by studying martial arts. Appeared in VIII.4.*

The martial arts have long been surrounded by an aura of mystery and the esoteric. It is therefore not too surprising to find that many martial artists profess to a belief in mysterious energies outside the understanding of Western science. Many martial artists talk about 'chi' (in Chinese martial arts) or 'ki' (in Japanese martial arts), a mysterious energy that allows those who have mastered it to achieve miraculous feats not possible by physical prowess alone. But real evidence for the existence of this mysterious energy is thin on the ground or non-existent. So why do so many martial artists apparently believe in mysterious energies?

Most of the martial arts we practise today came originally from the Orient, where belief in supernatural spirits and energies was, and is, very strong. In fact, it is almost impossible to disentangle the history of some of the older martial arts from the mythologies of the countries in which they developed. It is therefore hardly surprising that this belief in the supernatural should have suffused the martial arts. Also, the techniques of the fighting arts were, until very recently, jealously guarded secrets. An opponent knowing your techniques could easily have made the difference between life and death in an encounter. Inevitably, wherever there is secrecy, rumours and wild stories abound. It is human nature to exaggerate – breaking an inch of pine with a punch can easily become breaking ten inches of pine with a touch after 'Chinese whispers' have taken effect. Claiming to be able to teach not just fighting ability, but mystical powers as well must also have been a big help for instructors looking to recruit students. They were hardly likely to have discouraged such stories.

So why do many people continue to believe in these stories in the late twentieth century? First, because their instructors tell them to, and the instructor is a figure of considerable authority in most clubs. These assertions may be backed up with demonstrations. The complexity of human psychology and physiology allows for many 'tricks', such as the instructor making himself/herself 'heavier'. The usual form this takes is for a student to lift the instructor using their hands under the instructor's armpits or elbows. The instructor will then make himself/herself 'heavier' and the student has a lot more trouble lifting him/her on the second occasion. This can look quite impressive, but it is hardly a rigorous test. I believe it is attributable to simple physiology and psychology. Since the lifts are repeated in quick succession, the student is more tired the second time. Relaxing the shoulders also makes the upward force more difficult to apply. There is also a strong element of suggestion (in fact one skeptical instructor claimed that he had duplicated this feat by suggestion alone), since a test on your own student is hardly a fair test.

Laying claim to esoteric knowledge increases the instructor's standing. His senior students may be stronger, suppler, and faster, but they don't have as much esoteric knowledge. Who can resist making themselves more important? Martial arts instructors are only human after all. Students also have their own reasons for believing in mysterious energies. If they exist, then there is the possibility for an average person to become an immensely powerful fighter without a great deal of strenuous training (I wish!). One only has to look through some martial arts magazines with their endless reviews of wish-fulfilment chop-sockey videos and adverts to 'build big muscles fast' and 'be successful with women' to realize that the martial arts have an almost irresistible pull for the credulous. Mysterious energies promise a short-cut to a much desired end. If mysterious energies don't exist then this means that victory is likely to go to the man (or woman) who is the biggest, strongest, fittest, and has trained the hardest. People want to believe in the irrational, and usually these beliefs are completely sincere. One only has to look at the popularity of crystal healing, Tarot, horoscopes, psychic surgery, miracle diets, 'end of the world' cults, the Bermuda triangle, and UFOs to see this. Martial artists are no exception to this phenomenon. In fact, if they have been drawn to the martial arts by its mystical lure they are likely to be especially susceptible.

Belief in mysterious energies could also be seen as part of a trend towards more and more 'flowery' techniques in some martial arts. As the martial arts become divorced from their original drastic purposes and become more of an end in themselves, techniques lacking in substance are less and less likely to face the harsh reality of combat. It is interesting to note that belief in mysterious forces seems to be inversely proportional to the competitive nature of a martial art. I hear little reference to chi from judoka, kick boxers, and others who are forced to face the true effectiveness of their technique against uncooperative opponents. I have a hunch that proponents of even 'soft' arts (those that have minimal reliance on physical force) that are competitive (for example, tomiki aikidoka and tai-chi practitioners who push hands competitively) talk about chi a good deal less than those who practise only on cooperative colleagues.

Beliefs also have their own momentum. The more of yourself you invest in a belief the harder it is to change. A friend who practises judo told me an amusing story that illustrates this well. A practitioner of one of the more esoteric martial arts (which it would be invidious to name, so I shall refer to it as 'X') told him that 'X was better than judo' so he suggested they put this to the test. After a few minutes, the X exponent staggered off rather battered and considerably the worse for wear mumbling 'Well, I still think X is better!' If you have spent years developing mysterious energies, then admitting they do not exist means admitting you have wasted a lot of time; this is very difficult. In fact it is often easier to ignore contrary evidence than it is to change your beliefs (this is given the grand term 'cognitive dissonance' by psychologists). Beliefs have a habit of entrenching themselves.

So if mysterious energies don't exist why hasn't the myth been dispelled by now? Can't I disprove the existence of chi? Not really. If I could show that a particular feat could be explained without any need for chi a believer could easily say 'Chi doesn't work on skeptics', or 'Just because that martial artist doesn't have chi doesn't mean no one else has', or 'He was having a bad day', and so on. This is a game we are probably all familiar with and one the skeptic can rarely win.

Few would deny that the opening up of the martial arts and improved understanding of nutrition and physiology have allowed martial artists to make great strides forward over the last few decades. I think it is high time that some of the claims made for mysterious energies were subjected to similar rational analysis. I am not suggesting for a second that all those who profess a belief in mysterious energies are charlatans or that they are not good martial artists. However, they might become even better martial artists if they spent less time 'developing their chi'. Martial artists can perform extraordinary feats, but we don't need metaphysics to explain them. It is time that mysterious energies were relegated firmly to martial arts mythology along with 10-metre jumps into the air.

The Ten-Percent Solution
Barry Beyerstein

*It's commonly said that we use only 10 percent of the capacity of our brains, a claim that, if true, ought to inspire much research into how to unlock the rest. It also can be, and is, taken to imply that paranormal powers might be hiding in that unused 90 percent. But do we really waste most of our brain power? Tackling this question is Canadian skeptic **Barry Beyerstein** (1947–2007), who was a professor in the Department of Psychology and the Brain Behaviour Laboratory at Simon Fraser University in Vancouver, British Columbia. He was a co-founder of the Committee for the Scientific Investigation of Claims of the Paranormal (now the Committee for Skeptical Inquiry), chair of the British Columbia Skeptics Society, and a prolific writer. Appeared in X.2. An earlier version of this article first appeared in the **Rational Enquirer**, the magazine of the British Columbia Skeptics.*

In debates with advocates of the paranormal, I frequently encounter a ploy that rests on the widely quoted, but never supported, assertion that normal people only use 10 percent of their brains. So, the argument continues, if we don't know what the remainder of the brain is there for, it could be the repository for awesome mental powers that only a few adepts have mastered. This enlightened minority could be tapping their latent cerebral potential to accomplish levitation, spoon-bending, clairvoyance, precognition, telepathy, psychic healing, and other fantastica scarcely conceivable to mere mortals condemned to subsist on the drudge-like 10 percent. Of course, the one-tenth figure is itself debatable, but even if it were accurate, it would in no way entail the existence of psychic powers, which must stand or fall on their own demonstrable merits. The 10 percent myth is so prevalent that I have become curious about its origins and why it persists despite its inherent improbability.

Attack of the factoids

As someone who spends much of his professional life pondering how the brain works, I am quite willing to admit the extent of our ignorance about how this kilo and a half of grey matter manages to produce thoughts, feelings, and behaviours. Nonetheless, I am at a loss to understand how my debating adversaries came to know with such pontifical certainty that we normally use only 10 percent of it. To the best of my knowledge, this alleged 'fact' appears nowhere in the literature of neurophysiology or physiological psychology. On the contrary, it is at variance with most of what we do know about the brain. The 'dormant brain' thesis seems to be another of those 'factoids' that accumulate a patina of believability through mere repetition. It has become firmly ensconced in the conventional wisdom, though no one who has cited it to me has ever been able to state who first said it or what evidence there is in its favour.

Logic alone should give pause to the 10-percenters. When asked if the 10 percent figure is true, I often respond, 'How well do you think you would continue to function if 90 percent of your brain were suddenly incapacitated?' The typically dismal responses implicitly concede the implausibility of the claim. We all know stroke victims who have lost considerably less brain tissue and are severely debilitated.

Furthermore, virtually all educated people now accept that the human brain is the product of millions of years of evolution. Given the conservatism of natural selection, it seems highly unlikely that scarce resources would be squandered to produce and maintain such an under-utilized organ. The brain is costly to run, consuming approximately a quarter of the metabolic resources of the resting body. How long would you endure paying huge power bills to heat all ten rooms of your home if you never strayed beyond the kitchen?

Safety in numbers

The brain has evolved a fair bit of redundancy in its circuitry as a safety precaution, but little, if any, of it lies perpetually fallow. The armamentarium of modern neuroscience decisively repudiates this notion. EEGs, CAT, PET, and MRI scans, magnetoencephalography, regional cerebral blood flow measures, and so on, all show that even during sleep there are no silent areas in the brain (see, for example, Per E Roland, *Brain Activation,* Wiley-Lisa, 1993). Such tranquillity would be a sign of gross pathology. We also know from these technologies and from studying the effects of head trauma that the brain is not an undifferentiated mass. Rather, distinct functions are distributed to different regions of the brain. According to the 10 percent scenario, 90 percent of each of these distributed functional areas would have to be unused in order not to lose certain functions totally in a 90 percent dormant brain. This seems highly implausible in light of animal research where electrodes are inserted directly into the brain to map its microcircuitry and localization of function.

Henry Ford once said, 'Whatever you have, you must use it or lose it.' Muscles atrophy from disuse and so, apparently, do brain circuits. My own research and that of many others indicates that neural systems deprived of normal input either fail to develop or deteriorate permanently. If 90 percent of our brains were really idle, we would expect massive areas of degeneration but no such signs show up in normal people on the various scanners mentioned above. Of course, the 10 percent utilization figure could refer instead to storage capacity, processing speed, or some other index of brain activity (rather than simply to volume) but I know of no way to determine the theoretical limits of such processes in order to estimate the average person's efficiency. At any rate, research suggests that it is not lack of storage capacity that hinders performance most; the bottleneck is more likely to be difficulty in retrieving what we've safely stored.

Ten percent nonsense

If the 10 percent figure makes no sense neurologically, I would suggest that this presumed neural tithing in ordinary people is, instead, a metaphor for widespread human longings. It is comforting to believe that we all have this latent potential, and this may explain in part why so many people cling to this dictum of neuro-mythology. In addition, the remarkable ability of developing brains to reorganize and recover from neural damage may also have contributed to the plausibility of the belief. For instance, young children have been known to recover a surprisingly high level of functioning after loss of an entire cerebral hemisphere to injury or disease. This is far less than 90 percent of their brains, of course, but because dead nerve cells are not replaced after birth, these patients must be making do with what remains, suggesting there might have been some unused parts. In fact, it seems instead that the functions of the destroyed areas actually 'crowd in' alongside those the undamaged portions were already handling, rather than colonizing previously unused areas. Immediately following the trauma, such children experience devastating disruptions of behaviour and consciousness but, gradually, most abilities, including language, recover quite substantially. Unfortunately, this ability of the remaining neural tissue to assume the additional duties of destroyed parts wanes with age, as a visit to any neurological ward will quickly convince you. Even among those who suffer brain damage as young children and regain near-normal functioning, some deficits do remain, although it sometimes requires fairly sophisticated tests to reveal these shortcomings. The ability to achieve such a high degree of recovery seems to be largely lost by the time of puberty. Much recent research has been devoted to finding ways to suppress certain features of mature brains that largely prevent adult neural tissue from re-establishing functional neural connections after brain damage. Popularized accounts of the dramatic recoveries of some of these young brain damage victims probably fuelled the misconception that they never really needed the extra brain tissue in the first place.

This misapprehension was reinforced in an otherwise informative TV documentary that aired on the Public Broadcasting System and the Knowledge Network in North America. It featured the Sheffield University paediatric researcher John Lorber and an extraordinary group of his patients. Referred to Lorber because of fairly minor neurological complaints, these young adults were of normal or above-normal intelligence and were coping well educationally and socially. Astonishingly, CAT scans had revealed that their cerebral hemispheres had been compressed into a slab only a few millimetres thick. The compression had been caused by enlargement of the underlying fluid-filled ventricles. This had probably occurred insidiously as the normally circulating cerebrospinal fluid dammed up behind constricted outflow channels over an extended period. The condition is known as hydrocephalus and if it is of very early onset and left untreated it will cause the entire head to balloon out in a grotesque fashion because the infant cranium has not yet calcified. Severe mental and behavioural retardation typically ensue. In Lorber's cases, the cranium had presumably already solidified by the time of onset of hydrocephalus – trapping the cerebral hemispheres literally 'between a rock and a hard place'. The absence of mental retardation in these young adults, despite their tremendous neural shrinkage, led Lorber and the producers of the show to ask the misleading question that, unfortunately, became the title of the episode: 'Is the Brain Really Necessary?'

What Lorber's remarkable cases demonstrate is not, as the documentary coyly suggests, the irrelevance of the brain to our mental lives, but rather the amazing ability of the brain to adjust to massive disruptions, providing they occur slowly enough and early enough in life. CAT scans cannot reveal how much of the thinning of the cerebral hemispheres in Lorber's patients was due to cellular loss and how much to compacting of brain cells into less than their normal volume. In addition, there is reason to believe that the greater share of cell loss in such cases may be among the supporting glial cells rather than in the neurons that actually mediate mental functions. The fact that these patients can get by with reduced brain volume does not imply that they wouldn't have put any additional tissue to good use had if been retained. I also suspect that their degree of normalcy may have been somewhat exaggerated for dramatic effect. Nonetheless, Lorber's cases are an eloquent testimonial to the resilience of the young brain and its ability to reorganize and carry on after major insults. Mature brains subjected to more rapid increases in intracranial pressure, due to growing tumours for instance, certainly show much more drastic impairments. Lorber's CAT scans also serve the useful purpose of reminding neurologists and neuropsychologists that deeper structures in the brain (which are largely spared in these cases) contribute more to our mental abilities than our fascination with cortical structures sometimes leads us to think.

Origins

Although the origins of the Great 10 Percent Myth remain obscure, it has long been a staple of self-improvement courses like those of the Dale Carnegie organization. It remains a popular selling point for the hawkers of Transcendental Meditation courses and a variety of crackpot 'brain-tuner' devices so dear to New Age entrepreneurs. The myth has been around for a long time. For instance, Dwight Decker, in a 1994 internet posting to the *sci.skeptic* Usenet newsgroup, noted that in the foreword to Dale Carnegie's *How to Win Friends and Influence People* (1936), the journalist Lowell Thomas cites the 10 percent myth and credits it to the pioneering psychologist William James (1842–1910). One of Decker's sources said he remembered James discussing it in his magnum opus, *The Principles of Psychology* (1890), although Decker and I have both been unable to find such a reference. What gave rise to James's idea that we only use 10 percent of our brains, the source said, were anecdotal accounts of people who had suffered drastic losses of brain tissue due to accidents or disease, or who had been born with conditions (such as hydrocephalus) that left them with very little brain tissue at all. Yet they seemed to function more or less normally (obviously, cases such as those reported by John Lorber have been known to neurologists for a long time as well). Although he tried diligently, Decker was unable to locate such a passage in any of James's better-known writings. Perhaps James could have uttered it in one of his many public addresses and was merely quoted (or misquoted) elsewhere. Decker has also located references to versions of the 10 percent figure in the 1911 edition *of Encyclopaedia Britannica* and the 1929 edition of the *World Almanac,* all of which shows that the misapprehension was already widespread in the early part of the twentieth century. However it may have arisen, belief in 'the myth' obviously caught on: it was canonized at mid-century by no less a personage than Albert Einstein who once uttered it as a speculative reply to the constant barrage of questions about the source of his brilliance.

I believe this vision of the largely vegetative brain acquired at least some of its spurious scientific gloss from laypersons' misinterpretations of early neurological experiments with lower animals. Pioneering studies by Karl Lashley, for instance, showed that large portions of rat cortex could be removed with apparently little disruption in behaviour (later tests did find deficits that weren't obvious with the earlier research methods). In the same vein, confusion regarding certain terms used by early comparative neurologists may have compounded this misinterpretation. With evolutionary advancement, the cerebrum of mammals has enlarged greatly but a progressively smaller proportion of it is concerned with strictly sensory or motor duties. This was demonstrated in the 1930s by electrically stimulating the exposed cortical surface in a variety of species from different levels of the evolutionary tree. Because the current was unable to evoke overt responses from these increasingly large non-sensory and non-motor areas in the so-called 'higher' species with larger brains, those areas were referred to by some researchers as 'silent cortex'. Obviously, they did not mean that these regions were literally silent or unused. As we have seen, they are anything but silent – these so-called 'association areas are responsible for our most uniquely human characteristics, including language and abstract thought.

Areas of maximal activity shift in the brain as we change tasks and vary attention and arousal but there are normally no dormant regions awaiting new assignments.

A final speculation about the origins of the 10 percent myth is that it might have been derived from misconstruals of rightfully modest admissions by neuroscientists concerning the limitations of our understanding. Despite the huge amount that we have learnt about the brain, it is only honest to confess how much remains to be discovered. Such modesty would have been even more appropriate at the dawn of the twentieth century, when 'the myth' seems to have taken hold. Possibly, some early investigator's (probably optimistic) estimate that researchers only knew what 10 per cent of the brain does may have been misread as an assertion that we normally only need or use 10 percent of it.

Cerebral spare tire

In the end, I think this persistent curiosity boils down, once again, to the comforting nature of most occult and New Age beliefs. It would be nice if they were true – death would have no sting and there would be no shortcomings in life, materially or mentally. The 10 percent myth suggests we could all be Einsteins, Rockefellers, or Uri Gellers if we could just engage that ballast between our ears! This 'cerebral spare tire' concept continues to nourish the clientele of 'pop psychologists' and their many recycled self-improvement schemes. As a metaphor for the fact that few of us fully exploit our talents, who could deny it? As a spur to hope and a source of solace it has probably done more good than harm, but comfort afforded is not truth implied. As a refuge for occultists seeking the neural basis of the miraculous, the probability is considerably less than 10 percent.

The *Mary Celeste* Revisited
Alan Hunt

What happened to the ship Mary Celeste (not to be confused with Sir Arthur Conan Doyle's entirely fictional Marie Celeste), found floating empty in the Atlantic Ocean in early December 1872, is an enduring maritime mystery. In writing about it for an earlier issue (VII.6), London writer Brian Haines was unable to provide an explanation. Alan Hunt, a London writer, part-time lecturer at City University and the Working Man's College, a former civil servant at the Department of Education and Science, took up the challenge. Appeared in VIII.5.

The *Mary Celeste* remains a considerable mystery of the sea. It is surely extraordinary that a ship in reasonably good shape should have been abandoned by her crew for the hazards of a small boat on the open seas. It is surprising to realize today how small these ocean-going sailing ships really were. The *Mary Celeste* was little more than 100 feet long with a tonnage of approximately 280. The brigantine left New York Harbour on 5 November 1872 with a cargo of 1,700 (or 1,701) barrels of alcohol. This would not have been drinkable.

The master of the *Mary Celeste* was a Captain Briggs, who was a part-owner of the ship (possessing one-third of the shares in a small consortium that owned the ship). The captain's wife and small daughter were aboard along with a crew of seven. It has been reported that on the night before leaving New York, Briggs and his wife dined with a Captain Morehouse of the *De Gratia*. The seamen were old friends. During the loading of the *Mary Celeste*, the long boat, which normally hung on davits over the stern, was damaged. One small boat remained, which was lashed on top of the main hatch.

The *De Gratia* left New York a week later, its first port of call being Gibraltar, the same as that of the *Mary Celeste*. On 5 December, the *De Gratia* sighted a ship in difficulties. Getting no response, three of the crew boarded the troubled ship, which proved to be the *Mary Celeste*. It was deserted. There were no lifeboats, and there was water in the hold. It was decided that the water could be pumped out and the ship sailed to Gibraltar, the purpose being to collect salvage. The *Mary Celeste*, with its crew of three, arrived at Gibraltar on Friday 13 December, one day after the *De Gratia*. The claim for salvage was referred to the Admiralty Court, the President of which was a Queen's Advocate by the name of Solly Flood, who suspected an insurance fraud. Three months later, salvage was awarded but at approximately one-fifth of the value of the ship and its cargo. Some plausible solutions may be summarized as follows:

1. There was a criminal conspiracy to perpetrate an insurance swindle.
2. There was a mutiny. The Captain, his wife and child, and the Chief Mate were killed and thrown overboard. The mutineers abandoned ship and for obvious reasons never later revealed themselves.
3. The *Mary Celeste* was abandoned in a state of panic.

It makes most sense to me to seriously consider informed opinion of the time rather than wild theories concocted by non-experts at a much later date. Such commentators have nearly always given Flood a bad press. It is my guess that Flood was nobody's fool. He had a good knowledge of the kind of skulduggery that could happen on the high seas.

Flood seems to have considered solutions (1) and (2), and the inquiry at Gibraltar dragged on for three months. It is possible that Flood believed that some of the missing crew would appear alive. The strongest argument against Captain Briggs being involved in an insurance fraud is that he was part-owner of the *Mary Celeste*. This is not as simple as it sounds. He had probably borrowed the money for his third share in the syndicate owning the *Mary Celeste* from a man named Simon Hart who is later quoted as part-owner. The owner of the other two-thirds was a Captain J. H. Winchester, who went to the Gibraltar inquiry to protect his own interests. Winchester, after giving testimony at the inquiry during an adjournment, went to Cádiz, ostensibly for pleasure, giving the impression that he would return to Gibraltar. Captain Winchester turned up in New York a month later. The family of the missing Chief Mate Richardson thought that either a mutiny or a criminal conspiracy held the clue to the disappearance of the crew. It should be remembered that it was an age when ship-owners often sent men to sea in 'coffin' ships hoping to claim insurance.

Following the completion of the inquiry, the *New York Sun* of 12 March 1873 stated under the headline 'The Abandoned Ship' that the explanation was 'No Mutiny but a scheme to defraud the Insurance Company'. A reporter claimed that the *Mary Celeste* had been improperly cleared and sailed under false colours after leaving port. Reference is made to the proceedings of the inquiry about a ship or vessel 'supposed to be the *Mary Celeste*'. It seems unbelievable that those who boarded the *Mary Celeste* did not seem to identify the ship until they had boarded her. Was her name not painted on the stern? No evidence was given that she was flying the United States flag, and no mention is made of the flag in the detailed inventory.

The inquiry took such a long time that Captain Morehouse decided that his cargo should be delivered to Genoa. He put Deveau in charge of the *De Gratia* while he remained to fight the salvage claim. Deveau was of course one of the principal witnesses, whereas Morehouse had remained on the *De Gratia*. Although Deveau did return to Gibraltar this was not true of one of the crew who had boarded the *Mary Celeste*. He was said to have damaged his back while unloading in Genoa and was not fit to return. Flood was furious. He could not believe that the *Mary Celeste* had remained on course after being abandoned on 25 November. He was aware that Briggs and Morehouse were old friends. The Naval historian J. G. Lockhart has said that they dined together the night before the *Mary Celeste* left port. There would seem to be evidence to support some kind of insurance swindle.

The evidence to support a hasty abandonment of the ship seems even stronger. Missing from the abandoned ship were the chronometer and sextant, as well as a navigation book. The boat that had been lashed to the main hatch had been taken. Flood could not believe that an unmanned ship could have remained on course for eleven days. But what if the log had not been kept up to date? If the weather was bad the crew may have been so busy that they intended to make the log up later. Perhaps the skeleton crew on the *Mary Celeste* would not make up the log until they neared Gibraltar. All the evidence supports the idea that the *Mary Celeste* was abandoned in a hurry. Although the Captain's navigational instruments had been taken, the bulk of the crew's personal possessions had been left behind. This suggests a hasty leaving, or a belief that they would return, or both. It is likely that the small boat was attached to the *Mary Celeste* with the intention of returning when the immediate danger was over. We know that the ship's boat was not attached in the normal manner. We might guess that at some point the towing rope snapped, leaving the unfortunate occupants adrift in the open sea.

There are two theories to explain the sudden desertion of the larger ship. The most usual of these is that Captain Briggs feared an explosion might occur. The cargo of alcohol may have become volatile. This sometimes happened when ships of such type passed through varying temperatures. A process called 'dunnage' could occur, when ice melted in warmer temperature and released fumes. This was accompanied with loud crackling which might be mistaken for fire below. One hatch at least had been removed on the *Mary Celeste*; it may have been deliberately removed to allow fumes to escape, or been blown off. Captain Winchester supported the alcohol fumes theory, as did the widow of Captain Morehouse when quoting her dead husband's opinion in 1926.

The other theory to explain the hurried leaving of the ship is that the *Mary Celeste* became 'becalmed' and was in danger of being carried onto to rocks by treacherous currents. Captain Morehouse has also been quoted in support of this theory as has Captain James Briggs, the brother of the missing captain.

Should it be thought unlikely that an experienced captain would leave a larger boat for the open seas in a small boat, it is interesting to consider that in 1919 the schooner *Marion Douglas* was abandoned off Newfoundland yet managed to cross the Atlantic, and was towed in for salvage after being found off the Scilly Isles. Even more recently, and more amazingly, a Greek tanker, on New Year's Eve 1978, was thought to be in trouble. Thirty-seven of the crew took to the boats and perished in the sea. Three members stayed on board and survived.

There is another point of interest. The mystery of the abandoned ship is older than the *Mary Celeste*. As we have today 'urban myths', so there are traditional myths of the sea. *The Times* of 6 November 1840 is said to have reported that a large French vessel, *The Rosalie,* was found abandoned by a coaster, on or about 26 August. The greater part of her sails were set and she did not seem to have sustained any damage. The cargo was still in perfect condition although there was about three feet of water in the hold. This is about the same as in the case of the *Mary Celeste* although this may well have been average for the typical sailing ship. There was a cat, some fowl, and a canary on board. Everything pointed to a hasty abandonment of the ship, no member of the crew being on board. The truth of this story may be doubtful but it does seem to indicate an earlier example of a myth which is later echoed by the *Mary Celeste*. The recent version was circulated by the indefatigable Charles Fort. Lawrence Kusche, in his *The Bermuda Triangle Mystery – Solved*, reveals that Lloyds of London could find no record of such an incident; nor could the Musée de la Marine in Paris.

We are left with the tantalizing possibility that the story of the deserted ship had been told in the bars in the ports where seamen gathered for many years before 1872. Did a group of conspirators take this myth and give it a spurious reality in an ingenious attempt at an act of piracy or an insurance fraud?

Behind the Red Planet
Paul Chambers

*Some myths owe their existence to imperfect technology. As **Paul Chambers**, author of a number of books about the paranormal, explains, the Martian 'canals' and the 'face on Mars' are two such. Higher-resolution telescopes and better quality photography showed these up for what they were: artefacts of the human ability to see patterns where none exist. Keep this in mind every time you see a TV show where the heroes apply fantasy 'computer enhancement' techniques to turn a few pixels of a fuzzy, low-resolution CCTV image into a high-resolution, zoomed-in image that shows the words written on a pill in someone's hand in ultra-sharp relief. Appeared in XII.3-4.*

In April 1998 NASA's Mars Surveyor probe returned a number of high-resolution photographs taken of features on the northern Cydonia Plain of Mars. For over 20 years these photographs had been eagerly awaited by both occultists and astronomers and it was hoped that they might settle a long-running debate about whether an alien intelligence had left its mark on the surface of Mars. In the event, the new photographs not only settled this outstanding question, but also proved to be the final chapter in a modern story that shows a strange parallel to a similar debate that occurred over a hundred years ago.

Since the late 1970s a minor cult has developed around a series of photographs taken by the Mars Surveyor's predecessor, the Viking mission, which spent nearly six years mapping the Martian surface using two orbiting satellites. This cult is centred around a landform that was photographed by Viking on the northern Cydonia Plain of Mars. This feature resembles a human face and has been heralded as proof positive that extraterrestrial life once existed in our solar system. Indeed, the whole affair has become quite an industry which is collectively known as the 'face on Mars'.

Now that, as we shall see, the face on Mars controversy has been resolved to the satisfaction of most, it can be seen that the whole saga bears a remarkable similarity to one of the most embarrassing episodes in astronomical history, that of the canals on Mars.

The canals on Mars

The term *canali*, meaning waterway in Italian, was first used by Angelo Secchi in 1858 to describe a series of features on the Martian surface that he assumed to be large rivers or inland seas. In 1877, another Italian astronomer, Giovanni Schiaparelli, produced the first detailed map of Mars which included a number of dark straight lines that criss-crossed their way across the lighter regions of the planet. In common with Secchi, he believed them to be waterways and also called them *canali*. The *canali* caused much debate among the astronomy community of the time. English and Irish astronomers generally refused to believe in their reality, while Americans and continental Europeans not only believed in them, but spent hours trying to map them. At no point did anybody try to suggest that they were anything other than natural features, and it was not until 1894, when Boston businessman Percival Lowell took an interest, that they were connected with an extraterrestrial civilization.

Lowell, in common with many English-speaking astronomers, had mistranslated *canali* into the word canal, which implied an artificial origin for the structures. Using an observatory that he had built himself in Arizona, Lowell set about mapping and measuring the canals. Within a year he had produced a book, *Mars*, linking the canals to a dying race of Martians who had built the canals to transport melt water from the planet's polar ice caps to more fertile ground around the equator. In subsequent books *(Mars as the Abode for Life, Mars and its Canals)* Lowell claimed to be able to see the seasonal spread of vegetation following the melt water down the canals and even the cities that the canals were feeding. Eventually, Lowell surmised that the transformation of Mars from a once exotic and watery world into a dying desert held an omen for the Earth which, he concluded, would one day end up as barren and desert-like as Mars.

At every stage Lowell would use calculations, based on his telescope observations, to reinforce his theories, most of which were hopelessly wide of the mark, including his famous description of the Martian climate as being 'like that of southern England'.

He was also quite capable of changing his theories to suit the latest scientific opinion about Mars. For example, when it was discovered that the dark regions of Mars could not be vast oceans as was previously thought, his theory changed to make them dried-out ocean basins which had dark layers of vegetation growing in them. Lowell had many backers but, unfortunately for him, few of them were astronomers and many of them tried to steal his glory by coming up with more and more outrageous theories, particularly to do with contacting the Martians, until no astronomer would touch the issue with a barge pole.

The end of the canals came about due to a combination of things. One of these was Lowell's claim to have seen structures similar to the canals on Venus – something that was blatantly impossible due to the high temperatures there. Shortly after this, in 1900, Edward Maunder and John Evans devised an experiment which proved that when a series of loosely spread dots on a sheet of card were viewed from a distance they joined together to form canal-like networks. After this it was quickly realized that the poor optical quality of telescopes was causing smaller features on Mars, such as canyons and craters, to join up to give the impression of canals. This was confirmed in 1965 when Mariner IV sent back the first pictures of the Martian surface with not a canal or Martian to be seen.

The face on Mars

In 1976, ninety-nine years after Schiaparelli published his *canali* map, the Viking orbiter returned a picture of the northern Cydonia Plain to Earth. A NASA technician noticed that one of the features on the plain resembled a human face and, with NASA ever keen to generate publicity for its costly ventures, the photograph was released to the press as a curio. Very quickly, rumours started up about the face that linked it to pyramid-shaped features to the west of it. To scotch the rumours NASA acted quickly, claiming that the face had been photographed from a different angle and was nothing more than a hill.

The issue was dropped until, in 1982, two engineers searched all 68,000 Viking photographs looking for further evidence of the face. They found seven in total (two high-resolution, five low-resolution), all of which showed the face as it had first been published in 1976. Although this was probably because the angle of the sun was approximately the same when these photographs were taken, they wrote a book linking the face to ancient Egypt. As with the canals, it took a flamboyant publicist to move the issue of the face from relative obscurity into the public domain.

Richard C. Hoagland, a journalist, examined the NASA photographs and saw not just the face, but a whole series of artificial features on the Cydonia Plain. These include a city of pyramids, a spiral dome (called Tholus), one large isolated pyramid (called the D and M pyramid), the face, and a linear feature called the cliff.

In a scenario that seems to draw much from Arthur C. Clark's *2001: A Space Odyssey,* Hoagland declared that the Cydonia landforms were built 500,000 years ago by a race of transient aliens who had left a message for humanity in their ruins. By drawing straight lines between the Cydonia landforms, Hoagland found a geometric significance in the angles between them and deduced that the ruins were indicating that the latitude of 19.5° (the latitude that corresponds with the intersection of three vertices of a polar-oriented tetrahedron and its circumsphere) was significant. On this latitude on Mars is Olympus Mons, the solar system's largest volcano, while on Earth can be found the Hawaiian volcano chain. On other planets this latitude was associated with features such as Jupiter's Red Spot and the Great Dark Spot of Neptune. Hoagland now believes that this latitude marks the location of a vortex that can provide the Earth with infinite power once we have learned how to utilize it. In the meantime, the face on Mars bandwagon is rolling on with the feature now being linked to ancient astronauts, government conspiracies, and, most bizarre, proof that Elvis has visited Mars! I won't comment on David Percy's assertion that the features on the Cydonia Plain match those of the Avebury Circle – or Eric Crew's assertion that they form a map of our solar system.

Compare and contrast

The similarities between the two episodes are quite uncanny, something that owes more to the stupidity of human nature than any supernatural synchronicity. For a start, the controversy behind both began almost exactly one hundred years apart and look set to be resolved nearly one hundred years apart as well. Each case was initiated by an announcement from an astronomer that was picked up by amateur pseudoscientists and interpreted as being evidence of life on Mars. This was then taken, reinforced with further, less convincing evidence (for example, the seasonal spread of vegetation with the canals and the pyramids near the face), and then heavily promoted to the general public in a series of books and lectures by a highly charismatic personality who claimed to have the backing of science but in fact did not. Once in the public domain, the issue was added to by other interested parties until what was originally a simple astronomical observation ended up reading like a Hollywood science fiction script. The canals went from being rivers to a vast network of artificial waterways and cities feeding a dying planet, while the face went from being an amusing example of simulacra to evidence of an ancient race of aliens trying to communicate their secrets to humanity using planetary geometry.

Perhaps the reason behind the similarity in the rise to prominence of both issues is the rather hazy nature of their evidence. The canals were only ever viewed distantly through telescopes and, although the issue was effectively resolved by 1900, their existence could not be fully denied until Mariner IV visited the planet in 1965. A major problem with the canals was that not everybody could see them. In order to overcome difficulties people were having in seeing and interpreting the canals, Lowell and others would draw endless maps of them that were very subjective – impossibly detailed given the quality of telescopes at the time.

Similarly, the landform that makes the face on Mars is only 1.8 km in diameter and at the edge of the Viking's photographic resolution. On the original photographs the face is a very blurred and indistinct feature whose interpretation is open to question. Many of the other features on the Cydonia Plain, including the city, Tholus, and the D and M pyramid are smaller than the face and even more out-of-focus. To overcome this, many computer enhancements have been made of that region of the Cydonia Plain which have sharpened the shadow boundaries, increased the contrast, lessened the grain, and filled in details missing on the original photographs. All of this makes the images look sharper and gives the landforms straighter lines and darker shadows and therefore makes them look more artificial.

Subsequent attempts to remove the shadows and to alter the angle of view of the face are computer-generated reconstructions which, considering the limited of amount information in the original Viking photographs, have little basis in fact, although many people still view the results of statistical analyses as being definite conclusions, which they most certainly are not. Statistics, particularly multi-variate techniques such as fractal analysis, are designed to help researchers look at specific areas of their data more closely, not to give definite answers. In the case of the Cydonia analysis, this means that the fact that Mark Carlotto's fractal analysis highlighted the face and other features does not mean that they are artificial, but merely that they fit the criteria laid down in the algorithm of the original computer program. Also, it is unusual that the fractal analysis does not highlight any of the meteorite craters that litter the Cydonia Plain. Being perfectly circular, these should achieve a high score using fractal analysis but do not. Apart, that is, from one small and rather unremarkable crater that Carlotto calls 'the bowl', and which, he feels, may have some similarities to 'a Mesoamerican pyramid'.

Mysteriously, a much better defined crater, located a kilometre or so to the east of the face, is not highlighted at all by the same analysis.

In addition to enhancing their visual evidence, the supporters of both the canals and the face have used mathematics as a means of reinforcing their theories. Percival Lowell added thick appendices to his books on Mars, which were stuffed full of mathematical equations that, according to him, proved everything from the rate of cooling for all the planets to the composition and pressure of the Martian atmosphere. Almost without exception, everything Lowell calculated has now been proved wrong.

In order for his canals to exist, Lowell needed his equations to prove that Mars was a habitable planet. Since then, however, the large amount of data sent back by the Viking, Pathfinder, and other probes showed Mars to be an inhospitable place with sub-zero temperatures, a thin atmosphere with no ultra-violet screening and, most importantly, no liquid water. As supporters of the face are using NASA data, they cannot argue that the surface of Mars is currently a pleasant place to live. How, then, could there be a living alien civilization up there now? To overcome this, Hoagland used astronomical alignments to calculate that the face was built 500,000 years ago and that its builders had left geometric clues in the landscape.

Hoagland's use of geometry on the Cydonia Plain is interesting. It should be obvious to anybody that using straight lines to join random features on a map will produce geometric shapes. Join any three objects and you get a triangle, superimpose geometrical shapes onto non-linear landforms (such as a pentagon that was superimposed on the so-called 'D and M pyramid') and you end up with rigid geometrical shapes on paper where none exist on the planet's surface. Geometry, after all, is a branch of mathematics concerned with the properties of lines, curves, and surfaces and therefore once you have geometrical shapes it is relatively easy to find a mathematical significance within them. The latitude of the sites, so highly regarded by Hoagland, is also a function of planetary geometry and again it is easy to find mathematical significance in them.

Why is the use of mathematics so crucial to both the canals and face? The probable answer is because it appears to add independent scientific evidence to the arguments and because these theories are difficult for a non-mathematician to argue against. Many areas of the paranormal are shored up with apparently complex theories that use quantum physics, mathematics, or genetics that non-specialists find hard to argue against. If, however, a specialist does place convincing arguments against a paranormal theory they can always be accused of being part of the international scientific conspiracy against extraterrestrial intelligence. In the case of the face, the nature of the published evidence makes it hard to verify the mathematical claims and Mark Carlotto even wrote in his section on mathematics, 'Please note that the diagrams in this section are included for illustrative purposes only, and are not sufficiently precise to serve as a basis for testing the claims presented here.'

Although there are other more minor similarities between the canals and the face, there is one further similarity that, to my mind, seals their fate.

In the 1890s, at the height of the public interest in the canals, five mediums (independently of each other) claimed to have mentally visited Mars or to have spoken to Martians. Without exception, they reported a desert world inhabited by a dying race of aliens, some of whom were building canals to try and save themselves. These descriptions are identical to those then being promoted by Percival Lowell in his best-selling books on the canals on Mars.

One hundred years later, in the 1990s, we have a similar group of psychics, now called remote viewers, who claim to have visited Mars and in particular the Cydonia Plain. This time they have not found any trace of the canals or dying aliens, but instead large pyramids 'laid out in a specific geometric pattern' that were built by beings that were 'moving through our solar system and had to move onto a different location'. These are pretty accurate descriptions of Hoagland's (and others') theories concerning the face. In other words, the mediums and remote viewers are merely reflecting contemporary occult thinking about life on Mars.

Like the canals in their day, the face on Mars affair is rapidly gathering more and more unsubstantiated and esoteric theories, making it a scientifically untouchable subject. Negative attention meant that debate about the canals was abandoned by the astronomical community and the subject was left to amateurs and pseudoscientists. The same is now true of the face with few, if any, planetary scientists even bothering to comment on the issue at all.

The issue of the canals was settled to the satisfaction of most astronomers in 1900 with Maunder and Evans' experiment. The face on Mars was solved to the satisfaction of all astronomers in 1998. Given this, what will become of the considerable number of people currently financing themselves with their claims of extraterrestrial life on Mars?

Some have already claimed that NASA has conspired to remove vital information from the Mars Surveyor photographs, but most, to be frank, have simply ignored the newer photographs in favour of the older Viking ones. In 1998, Graham Hancock produced the number one bestseller *The Mars Mystery*, which, despite hastily added comments about the Mars Surveyor results, advocates alien intervention in human affairs. Fuelled by Hancock's success, a new generation of Mars books followed in 1999.

Other members of the face on Mars community have simply moved onto bigger and better topics. A new campaign claims that the moon-landings were faked, while others believe that evidence of extraterrestrial cities has been air-brushed out of the Apollo photographs. The world of the paranormal seems able to support such contradictions, and reasoned arguments against them have little or no effect.

3

What ever Happened to ... ?

There are fashions in belief as there are in everything else. How often do you hear now about biorhythms, crop circles, the Cottingley Fairies, the Fox sisters, the Turin Shroud, or Carlos Castaneda? Yet all of these commanded many headlines in their day.

Sometimes, ideas fall out of fashion because they've been thoroughly debunked. Crop circles, for example, got a lot less interesting when Doug Bower and Dave Chorley confessed to making many (if not most) of the most famously mysterious formations. In other cases, such as spirit photography and physical mediumship, more widespread familiarity with the technology they rely on dates them as quickly as the computer-generated special effects in a 1990s movie.

Since learning from other people's mistakes is the cheapest way to learn from experience, this section takes a retrospective look at some of the excitements of the past.

The Summer of '91
Martin Hempstead

*In the late 1980s to early 1990s, crop circles were an annual summer phenomenon, practically tailor-made for a press hungry each year for stories to fill space during the 'silly season'. Every year the circles got more elaborate – and in response so did the theories attempting to explain them. **Martin Hempstead**, a physicist and member of the Wessex Skeptics, was one of an indefatigable team who tried to make sense of the phenomenon in the midst of all the media excitement. By the summer of 1991, the Wessex Skeptics had become frustrated with the group's lack of progress at debunking cerealogists' increasingly wild theories about the circles' origin, and decided to take matters into their own hands. This account is taken from a much longer talk Hempstead gave at the fundraising dinner at the third Euroskeptics Congress, held in Amsterdam in 1991, only a few weeks after Doug Bower and Dave Chorley admitted they'd made many or most of the best-known formations. By 1994 it was possible to write the history of the crop circle phenomenon as a hoax, although it took some years longer for interest to fade. Probably no one misses the theories about intelligent plasma vortices or extraterrestrial origins, but there's one thing about crop circles almost no other paranormal phenomenon can say for itself: they sure made great photographs. Appeared in VIII.1–2.*

Impatient with our lack of progress, in the summer of 1991 we finally decided on a high-risk strategy. This was to hoax our own circles, and see if the experts could tell the difference. This was high-risk, because failure might prove nothing more than our own incompetence, yet discredit the skeptical viewpoint.

First we had to practise the techniques. With the assistance of *National Geographic,* visiting England to make a film about crop circles, we rented a field from a friendly farmer (a rare commodity in Wiltshire these days) and made a pictogram. In broad daylight, on a sunny Saturday afternoon. We were buzzed by planes, helicopters, and microlites. Even this level of observation did not stop certain members of the Centre for Crop Circle Studies from declaring it genuine – in fact one gentleman did so when overflying it a couple of days later. Other members, while aware the main pattern was artificial, became convinced that a ring had appeared mysteriously some time later outside our main circle. Furthermore, this ring was said, darkly, to be 'too narrow to be made by trampling'. In fact, it was made just that way, and only minutes after the main circle. I am still not sure that we have convinced them all that we made it!

What were our techniques? Mostly simple and obvious ones, really. A bit of string held by a central person while another described a circle. Trampling. Sticks and rollers to lay the corn. Sighting on a distant object to make the straight corridors. We found that it was not especially difficult to get through the corn without leaving a trail, particularly if you walk along the seed lines and turn around every metre or so to re-entangle the plants by brushing them gently with a stick. We concluded that a garden roller was the best tool, since if used with care it would lay the corn without unnecessary damage. We determined to try again, this time for real.

Fortunately, we were successful, though not at first. Our first attempt was thrilling, and performed without the farmer's permission (we did send the farmer compensation anonymously a week or two later). We wanted to see if hoaxing was possible under the pressure of fear of being caught; we also wanted to avoid asking a farmer to lie, as he or she would need to do if the test were to be effectively blind to the experts. We picked a field on top of a hill near Marlborough. It was a beautiful, crisp night, and the sky was clear with a full moon. Every sound frightened us. Many cars passed, causing us to spend much of our time crouching down in fear of detection. We got hot, tired, and frustrated – our chosen field was muddy and had very deep tramlines. We changed our plans, dropping our elaborate pattern and doing just a huge circle with a ring and a small circle some way off. And we were rumbled – a car stopped! Some people got out, but they soon left, and we thought we had got away with it. Only later did we discover we had been spotted. As we squatted in the damp at the edge of the field, waiting for our getaway car we were filled with undeserved euphoria at our imagined success. It truly was a beautiful night, and we were rewarded for our endeavours by the sound of a female fox screaming its chilling, almost human, cry.

Even though we were discovered by circle watchers, and word got around very fast, we were not stopped or apprehended, which was interesting in itself. Some members of CCCS did not get the news in time, and declared the circle genuine. Many members of the public were impressed, and a few unwitting dowsers found their rods stirring.

Why crop circles should dowse is unclear – something to do with earth energies or ill-defined electromagnetic anomalies, apparently. I have witnessed the replication problems of the dowsing technique at first hand. At Alton Barnes last year, I watched with some amusement as a couple of dowsers compared notes in one of the circles. The woman had found a distinct vortex, and her rods were whirling to back her up, whereas the man had found the same spot to be devoid of activity, and his pendulum hung limply. That dowsing is so heavily implicated in circles 'research' is just a symptom of the subjective nature of these investigations.

But I digress. Chastened with failure, not because our circle had failed to meet the experts' criteria but rather because they were not forced to work blind, we were a bit lacking in eagerness to try again. But the despondency soon passed, and we started plotting again. We were to be filmed for the TV program *Equinox,* and we decided to get the permission of a farmer this time.

We were lucky enough to find just the man we needed – someone who would be willing to dissemble to all and sundry and be convincing with it!

Once again, things started off badly and moved further and further from our well-laid plans. We had scouted the terrain beforehand, checked the tramlines and prepared an appropriate plan. But when we got there, we found that much of the field had, ironically, been laid low by wind damage, and we had to redesign fast. Our problems were doubled when the TV crew did not maintain an appropriate demeanour for the situation; they barged through the corn, interviewing us as we worked and flooding the field in light. Since Wiltshire was infested with circle spotters, we were sure we would be found out. As if to make sure that even if the TV crew failed to give the game away, word would still get out, we accidentally left some string in the field. Fortunately, the farmer removed this the next morning.

We were again despondent; one of us had laid the corn the wrong way, pointing towards the centre of the circle, and the TV crew had trampled through the corn. We were sure that we had made a crude hoax, and that nobody would be fooled by it. Boy, were we wrong! We were still guilty of overestimating the objectivity of the experts.

It took a while for the experts to find it, because it wasn't visible from the road, but within two weeks we had proven that it was possible to mislead the experts, including some who had so far remained immune from the taint of error. Busty Taylor of CCCS found it genuine, and emphasized the departure of the large central pattern from true circularity as the mark of authenticity.

Terence Meaden, who had publicly resisted the possibility that he could be mistaken in his judgement of circles, not only found our fabrication credible, but that it 'fit perfectly the scientific theory I have been putting forward for the last ten years', and was '100 percent genuine'. He stressed how many hoaxes he had seen, and marvelled at the classic layering patterns (another mark of authenticity, according to the experts). He was interviewed in the circle, and brought reporters to see it. A medium flown in from Paris by a producer from Paramount found the energies overwhelming – she developed a headache and had to leave. Dowsers' tools went wild in the circle. (Of course, we can't deny that a lot of psychic energy may well have been trapped in the circle – there was quite a lot of cursing and swearing the night we made it!)

This was not the first time the experts had been misled – Pat Delgado and Colin Andrews had several times in the past been wrong in their claims that circles are genuine – but it was the first that we knew of for Terence Meaden, and proved that the features alleged to be impossible to simulate were in fact quite easy to reproduce. We are now of the firm opinion that there is no substance to the experts' claims that they can distinguish a category of circles for which hoaxing is impossible.

Admittedly, we have never entered a 'fresh' circle, one that has had no sightseers. We have been told by Meaden of a complete absence of collateral damage in these cases. If this is true, we could probably not reproduce them with our present techniques. We always found a small number of damaged plants, in which the stalk was bent in more than one place. On the other hand, damaged plants do not prove hoaxing – in one field, for example, we observed that even in stands of fresh corn some of the plants were damaged. Moreover, it is always possible to remove them, if one is sufficiently patient.

So this was the situation at the end of August 1991– we knew that the experts could be fooled and had, as far as we could tell, no method for reliably distinguishing 'true' circles. We had preliminary evidence that crop circles had not existed for very long. We also knew that our organizational skills needed a little polishing!

Pearce 1 bottom right: He's "aligning" the compost bags again. (Appeared 13.3-4).

Explaining the Shroud: Steve Donnelly Interviews Joe Nickell

When the Turin Shroud was put on display in Turin Cathedral in 1978 more than 3.5 million pilgrims flocked to see it. In 1988, the Holy See agreed to permit the shroud to be independently carbon-dated by three teams, in Oxford, Zurich, and Arizona. The results indicated clearly that the shroud is a piece of linen woven between AD 1260 and 1390, dates that match the shroud's first known public appearances. Most skeptics consider that the image on the shroud of an apparently crucified man was unambiguously proved to be a medieval forgery, albeit one clever enough to form a lasting image with some of the properties of a photographic negative. Others, however, continue to argue that the shroud is between thirteen hundred and three thousand years old. Two weeks before the official 1988 announcement of the carbon-dating results, **Steve Donnelly** *interviewed Joe Nickell, a research fellow for the Committee for Skeptical Inquiry and author of* **Inquest on the Shroud of Turin,** *for the BBC Radio 4 programme* **Science Now.** *This is an edited transcript. Appeared in II.6.*

SD: The aspect of the shroud which is in the news at the moment is the carbon dating, but what I'd like to talk about are the various hypotheses which have been put forward to explain the image. The reason for this is that, assuming that the question of the dating has been settled, I think the question in everybody's mind is going to be, how did the image get there if it wasn't by miraculous means at the time of Christ? Could you tell us a little about the various hypotheses that have been put up over the decades or over the centuries to account for the image?

JN: Of course, the shroud first came to light in the Middle Ages and the earliest report is a bishop's report to Pope Clement that the forger had been found, and had confessed, and so the earliest claims are that the shroud image was cunningly painted. But when the shroud was first photographed by Secondo Pia in 1898 it was found that the darks and lights on the negative were reversed. That is to say that when you looked at the glass plate negative you saw a positive rather than a negative image, and so the modern era of shroud studies really began there with people asking how it could be possible for a forger to produce a photographic negative in the Middle Ages. Actually, the question is a little bit of a bogus one because it isn't a true photographic negative. There are blank spaces in the image that would not be in a photographic image. Also the colour of the hair is reversed, so that in a positive image Jesus looks like a white haired and white bearded old man. But putting that aside, the earliest obvious theory that would be consistent with the shroud being genuine was that it was simply an imprint made from the body being covered with the burial spices myrrh and aloes, and that this had caused an imprint on the shroud. The problem is, as I've found by experimenting along those lines, that you get a severe wraparound distortion.

That is, when you press a cloth around a three-dimensional form like the human face with the nose sticking out the way it does, you get severe distortions with elongated eye sockets and other distortions that are really rather grotesque.

SD: So it's a bit like a projection of the Earth's surface onto a flat plane?

JN: It is a mapping type problem, yes, and it is such a severe problem there is no way of getting around it. Also, people realized later that there were places which had been imprinted which would not have been touched by a draped cloth. So a fellow named Paul Vignon suggested that there must have been some form of imprinting across a distance. He postulated the so-called vaporograph theory which included the notion that body vapours – weak ammonia vapours from morbid body sweat – might have interacted with the burial spices on the cloth to produce a so-called vapour photo.

SD: But it seems to me that this would not give rise to a very detailed image.

JN: Right. In fact I experimented with that technology. I used a sculpture, coated it with ammonia, and used a cloth treated with phenolphthalein and draped it over, and of course what I got is what most scientists could extrapolate would happen – a big blur. And that theory has been negated now and no one pays any attention to it. Then, because of the faint brown or sepia colour of the image, which is approximately the colour of a scorch, people suggested that maybe it was caused by a burst of radiant energy at the moment of resurrection. The problem with that is that the image on the cloth is very superficial. It does not penetrate through the fibres to the back of the cloth. And while this was used to argue that it was not a painting it also argues against radiation because there is no radiation known that would travel the varying distances from body to cloth, and as soon as it hit the cloth drop to zero.

SD: So, any kind of radiation, ultra-violet for instance, wouldn't just scorch the very surface of the fibres. You're saying it would penetrate?

JN: That's right. But also, there are problems with the fact that the image would really have to be focused in order to get an image that's not blurred and distorted. What one is doing when one goes down that path is just invoking a miracle. And so the question then is whether there is any reason to invoke a miracle. Is the *prima facie* evidence of a nature that we should give up other explanations? And my position is that we know from a body of evidence that the shroud was produced by an artist in the Middle Ages.

SD: What scientific analysis, other than the carbon dating, has been carried out on the image and blood-stained areas?

JN: An earlier series of tests was done by a once-secret commission which later produced a report, although it has been very difficult for people to obtain copies of the original report. But we do know that they took threads out of the shroud from the so-called blood-stained areas and these went to forensic laboratories in which internationally known forensic experts tested them using all the standard tests, then the more specific tests for blood and blood compounds, and the fibres failed all those tests. The Church authorities did not like this, apparently, so they issued a rebuttal report, but later the Shroud of Turin Research Project visited Turin and they lifted sticky tape samples from the fibres just by placing the tape on the cloth, peeling it off and mounting these on microscope slides. The samples were first analysed at the world-renowned McCrone forensic laboratories in Chicago. Immediately, they found traces of various substances identifiable as paint pigments. They found red iron oxide of a type used in the pigment red ochre and smaller amounts of vermilion and rose madder.

SD: Are these all pigments that were used in medieval times?

JN: Right. Even some pro-shroud analysts found traces of the vermilion but much smaller traces than McCrone. One of the big questions was whether that red iron oxide was primarily on the image area or not. McCrone's results, in a blind study, demonstrated that the iron oxide was on the image areas and very little on the off-image areas. McCrone then took the view that the image was a painting. I have a problem with that viewpoint because again the body image is superficial and does not soak through the cloth whereas the so-called blood areas do soak through. Later tests after McCrone (although by pro-shroud people which makes a bit of a problem for objectivity) seem to have found that there is very little pigment or very little iron oxide, and that what you see as a body image is really just a yellowing of the cloth. So what I think might have happened is that a powdered pigment was rubbed onto the fibres and over time that has caused a yellowing just by its presence on there. That is, by being slightly acidic it has stained the cloth over time and most of the powder has been sloughed off.

SD: You have written a book entitled *Inquest on the Shroud of Turin* on your investigations into the shroud, and in the book you write about a type of rubbing technique which you have used to produce an image very similar to the shroud image. Can you tell me a bit about this and whether you feel that a medieval forger would have had the skill required to produce such an image?

JN: Joe Nickell, master forger! Well, when I began to realize that wraparound distortion was a problem, and when I found out about the lack of history, the forger's confession, and so forth, and also the presence of some reddish granules – although at that time we didn't know what they were – I began to seriously consider the possibility of artistry. I had eliminated contact imprinting. I had eliminated vaporography. The miraculous theory, of course, could not be tested and I felt was not yet warranted until we had tried everything. So I then took the other category of possible solutions – artistry – and began to work on it. Immediately, it occurred to me that a full three-dimensional sculpture would not work. But there did seem to be evidence that it was not a painting and that it did have three-dimensional information – there have been microdensitometer tracings and other studies that show that the darks and lights of the image are consistent with some kind of three-dimensional form.

SD: Can we just recap on why you felt it wasn't a painting? This was due to the lack of penetration of pigment into the fibres?

JN: Right. There was no evidence of capillary action where there would be a soaking of a fluid medium into the fibres of the shroud except in the blood areas. There also were no brush marks, and of course there was the phenomenon of light and dark reversal which would be another unusual characteristic for a painting. And there were other indications. For example, there were various flaws in the image that were interesting. There were the blank spaces we talked about earlier and a number of things that indicated to me that we might be dealing with some kind of imprinting technique from a bas-relief – a low sculpted relief, not a full three-dimensional relief, but not a flat plate like an engraving. So my first experiments were to try to make an actual print by coating the bas-relief and pressing cloth to it.

SD: So you're talking about a fairly familiar technique – brass rubbing?

JN: Well, that was the next step. Printing was a possible technique but it had some serious drawbacks. So I then tried a technique, as you pointed out, analogous to brass rubbing except that usually we put a paper on a flat surface and rub it. In this case, I was using cloth and a curved form, but by wetting the cloth and moulding it to the bas-relief I was able to form the cloth to the relief, rather like a mask. Then when the cloth was thoroughly dry I took a dauber and some powdered pigment and rubbed it on carefully in strokes. When I did this the dauber hit the prominences and left the recesses blank, and since the prominences in a positive image, like a face, are in highlight, my technique produced the prominences as dark areas. So it made a systematic quasi-negative image just like the shroud image. It had the darks and lights reversed, the hair was still white in the positive image, there were blank spaces and tonal gradations, and, in all, there were some thirty points of similarity between my images and the shroud images at the visual or macroscopic level and even at the microscopic level. The only differences, I believe, are those due to the effects of six hundred years, during which time the image would be expected to have yellowed the cloth and most of the powdered pigment would have sloughed off.

SD: How confident are you that you have arrived at the technique which was used in the fourteenth century to do the forgery?

JN: I have a very high degree of confidence. It is very unlikely, in my thinking, that the shroud is an ordinary painting. There are serious problems with that, although there are ways around the difficulties. For example, if you wanted the pigment not to soak into the cloth you could give the cloth a coat of a sealer of some kind. The problem there is, why would you have the blood areas soaking through? Why would parts of it soak through and parts not? But it is also very difficult for a person to paint a negative image. It's easy enough to copy one if you have one in front of you. In other words, an artist can look at the shroud and copy it but, you see, he is sort of cheating because he has a negative already made for him to copy. It's harder to take a positive image and translate it into a negative, whereas my technique does it automatically. And then I would point out that the technique I used duplicates a number of these very particular flaws and peculiar characteristics, and while those might be imitated by a counterfeiter, the question would arise, why would you put these particular distortions, faults, and flaws in? Whereas the answer for me for my technique is because that's what my technique does. It just naturally produces them – blank spaces for example.

SD: So you're saying, for instance, that when a negative photograph is taken of the shroud image and gives an apparently positive image the fact that the beard and hair come out white is a natural function of just the way it has been done?

JN: Yes, you see, when we look at an ordinary photographic negative we're looking at colours like brown hair which is dark because of its colour. But when we make a rubbing from a bas-relief, that which is raised will be dark, regardless. So the hair becomes dark on the original image but light on the apparently positive photographic negative, so there is that reversal of form. Now it may be that an artist, since rubbings were beginning to become common during the Middle Ages, had studied some rubbings and then did a painting imitating them. I would point out too that there is evidence that the shroud image was once much darker than it is now. So it does appear that the image is losing pigment over time and so the problem is that when we try to figure out exactly what the artist did there is so little left of the original painting or printing that all we have is a residual stain and that does complicate it. Plus the fact that skeptical people with artistic training have really not been allowed access to it.

SD: Given the results of the carbon dating that seem to indicate clearly that the shroud dates back to the fourteenth century and not the first century, and given your findings on a fairly convincing method by which the shroud may have been forged, do you think this will kill forever speculation about the authenticity of the shroud?

JN: Well, it's difficult to say. There may be some really pathological believers who simply can't accept what everyone else will be able to accept. But when you look at the totality of the evidence, and you look at the age of the cloth, which is now apparently established with a very high degree of accuracy as the same time as the forger's confession, and you realize that this is supported by the lack of historical record, the method of wrapping the body which is contrary to Jewish burial practice, and the evidence from the paint pigment, the fact is that, although we may disagree slightly about the method of artistic simulation, the skeptics have maybe too many techniques on their side whereas the believers have none. And so the evidence is just overwhelming and if all issues were this clear life would be much simpler.

What Hath Carlos Wrought?
Robert McGrath

*The early 1970s tales of anthropology PhD candidate Carlos Castaneda's interactions with Don Juan, a mystical teacher he supposedly encountered in Mexico's Sonora Desert, were very widely read – and almost as widely believed, at least as spiritual metaphor if not in literal detail. Many may have wondered whether Castaneda, writing in the first person, had actually accessed new realms of perception while learning magic and the way of a warrior from Don Juan. Few questioned whether Don Juan existed. Unlike Castaneda's publishers or doctoral committee, **Robert McGrath**, a computer scientist in Urbana, Illinois, with undergraduate and postgraduate degrees in anthropology and psychology, was one of those few. Appeared in VII.2.*

Those definitely were the days. I remember it well: in the spring of 1972, my first real college seminar. The topic was 'Contemporary Issues in Anthropological Theory'. Present were one professor, a half-dozen seniors and graduate students, and one precocious sophomore – myself. One of the readings was the controversial new book *The Teachings of Don Juan* by Carlos Castaneda. In my paper, I firmly declared the book to be fiction. The more mature scholars were less certain and more cautious. My judgement that day was based on general skepticism and, I would like to think, good taste in literature. Imagine my pleasure years later when I discovered that I was absolutely correct in my estimate, and that it would be shared by many. Enough brilliant guesses like that and people will think I'm a genius!

The Teachings of Don Juan: A Yaqui Way of Knowledge, by Carlos Castaneda, and its many sequels claim to be a report of the experiences of an anthropologist who, during the early 1960s, established himself as the student of a shaman. 'Don Juan', the shaman, is said to be a Yaqui Indian from Sonora, Mexico. The narrative is presented in dialogues and first-person reports of the anthropologist's experiences. And such experiences! As an apprentice shaman, 'Carlos' is introduced to magic rituals and the entire world view of Don Juan. The rituals included smoking powdered hallucinogenic mushrooms, the experience of which is vividly recounted. Besides drug trips, Don Juan teaches much 'ancient wisdom' of the 'warrior's way', about 'power', 'stalking', 'enemies', 'luminous beings', and other wonders to be encountered in 'non-ordinary reality'. If the narrative is to be believed, Don Juan has access to realms of perception and action unknown to Western science.

If this book were presented as fiction or as allegory it would be a remarkable document. However, it is said to be based on actual anthropological observations, and field notes are supposed to exist documenting the story. Furthermore, Castaneda was awarded a PhD in

Anthropology from the University of California at Los Angeles (UCLA) for this work. With the seeming scientific validity of the story, the book has been hailed by college students and the counter-culture, and also saluted and praised by the establishment media. Many anthropologists and other scholars have embraced the book, it has been cited and used as a textbook, and the Goddess only knows how many theses and term papers have been written about the book and its sequels. They have sold millions of copies in the 'anthropology' section of bookstores, and are catalogued in libraries under 'Yaqui Indians – Religion and Mythology'.

But, there have been skeptics. There are *always* skeptics. In particular, many anthropologists are skeptical of the work, especially those with knowledge of psycho-pharmacology, the Sonora Desert, or the Yaqui Indians. These skeptics found Castaneda's work incorrect, impossible, and derivative.

One of the most convincing skeptical studies of the 'Carlos Castaneda' affair is *The Don Juan Papers*. Edited by Richard de Mille, this is a collection of essays and commentary on the Don Juan books, the hoax that they represent, and its implications. About half the book is written by de Mille himself and the balance by other authors. If this book had simply debunked the Don Juan tale as a scientific hoax, it would rank as one of the great books of skeptical inquiry ever. But de Mille has done much, much more than that. He investigates not only the Castaneda books, but Castaneda himself, how and why the hoax was successful, the nature of skepticism and belief, the relation of religion and science, the psychology and sociology of science, and, I regret to say, a case of serious scientific misconduct.

Let's begin at the beginning. *The Teachings of Don Juan* (and the books which followed) is presented as a report of ethnographic field research. However, the raw field notes have never been published, nor have they been made available to other investigators. Nor, indeed, were they ever seen by *most of the members of Castaneda's doctoral committee*.

The contributors to *The Don Juan Papers* show conclusively that the field notes have not been seen because the fieldwork could not have occurred. The evidence is overwhelming that Castaneda's 'fieldwork' was done in the stacks of the UCLA library. The description of the desert, its wildlife, and even the mushrooms that figure so heavily in the story are all flat *wrong*. 'Don Juan' knows few words of Yaqui (and misuses those) and the teachings are a mishmash of Zen, Wittgenstein, and other philosophies that have nothing at all to do with any Native American culture, let alone the Yaquis. In fact, de Mille traces dozens of sources used, including real ethnographies, works of social science, philosophy, metaphysics, occultism, and Edgar Allen Poe.

If Castaneda had simply produced a collage of borrowed texts, the story would end there. But he is no simple plagiarist. For one thing, he cleverly twists his sources to slightly disguise them. For another, his books are artfully constructed to look just like a real ethnographic report, and they have been taken as such by many. Castaneda's books are not parody, they are allegory. De Mille claims that there is *not one single word of truth in the books*, that there is no kernel of fact, and that they are pure artifice. They are, if de Mille is correct, an elegant and exquisite anthropological hoax, perhaps the biggest since Piltdown Man.

To understand the Piltdown hoax one must understand the palaeontology, anthropology, and nationalist rivalries of the time. To make sense of the Don Juan hoax it is necessary to have a similar background of academic social science and popular culture of the 1960s and 1970s. *The Don Juan Papers* provides part of this understanding, but as a nearly contemporary response to the hoax some of the story it tells may be difficult to follow it you weren't 'there' yourself. Besides providing the crucial debunking of the fake fieldwork, the contributors to *The Don Juan Papers* discuss the credulity and outright misbehaviour (de Mille calls it 'Sonoragate') of Castaneda's publishers, and his academic and popular supporters. The collection contains some 'conversion' documents – comments by people who once believed Don Juan and his teachings were literally true and now realize that they were fooled. These documents are interesting because they provide insight into why people believed Castaneda so easily, and fascinating for the fact that so many still value the teachings even after admitting that they are a blatant and dishonest fraud.

Another vital contribution of *The Don Juan Papers* is the 'debunking' of Castaneda himself. Not only are his books fabrications, but his entire life is concealed behind lies. This in itself is not that unusual, but Castaneda's lies are of a special sort: he is amazingly adept at mirroring back a person's expectations, so that each one who talks to him sees only their own conceptions 'reflected' back to them. De Mille has called Castaneda 'the Rorschach man', after the ink blot test. *The Don Juan Papers* documents what little is known about Castaneda's 'real' life and builds a (somewhat sad) profile of the psychology of a master hoaxer. This part of the story is, for me, even more interesting than unmasking the hoax, and *vastly* more interesting than the Don Juan books themselves.

The Don Juan books were a founding influence on the 'new shamanism' and are much beloved of poets, neo-pagans, and many New-Agers. Spin-offs and rip-offs have sprung up. I have even read that there is a man who 'channels' Don Juan, producing new teachings never heard by 'Carlos'. What, indeed, hath Carlos wrought?

Rendlesham: Britain's Roswell
David Clarke

'Britain's Roswell', people like to call it. At 3 am on 26 December 1980, three American servicemen patrolling near the joint RAF Bentwaters and RAF Woodbridge base saw mysterious lights in Rendlesham Forest. The lights were seen again the next night. Of all British UFO sightings, this one was by far the most celebrated, and the proximity to the military base and lack of an immediate explanation put Rendlesham on the front pages of the tabloids. Astronomy writer Ian Ridpath (who has posted many documents concerning the case on his site at www.ianridpath.com) and forester Vincent Thirkettle were the first to propose the explanation that the lights the servicemen saw were, surprisingly, the beam of the Orford Ness lighthouse six miles away. Ridpath's explanation was greeted with considerable skepticism, even ridicule, by UFOlogists (some of whom accused him of conjuring up 'flying lighthouses'), but a personal visit with Ridpath to Rendlesham in the mid-1990s showed clearly that the open winter landscape coupled with the shape of the terrain make it not only possible but the most likely explanation.

The 1987 Channel 4 documentary **Is There Anybody There?**, produced by Karl Sabbagh, examined the Rendlesham case and demonstrated persuasively how confusing and spooky lights can look at night in an unfamiliar location. But it wasn't until the early 2000s that documents came to light that made it plain that Ridpath and Thirkettle were right. James Easton, an investigative journalist and feature writer for **Fortean Times**, made public not only those documents but also personal information from Kevin Conde, who said that some aspects of the sightings – mysterious lights – were part of a hoax he perpetrated using multi-coloured lights on a car driven slowly through the fog.

In 2004, **The Skeptic** ran a special issue on Rendlesham that included three long articles putting (we hope) the case to rest. In the first, Easton laid out the evidence he had developed; this piece also appeared in **Fortean Times**. Easton has since disappeared from the scene and the websites he maintained on the subject have vanished, but you can still access his information via the **Fortean Times** site, the Internet Archive, and Ridpath's site.

A second article came from well-known UFOlogist and book author Jenny Randles, who recounted the long, slow process of investigating the case and dissected the more sensationalist claims made about it. Among other points, Randles noted that it is often not in the interests of UFOlogists to solve the biggest UFO mysteries. Skeptics typically only become involved after the cases have made headlines; by contrast, she first became involved in investigating Rendlesham in early 1981, when the story was still just second-hand rumours. It was not until late 1983, when the story landed on the front *page of the* **News of the World**, *that Rendlesham became widely known. Randles has written two books and a lengthy chapter about Rendlesham.*

Randles also lays out some rules for investigating UFOs that might surprise some skeptics. As many as 95 percent of UFOs have prosaic explanations, she writes; therefore, UFOlogists should approach cases with the assumption that ultimately it will be solved and start with the simplest possible explanation.

The third article, which follows here, talks about two aspects of Rendlesham that are less well documented. **David Clarke**, *a teacher in the School of English at the University of Sheffield and author of a number of books on aspects of supernatural belief and contemporary legend, particularly UFO mythology, asks why UFOlogists remain so willing to believe in a government cover-up. Appeared in XVII.2–3.*

There are two basic categories of UFO lore: alien abductions and conspiracies. Central to UFO lore is belief in a conspiracy by 'the Government' – and primarily those of the USA and UK – to withhold the 'secret truth' from the general public. This 'truth' being an admission that the authorities have proof of the alien presence on earth, in the form of the wreckage of a spacecraft and the bodies of its crew. The ultimate expression of this modern legend is the Roswell incident, but the *idea* of an official cover-up has become widespread in popular culture. The 'landed Martians' is such a well-known story that it was included in Professor Jan Brunvand's list of modern legends about governments in his book *The Choking Doberman*.

Brunvand says he received a lot of angry letters for comparing UFO cover-ups with urban legends. Indeed, many 'serious UFOlogists' are horrified at attempts to study these stories as the modern equivalents of fairy tales and ancient legends. However, there are similarities between UFO cover-up narratives and modern legends such as the vanishing hitchhiker: stories heard as rumour and gossip. Those who pass on the story believe it really happened to a friend of a friend, and the story is given immediacy and legitimacy by the inclusion of 'real' names and places. With the arrival of the internet, new versions spread with dizzying speed around the world, spawning new variations upon the original theme.

While Roswell is the seminal story, the Rendlesham incident is often cited as 'Britain's Roswell'. They are composed of two distinct entities: the popular myth and the few certain facts. In both cases, the two constituents have taken an independent life of their own, and continue to grow apart in ever more distant directions.

Central to the Rendlesham incidents is the testimony of a group of USAF security policemen who reported mysterious lights outside the perimeter of RAF Woodbridge, in Suffolk, on two occasions in December 1980. The most senior officer was USAF Lt Col (later Col) Charles Halt, who was the Deputy Base Commander of RAF Woodbridge. It was Halt who prepared an official memorandum summarizing these incidents for the attention of the British

Ministry of Defence (MoD). At that time, Woodbridge and its twin base at Bentwaters were tenanted by USAF as part of their air defence responsibilities in Europe. Halt was, at face value, an experienced officer who was held in high regard by his superiors.

The Ministry of Defence and the Rendlesham incident

UFOlogists first learned that a UFO incident had occurred in the forest adjoining the twin RAF bases at Bentwaters/Woodbridge early in 1981. Although the bases were loaned to the USAF, responsibility for events off-base – and indeed defence of surrounding UK airspace – rested with the Ministry of Defence. Almost immediately, speculation was rife in the UFO community about an official cover-up.

In 1980 an air staff secretariat known as Defence Secretariat 8 (DS8) was the only government agency officially acknowledged as having an interest in UFO reports. Policy documents released at the Public Record Office (PRO) reveal that UFOs were the lowest priority among the many other operational duties handled by DS8. A single member of staff (usually an Executive Office or Higher Executive Officer, both junior posts) spent a small proportion of his or her time examining reports received, purely for evidence of 'defence significance' (that is, for evidence that the UFOs were intruder aircraft). Essentially this policy had remained unchanged since 1958 when DS8's predecessor S4 (Air) accepted responsibility for responding to all inquiries concerning UFOs. On accepting the burden, a senior civil servant suggested that responses to questions on the subject should 'for the most part be politely unhelpful'.

There has been much speculation in UFO circles that DS8 and its successors were merely a 'shop window' for a more covert MoD investigation team. PRO records suggest this perception is the result of a misunderstanding. Since 1958 S4 (Air) and later DS8 routinely copied all the reports they received to two other military and scientific branches of MoD. These are a defence intelligence unit, DI 55, and an RAF Ground Environment branch, which is responsible for the air defence radar. Records show that neither was interested in UFOs outside of a limited defence remit, and had rarely made inquiries of their own in recent years.

The MoD has historically said little or nothing in public concerning the extent and nature of its UFO investigations. Its policy of playing down the subject was in sharp contrast with the USAF, which maintained a highly public UFO project (Blue Book) until 1969. Even after the closure of Blue Book, American UFOlogists were able to use their country's Freedom of Information Act (FOIA) to obtain access to documents produced by a variety of official agencies. It was via the US FOIA in 1983 that a copy of Col Halt's memo was obtained by an American UFOlogist, and released into the public domain.

Until recently, it was impossible to obtain information from the MoD concerning what they did, or did not, know about specific UFO reports. The Ministry maintained that all correspondence with members of the public was confidential, and files could only be released after 30 years had passed under the Public Record Act. Under the current 'thirty-year rule', files on the Rendlesham Forest incident would not have been made public until 2011.

When UFOlogist Jenny Randles, with Brenda Butler and Dot Street, began to investigate the story early in 1981, they were informed that Halt's report was 'passed to staff concerned with air defence matters who were satisfied that there was nothing of defence interest in the alleged sightings'. From 1981 until 2001 this bland statement remained the standard official response to all inquiries about the incident. While adequate for media and public consumption, it encouraged some UFOlogists to believe a cover-up was under way.

As Britain did not have a FOIA (a partial equivalent took effect in January 2005), little progress could be made with the Ministry of Defence until very recently. In 1994 a Code of Practice for Access to Government Information was introduced that provided limited access to material closed under the thirty-year rule. Paradoxically, although the UFOlogists who were promoting the case claimed they were determined to discover 'the truth' about Rendlesham, until 2001 no one made use of the new legislation to request access to official records. During the research for my book *Out of the Shadows* (Clarke & Roberts, 2002), I made an application under the Code for access to records that were relevant to the case.

In May 2001 the contents of an MoD Air file – 150 pages in length – were released. The file was unclassified and contained nothing 'secret' or 'top secret' as the UFOlogists had claimed. Five documents were initially withheld, two on the grounds of 'defence, security and international relations' and three briefing documents because they contained 'internal opinion, advice, recommendation and deliberation'. Speculation was immediately rife within the UFO community about the nature of their contents. One magazine editor declared they were withheld because they contained 'top secret' information about the case, or revealed the much sought-after 'smoking gun'.

All five documents have now been released on appeal, the first two in October 2001 and the remaining briefings early in 2003. They contained nothing remotely 'top secret' and the reasons for their retention had more to do with civil service bureaucracy than they had with the desire to conceal any 'secret truth'. Their significance lay in the mystery that surrounded their content.

The smoking gun?

Jenny Randles acknowledges that the file 'tells us much more about the MoD than it does about the events in Rendlesham Forest'. A small amount of material relates to the official investigation of Halt's report – if it can be so described – between 1981 and 1983. The vast majority of its content consists of long and often tedious correspondence between Sec(AS)2, the MoD secretariat which replaced DS8, and members of the public between 1982 and 1994. The later material documents the MoD's often tortuous attempts to avoid answering specific questions and its desire to avoid unwelcome publicity on the subject.

The file contains evidence that the MoD was not officially aware of the incident until DS8 received a copy of Lt Col Halt's memo, forwarded by the British base commander, early in January 1981. By the time action was taken – in the form of circulating the paperwork to other branches – a month had passed and 'the scent was cold'. In February checks were made with the radar cameras at Eastern Radar (RAF Watton) and the Central Reporting Centre at RAF Neatishead in Norfolk. This found 'no entry in respect of unusual radar returns or other unusual occurrences'.

Unfortunately, on both occasions the MoD were reliant upon the dates of 27 and 29 December for the UFO events in Rendlesham Forest supplied by Col Halt in his memo. Both dates were incorrect, a mistake that could have been easily rectified. All the evidence suggests no follow-up request was ever made to Halt or his USAF superiors by the MoD. This lack of official interest was confirmed by the Group Captain, Neil Colvin, responsible for Air Defence at MoD in 1981. In a letter dated 3 February 2003 he wrote: 'I remember the alleged sightings by US airmen at Bentwaters [sic]. I recall that we could not explain them but were very skeptical of the reports. We were not privy to the actual evidence of the sightings by the personnel concerned, nor did we have the opportunity to interview the individuals involved.'

Cover-up or cock-up?

Possibly the most astounding revelation contained in the file is that it was not until 1983 – two years after the events – that the MoD obtained the correct dates. These were supplied not by the USAF but came from a member of the public! Shortly after Halt's memo was published by the *News of the World*, astronomy writer Ian Ridpath made inquiries with Suffolk Police and was able to confirm from their records the correct date for the initial sighting by the airmen. Ridpath wrote to advise DS8 on 14 November 1983 that police had first been called to the scene in Rendlesham forest at 4.11 am on 26 December 1980. He added: 'They said that all they could see was the lighthouse [at Orford Ness]. They were called out again at 10.30am on Dec 26 to examine the reported landing marks. There seems little doubt that the date of Dec 27 given in Col. Halt's letter is wrong. This also casts doubt on the second date he gives for the later events.'

As a result of this, DS8 wrote to the RAF Base Commander, Squadron Leader Donald Moreland, asking if he could recheck the dates. Moreland's reply, dated 25 November 1983, compounded the errors and demonstrated the complete lack of interest the MoD had in the events of 1980. He wrote: 'The incident is now almost 3 years old and no one here remembers it clearly. All we have is Lt Col. Halt's letter dated 13 January 1981.'

This was hardly the 'smoking gun' imagined by the UFOlogists. If an event of world-changing status had occurred at the base just two years earlier it was odd that 'no one here remembers it clearly'.

A similar lack of interest related to claims of higher than expected levels of radiation recorded by Col Halt in the area of the forest visited by the UFOs. Early in 1981 the MoD asked its defence intelligence specialists to comment on the data recorded in Lt Col Halt's memo, but made no attempt to establish independent confirmation of them. R. C. Moorcroft at DI 52, responding to DS8 on 23 February 1981 to the question, noted: 'Background radioactivity varies considerably due to a number of factors ... If you wish to pursue this further I could make enquiries as to natural background levels in the area.' There is nothing to suggest that any further action was taken. The radioactivity issue was not raised again until 1994 when Nick Pope, who was then Executive Officer at Sec(AS) 2, took the matter up with Giles Cowling at the Defence Radiological Protection Service, a branch of the Government's Defence Evaluation Research Agency (DERA). Pope's handwritten notes of his discussion with Cowling, dated 15 April 1994, form the last enclosure in the file. Pope – who subsequently described these notes as 'the first and only official investigation into this aspect of the case' – ends with the comment 'The level of 0.1 is completely harmless.'

Oddly, in the light of his own handwritten reservations, by 1996 Pope was describing the alleged radiation traces as 'the most tangible proof that something extraordinary happened there [Rendlesham Forest]'.

'UFO lands in Suffolk – that's official!'

In October 1983 the *News of the World* broke the story contained in Lt Col Halt's memo and the MoD Press Office began to receive calls from the world's media. DS8 prepared what it called a 'Defensive Press Line' anticipating the questions that might be asked. The most amusing comment noted that the MoD and USAF 'both referred callers to the other ... [this] will have done nothing but confirm suspicions held in UFO circles that we are engaged in a cover-up.'

When in 1984 the retired head of DS8, Ralph Noyes, contacted his former colleagues to ask for clarification of their position he had to send two reminders before receiving a standard reply. This delay contributed to Noyes' increasingly public pro-UFO stance and by 1987 he came to believe that the MoD had indeed lied about the incident. He was joined by a former Chief of Defence Staff, Admiral Lord Hill-Norton. The Admiral, who became a UFO believer in retirement, also took up the case and reached the same conclusion. Ironically, while supporting the idea of a high-level conspiracy, the Admiral asks us to believe that he was not part of it, and that the subject 'never once crossed his desk' during his service as CDS!

The most recent MoD briefing on the Rendlesham Forest case contained in the file was compiled by Britain's self-styled Fox Mulder, Nick Pope, in 1994. In this Pope followed the standard MoD line that 'no evidence was found of any threat to the defence of the United Kingdom and no further investigations were carried out ... no further information has come to light which alters our view that the sightings of these lights was of no defence significance ... in the absence of any hard evidence, the MOD remains open-minded about these sightings'.

Pope served the standard three years as a junior officer with Sec (AS) 2 from 1991 to 1994. After leaving this post he produced a book, *Open Skies, Closed Minds*, that took a pro-UFO stance. He maintains there was no cover-up of the Rendlesham incident but rather 'a lack of action' by the MoD. In 2000 he provided the foreword to Georgina Bruni's book on the Rendlesham incident, *You Can't Tell the People*. Although this book's author strongly believed in a cover-up by the British and US Governments, Pope failed to appreciate the contradiction in his stance. During an interview I recorded with Pope in 2001 it became clear that he had abandoned the objective viewpoint he displayed while working for the MoD. When asked for his current belief about what happened at Rendlesham he told us: 'As you know, despite the fact that I am a non-conspiracy theorist and a rational guy, you know that I am a believer in the Extraterrestrial Hypothesis and I will go with the ETH on this one. Am I allowed to give my answer as an extraterrestrial spacecraft? That's the answer I'm going with on this case.'

Conclusion

As the MoD maintained from the very beginning, there is nothing in the file to support claims that a cover-up had taken place to hide evidence of UFO landings in Suffolk. Rather than being a 'smoking gun', the file's contents chart the growth of a modern legend from birth to full maturity. As is the case with Roswell, the established facts have only a loose connection with the mythology that has grown up around the case in the UFO literature.

Folklore and UFO lore share the same kind of evidence: the testimony of narrators describing extraordinary experiences. In UFO lore reports made by military witnesses, particularly senior officers, are accredited with special status. The existence of official documents describing extraordinary events is the UFOlogical equivalent of the 'holy grail'. This is where the circular arguments that bedevil UFO lore begin.

The UFOlogists want to know the truth about a baffling subject and because the government is involved they assume, wrongly, that it must know all the answers. From the standpoint of believers in alien visitors, all that has to be done is to force the government to release 'the truth' and the UFO reality would be established to everyone's satisfaction. Unfortunately, to use the words of Daniel Webster, 'There is nothing so powerful as the truth and often nothing as strange.' When information is not forthcoming, or when it is released but does not provide the conclusive evidence demanded by believers, a deeper cover-up is suspected and so the argument becomes a circular one.

The idea of an official cover-up of the Rendlesham Forest UFO incident is belief-driven and can never be disproved, only proved.

Foreign Objects: Testing an Alien Implant
Susan Blackmore and David T. Patton

*In the early 1990s, a prominent British skeptic told me that alien abductions, then a new fad in the US, would never catch on as a belief in the UK because, essentially, British people are too sensible. He was, sadly, wrong – and there's no very good way you can prove someone **wasn't** abducted. You can, however, test any physical traces the 'aliens' leave behind, as **Susan Blackmore** and **David T. Patton**, then both members of the Faculty of Applied Sciences at the University of the West of England, Bristol, show here. James Basil, discussed here and whom I met when we both appeared on the same TV programme, claims to have been repeatedly abducted throughout his life, beginning at the age of five, leading me to suggest in a column that it would be helpful if he kept himself supplied with a kit so he'd be prepared to collect physical evidence. In this case, he apparently needed no tools, as the aliens helpfully left a small object in his mouth for Blackmore and Patton to study. Appeared in XI.3.*

James Basil is an 'abductee'. In 1992, at the age of 13, he had a terrifying experience in which he reached out in his bed and found he was touching another hand – a smooth lizard-like hand with curled fingers. After this he began to remember other experiences, including being floated across the hallway into a UFO outside his bathroom window. He later found himself back in bed, with two aliens, one male and one female, standing by his bed. Subsequently he had many other memories of abduction by aliens.

In March 1997 he came to interview me (SB) for a student media project. He asked for my views on alien abductions and sleep paralysis, and then revealed that not only had he experienced sleep paralysis, but was also an abductee – and in his opinion the two experiences were quite different. He also thought he could prove his experiences were real because the aliens had implanted a small object in his mouth, which he had subsequently removed. He asked me whether I would be interested in seeing the implant and possibly analysing it to find out what it was.

Physical evidence of abductions is extremely rare. In his 1981 book *Missing Time*, Budd Hopkins described the insertion of small 'implants' into abductees' noses, legs, and other body parts. In 1994, writing in his book *Abduction: Human Encounters with Aliens*, JE Mack reported several abductees who claimed to have 'tracking devices' inserted into their bodies by the aliens. Some abductees claim that the aliens do not want the implant removed or subjected to X-rays or scanning. Some of the implants have reportedly been removed from abductees' bodies but they usually mysteriously disappear according to DM Jacobs in his 1993 book *Secret Life: First Hand Accounts of UFO Abductions*. Mack reports one implant that turned out to be 'an interesting twisted fibre consisting of carbon, silicon, oxygen, no nitrogen, and traces of other elements' and others that were clearly of normal biological material. He concluded that 'it may be wrong to expect that a phenomenon whose very nature is subtle ... will yield its secrets to an epistemology or methodology that operates at a lower level of consciousness'. Many would not agree. This seemed like a unique opportunity to investigate putatively alien material.

The 'implant' is about 2mm by 3mm and dullish grey. Little can be discerned with the naked eye. After all, dullish grey metal could cover miniaturized alien technology – or more dullish grey metal. The obvious next step seemed to be electron microscopy but that is expensive and not available in the psychology department! So, with some trepidation, I sent out an email to everyone in our faculty asking for help. Within one hour I had already had three replies offering help and advice, and by the following day several more. The consensus seemed to be that the best non-destructive method would be to use the scanning electron microscope (SEM) and the attached X-ray microanalysis system which would give an analysis of the elemental composition. So on 9 April 1997 James and I visited Dave Patton.

First we examined the object through a stereo light microscope which revealed irregular edges and surface detail and colour. Part of the surface was covered with yellow-brown material which we assumed to be dried organic matter from Basil's mouth. The object was then mounted on an SEM holder using double-sided sticky tape and viewed using a Hitachi S-450 scanning electron microscope.

In a scanning electron microscope, electrons that are emitted or reflected when a very fine beam of electrons is scanned and rastered across a specimen (usually in vacuum) are collected to form a television-type image of the specimen. These microscopes can give very high magnifications, sufficient to resolve features as small as one millionth of a millimetre in the best instruments.

In addition to producing a magnified image, the beam can be focused onto one spot and X-rays, which are also emitted when the electrons strike the specimen, can be collected, analysed, and used to provide an accurate 'fingerprint' of the elements present in small regions of the specimen.

The object had a rough irregular appearance (Figure 3a). James was particularly interested in looking for fibres because of reported fibres on previous implants. A possible fibre is shown in Figure 3b. It is very small, about 2μm in diameter and somewhat irregular.

We spent about an hour just examining the surface at various magnifications (see Figure 3b). We saw several fibres and small rounded features on the surface, which James compared with other alien implants he had heard about. Nothing we saw looked like miniature technology or mechanical components, but then of course alien technology might be unrecognizable to human eyes. The final step was therefore to use Energy Dispersive X-ray Microanalysis (EDX) to determine the object's composition. Potentially this might reveal a combination of elements unlikely to be found on earth.

EDX was performed using an 'EDAX PV9100' system. The composition of the 'alien implant' is given in Table 1. This provided the answer we needed.

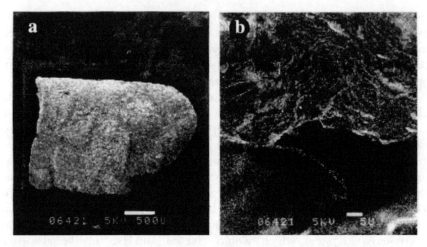

Figure 3 Scanning electron microscope images of the material 'implanted' in James Basil's mouth. *(a)* Low magnification view of entire 'implant' – scale marker indicates 0.5 mm. *(b)* Higher magnification view showing small fibre – scale marker indicates 0.005 mm.

Dental amalgam varies considerably in its exact composition but is typically 50 percent mercury with the other 50 percent being silver and tin, usually in the proportions 73 percent to 27 percent.

Our conclusion is that the 'implant' was a displaced dental filling coated with dried organic material. The fibre shown in Figure 3b could possibly have been initially on the surface and been partly detached during specimen mounting. The rounded objects could be dried organic, possibly cellular, material. Since the object was in James' mouth for about two weeks it seems likely that these features are organic and derived from him.

This investigation raises many interesting questions. First, how far should scientists be prepared to go in using their time and expensive equipment to test extraordinary claims? Obviously there must be a limit, but in this case we believe it was well worth the effort. If we are not prepared to help, the

Table 1 Composition of James Basil's 'implant' as determined by EDAX compared with the composition of standard dental amalgam.

Element	Implant % by weight	Amalgam % by weight
mercury	40.5	50
tin + silver	46.3	50
others (Ca, Cl, and Si)	10.7	

believers in UFOs and the conspiracy theorists are given more cause to claim they are being unfairly treated and that the 'scientific community' is biased against them. Judging from the very positive response, many other scientists at the University of the West of England agree. Also, we might have found the first-ever piece of alien technology on earth.

As James pointed out afterwards, the real question now concerns all those other implants.

4

Beyond a Joke

What harm can it do? People ask skeptics this all the time about all kinds of beliefs. When you're talking about astrology or spoon-bending, maybe it's reasonable to claim that skeptics are just being purist intellectual snobs to carp. Many, maybe even most, paranormal beliefs are mostly harmless, other than creating a sort of background noise that Simon Hoggart has called 'interference with the truth'. But the consequences of some claims are too serious to take lightly. Most of these are in the medical field: even a treatment as simple as faith healing can cost lives if believers favour it over medical care. Just as serious in their impact on families and the social fabric are false memory syndrome and memories of child abuse 'recovered' under hypnosis.

Miracle Cures: Only Believe
John Diamond

John Diamond (1953–2001) was a well-known Sunday Times *columnist and broadcaster married to writer and TV cook Nigella Lawson when, in 1997, he was diagnosed with throat cancer. He wrote frequently about his cancer and his experiences in treatment in his column and also in his 1998 book,* C: Because Cowards Get Cancer, Too. *As his situation worsened, readers' convictions that simple cures rejected by medicine could fix it poured ever faster into his mailbag. At his death he left behind a half-finished, scathing, and well-researched book on alternative medicine; it was published posthumously filled out with a smattering of columns and essays as* Snake Oil and Other Preoccupations. *In that book he wrote a simple summary of alternative medicine: 'It's not a question of alternative medicine not working, but of the classification not actually existing. There are interventions one can make which have some effect on illness and there are interventions one can make which have no effect at all. The former count as medicine, the latter don't.' Appeared in XVIII.3–4.*

For three years now I've been writing about me and my tumour in the *Times* magazine each Saturday. As the cancer has degraded from easy-peasey treatable through the various surgeon-confusing stages to its current apparently terminal state, so the number of readers who have written in with alternative cures has increased. I've had the lot: Girson therapy, naturopathy, megavitamin diets, laetrile, Essiac – any and every therapy listed in the Questionable Cancer Therapies section of the Web's invaluable Quackwatch site has been offered to me as a cure.

None of them work, of course. I'm no particular fan of the free market in general, but if coffee enemas really did work the wonders that Dr Girson's followers claim for them then every cancer patient would be using them. And, of course, every cancer doctor would be prescribing them. The single belief shared by almost all my correspondents is that there's a conspiracy among all those egotistical, money-grubbing doctors to keep these cures away from the suffering public. The truth is, of course, that it's precisely because so many doctors are egotistical and money-grubbing that if any one of them found a way of curing currently incurable cancers they'd use it tomorrow, claim their position as saviour of mankind, and never mind what the drug companies – their partners in the conspiracy according to my correspondents – said.

I don't deny that my correspondents have the best and kindest of intentions. They really do want me to be well. But what is remarkable is not that they believe in these cures but the extent to which they're willing to go to delude themselves in order to maintain that belief. What's equally remarkable is just how often the same phrases appear again and again in their letters.

The doctors only gave her x months/years to live ...

This is always in the preamble to a story of a miracle recovery as in 'Two years ago my aunt's doctor said she had only three months to live ...' Except that doctors never quite say that. A year or so ago I was told that my cancer was probably incurable but that a particular form of chemotherapy might put it into remission. How long did I have? Well, the doctor said, it was hard to say. Possibly three months, possibly longer. If the chemo worked then possibly a year or two. Subsequently friends asked me the same question I'd asked the doctors: how long? For a while I told them what I'd been told: I had three months to live. But, of course, I hadn't been told that. It was a possible interpretation of what I'd heard, but then so was 'a year' or 'two years' or 'who knows?'

If I, so resolutely opposed to alternativism, found it easy to translate the prognosis so dramatically, how much more likely is somebody who has embarked on some last-ditch cure or another to make the same translation and thus prove the efficacy of whatever snake oil they're dosing themselves with?

... and x months after he'd started on the treatment the tumour had shrunk by half!

Which always sounds impressive and invariably comes at the end of a story about somebody who'd been sent off home to die. The last time I got an email with this announcement in it I emailed back: if the patient had been sent home to die how come they were given the scan which showed that the tumour had shrunk? Scans are expensive and are generally given only to those the doctors think they can help.

It turned out, as it always does, that the patient had been using the treatment – Girson therapy in this case – alongside high-dose radiotherapy. She hadn't been sent home to die at all but had been told that if the radiotherapy didn't work then her time was limited. And indeed whenever I've bothered to check on one of these miracle cures which seems to have given remission or, rarely, a cure, it turns out that the patient has been taking it at the same time as some orthodox therapy. Why they should believe that it's the mad diet that works and that the radio- or chemotherapy has had no effect is beyond me.

The doctors were amazed by her progress – they even took pictures of her ...

In this country cancer doctors have to spend 50 percent of their time telling patients that they're going to check out earlier than they'd imagined. It must be a pretty depressing way to earn your living. No wonder, then, that when there's good news so many of them tend to hop and skip with pleasure. The chemotherapy I finished last year had a 33 percent chance of working and about a 25 percent chance, if it worked, of keeping me going longer than three months after it finished. When I started turning up at the various clinics some months after the three-month point, the doctors gambolled like beaming lambs. How marvellous this was! How remarkable! How clever I was! How clever *they* were! Quick: let's take some pictures for the academic press!

It was hard for me to remember in all of this that terminal still meant terminal. I can well imagine that if I'd been taking the snake-oil diet at the same time as the chemotherapy I'd have walked out of the clinic believing that something miraculous and rare had been achieved.

This isn't an alternative cure: it's been proved to have worked ...

The remedy I most often hear this about is damned Essiac. Essiac is an ancient American Indian recipe which was touted by a now-dead Canadian nurse and is the pride of Canadian alternative medicine. Despite the fact that the Canadian Health Board has found it lacking in certain curative essentials – like curing, for instance – it seems to be a generally held belief that Essiac is some sort of 'official' cure in Canada. I put this to one Canadian doctor who said that yes: hospitals in Canada do offer it. But only in the same sort of way that hospitals in Britain offer a chapel to pray in.

... although the doctors won't say he's cured ...

This is usually given as evidence of the general petulance of the medical profession when faced with a miracle cure not of their causing. What it invariably means is that the patient is in remission – which is something entirely different from a cure. So often proponents of alternative medicine use the same arguments for their own beliefs that they use against those of the medical orthodoxy. Thus, for instance, a single paper which suggests that homoeopathy might possibly have some effect on some minor ailment or another is taken as proof that homoeopathy works in all eventualities while a single paper suggesting that some orthodox cancer therapy might not be all it's cracked up to be is taken by them as equal proof that no orthodox medicine is worth considering.

It's the same with remission and cure. Tell an alternativist that the cure rate for cancer using entirely orthodox methods has quintupled since the turn of the century and you might well hear that this is a scam perpetrated by the orthodoxy because when they say 'cured' what they really mean is 'hasn't returned for five years'. Which is true enough: generally speaking that is the definition. But then, as it was the definition all those decades ago it seems a pretty fair comparison to make. On the other hand, those same complainants are usually pretty happy to see a year or two years' remission effected, as they believe it, by some nonce remedy or another as evidence of a complete cure.

So do I tell my correspondents all of this? Usually no. And for the same reason their doctors don't tell them it either. Being in the situation they're in isn't much fun. After all, I'm in it too. And while there's part of me which thinks the honest thing would be to tell the truth, why should I make things worse than they already are? If they're happy believing what they believe then that's fine by me. When these particular chips are down, you take what succour you can get. And in any case I'm pretty certain that if I told them otherwise they wouldn't believe me.

What's Wrong with Alternative Medicine?
Thurstan Brewin

*John Diamond presented the point of view of a patient. Presenting the point of view of a doctor is **Thurstan Brewin** (1921–2001), an oncologist, Fellow of the Royal College of Physicians and Surgeons, and a former chair of HealthWatch (www.healthwatch.org.uk). In this talk, presented at the fifth European Skeptics' Conference held in Keele in 1993, he explains the harm misplaced belief in alternative medicine can do and makes the case for 'opting out' of complementary therapies. Appeared in VIII.6.*

Taken literally, *alternative* medicine covers only those therapies recommended *instead of* mainstream medicine – and *complementary* medicine only those recommended *in addition to* mainstream medicine. And this is how some people use the terms. Recently both meanings have been blurred, so that they are almost interchangeable, but with 'complementary' the preferred umbrella expression, though 'natural' and 'holistic' are by no means forgotten – until someone comes up with yet another name. Fringe is the most useful term because it covers everything that is not mainstream, without attempting to describe it in any other way. It was the term advocated in the book of that name by Brian Inglis, editor of *The Spectator* and a great admirer of fringe medicine, so nobody should object to it, but it seems that many now do.

Similarly, the neutral term 'mainstream' is a better name than 'conventional', 'orthodox', or 'scientific'. Orthodox is especially misleading as it suggests that some particular belief or system is followed. This is what is often claimed by critics, but it's not true and never has been. The fact is that mainstream medicine is more pragmatic than fringe medicine, less tied to beliefs and theories. In my view the best of it is also actually *more*, not less, holistic (not in the mystical sense, but in terms of treating the patient, not just the disease) for it aims to help both the patient's physical problems, taking full advantage of all that has been discovered this century, and at the same time every problem that the patient has, physical or psychological, with maximum encouragement, relaxation, and peace of mind. Moreover, mainstream medicine, since it is not tied to any system or belief, is free to incorporate any really effective remedy at any time, whether or not its mechanism is understood.

However, the medical establishment is now, it seems, so anxious not to be thought patronizing or arrogant that it is bending over backwards to be polite and show respect to almost any kind of fringe medicine. It is now in bad taste to speak of quackery, except perhaps in the grossest kind of deliberate fraud. The 1993 report of the British Medical Association (*Complementary Medicine – New Approaches to Good Practice*) is a good example of this, containing hardly a word of criticism of *any* branch of fringe medicine, however far-fetched. And hardly a hint of pride in the considerable achievements of mainstream medicine. This to me comes close to a betrayal of all those doctors and scientists today and in the past with just as much desire as anyone else to put the patient first, but with a keen honest intellect and little respect for woolly thinking and flim-flam.

Diagnosis and treatment

It's much easier to prove that a procedure is bogus when it is used for diagnosis than when it is used for therapy. For example, looking at the eyes (iridology) or feet (reflexology) in order to tell what's wrong with other parts of the body – both methods are politely listed in the BMA report – can fairly easily be exposed as no better than palmistry or astrology. Some people are impressed when the answer turns out to be correct, but this is bound to be so quite frequently and the chance of its happening will further increase if age, or general appearance, or previous illness are taken into account. If the claims made for such tests are shown (perhaps by means of a little judicious deception, as used by the Consumers Association) to be worthless – adding nothing to the rate of successful diagnosis – then their advocates have no choice but to fall back on the old excuse used by some believers in the paranormal – that the mere testing of a remedy by skeptics can in some way inhibit the effect. At this point, further discussion or testing is unlikely to be rewarding.

Meanwhile, as with palmistry, astrology, and the paranormal, it is striking how many people *want* to believe it, *need* to believe it, get a *thrill* out of believing it – and will therefore exaggerate the accuracy of the diagnosis or prognosis given. It seems that part of human nature is in love with magic and that it is sometimes a relief to switch off our powers of reasoning and believe implicitly in such things, rather than just keep an open mind about unlikely possibilities.

As to treatment, one of the most remarkable things about the history of medicine is that until recently scarcely anyone saw that the best way to assess how much was being achieved was to compare results, Why was this basic common-sense approach not always obvious? However (as with 'league tables' purporting to measure the performance of schools, hospitals, and so on) if the groups being compared are not as alike as possible apart from the method of treatment, there is a big danger of coming to false conclusions. Hence – whenever nobody knows which of two treatment policies is best – there is a need to ask patients if they will agree to take part in a careful randomized comparison.

They lose nothing by doing so. On the contrary several studies suggest that they may gain something just from joining a trial. In fact, when doctors and nurses find *themselves* ill or injured, they should encourage this attitude by asking to be included in such comparisons. This is a very different matter to research aimed at new discoveries; or at a better understanding of mechanisms. It is simply comparing outcomes. It is answering a very practical question: which policy gets the best results?

In HealthWatch, we don't see how any reasonable person can argue against this in principle, no matter what the type of remedy, no matter what the theory behind it, and no matter to what extent treatment is individualized. Once you have two groups that are broadly the same apart from how they are treated, you can make any comparison between two policies that you like. All the advantages and all the disadvantages – physical and psychological, short term and long term – can be compared. Anything that anyone wants to compare can be compared. For example, alongside more objective aspects, there is no reason why the *percentage* of patients who merely *feel happier* than they did before the treatment cannot be compared. Whichever way you look at it, valid comparison is the key.

Is this approach really, as some critics claim, no more than just the current thinking of Western medicine and Western science? On the contrary, is it not rock-hard, inescapable logic ? And is it not the honest, common-sense way to get at the truth? And is it not surprising that for many centuries reasonable human beings worldwide have not urged that it should be done? If 'amazing' results occur after a particular form of treatment, *how often* do similar results occur (*a*) after this treatment, (*b*) after other treatments, (*c*) after neither? If there is a difference, we want to know which policy gives the patient *the best chance* of doing well.

To take one very small current example, how many of the thousands of women who take evening primrose oil for pre-menstrual tension are aware that a Swedish double-blind trial has found that this very popular 'alternative' remedy (with a name like that, how could it fail?) had no more effect than ordinary liquid paraffin? Perhaps customers should have a right to this sort of evidence before they decide how to spend their money.

Then why so many grateful patients?

The history of medicine shows all too clearly how easy it is for both doctors and patients to be convinced that a remedy is beneficial when, in fact, it is doing no good – or even doing harm. It has happened many times in mainstream medicine as well as in fringe medicine. There is no 'remedy', however worthless, that does not have its quota of grateful patients. This is due partly, but not entirely, to the placebo effect. In HealthWatch (which has an updated position paper on this subject, if anyone is interested), we fully recognize the powerful and vital subjective help that one or more kinds of placebo therapy can give, together with listening, understanding, encouragement, relaxation, and so on. However, though many people long to believe that equally powerful *objective* effects can occur – including measurable physical healing and cures that would not otherwise have occurred – the evidence for this, though important and interesting, is only slight.

It is often forgotten that there are at least three other explanations, quite apart from the placebo effect, for patients feeling convinced that a treatment has helped them. First, many medical conditions are self-limiting. Those people who always take a remedy of some kind – or always want their doctor to give them one, even if he or she doesn't think it is necessary – fail to appreciate this, because they have so little experience of it. Many, though they talk a lot of natural healing and self-healing, seem surprisingly reluctant to take no remedy in situations where this is appropriate. Ironically they often seem to have *less* confidence in this policy than do many in mainstream medicine.

Second, in many long-standing conditions spontaneous improvements and remissions – lasting weeks, months, or even years – are common. In fact, nobody is more keenly aware of the self-healing powers of the human body than the men and women who practise mainstream medicine. Third, belief that a remedy has been successful is often based on a false assumption – the assumption that without it there would have been no improvement, or steady deterioration, or perhaps even death. People love to say that they *know* they would now be dead if it wasn't for some fringe medicine remedy. But this may not be true at all: the same thing happens to patients who have had nothing but standard treatment.

Following the completion of mainstream medicine for a cancer, for example, all trace of the disease may be gone and the patient may now feel completely well (perhaps cured, but with no guarantee of this). Then fringe medicine of some kind is added – and if the patient does exceptionally well, that's great, but no prizes for guessing which treatment then tends to get the credit. 'Living longer than expected' is by itself worthless as evidence, unless it can be shown to happen *more often* after this extra treatment than without it. It is quite common in mainstream medicine for patients to do not just better than average but far better than average. It happens all the time.

Another reason for misplaced gratitude is when completely healthy people (in so far as any of us are ever *completely* healthy – it would be very surprising if we were, given the amazing complexity of the ingenious mechanisms that keep our bodies ticking over) are conned into thinking that if they want to stay well they had better have a fringe remedy of some kind. Many people do this for years, the total cost mounting up to large sums, which they can ill afford. Those who stay well would probably have stayed well anyway.

Two personal experiences

All doctors have been patients at certain times in their life. Though they don't often talk about it ('it's funny to think of the doctor being ill' is still sometimes heard in wards or clinics) some have had more experience of being ill or in pain than have many of their patients. Here are two very ordinary, commonplace experiences of my own that illustrate two of the points I've made.

The first time was when I was recovering from major medical surgery and had a day when I felt very ill, but no cause was evident, so I got nothing for it. No suggested explanation, no reassurance, no hopeful suggestion that I would probably feel better next day, no humour, no mock chiding for feeling sorry for myself (too much sympathy is as bad as too little), and no placebo. A brief word of encouragement, combined with a spoonful of pink peppermint water – something equally cheap and harmless – would have cheered me up. This is an example of modern hospital staff sometimes failing to live up to the traditions of simple old-fashioned common-sense mainstream medicine.

The second time was when after months of severe sciatic nerve root pain (possibly made a little easier by the soothing and comforting hands of a sympathetic masseuse, but that's all – no real change) I was given a very gloomy prognosis by a senior neurosurgeon. However, *without any remedy of any kind*, it then all cleared up and I had no trouble whatever for the next fifteen years. The point here is that had I visited, say, an osteopath or chiropractor or acupuncturist, what happened would have been regarded by many people as impressive evidence for the effectiveness of alternative medicine.

Contradictory theories

To return to the 1993 BMA report, many of the dozens and dozens of different types of fringe medicine are based on some all-embracing theory regarding the way in which one part of the body is supposed to influence all other parts; or on some vague idea of imbalance and loss of harmony; or on the need to cleanse the body, or on the importance of unblocking channels of energy. In the past these sorts of theories were popular in mainstream medicine. But as soon as science and reason and hard work solve a problem and the real cause is discovered (of malaria, for example, which used to be thought due to 'bad air', hence its name) is such guesses are no longer needed.

Most fringe theories contradict each other, but the BMA is too polite to point this out in their report, contenting themselves with urging a register of all groups, so that after training they become 'competent' and have the necessary 'good practice'. Not wanting to offend anyone or sound patronizing, they make little or no attempt in this report to demarcate the absurd or the undesirable. Isn't it rather probable that the *competent* and *skilled* 'good practice' of nonsense, *following a course of thorough training* in nonsense, will remain nonsense?

Some branches of fringe medicine are now behaving in a much more honest and realistic way. Most osteopaths and chiropractors, for example, seem now to have quietly given up the claim that they stuck firmly to for more than a hundred years – that spinal manipulation was capable of curing or alleviating almost any disease in any part of the body. Since half the population suffers from intermittent backache, just sticking to that problem alone can no doubt keep them busy and earn them many grateful patients. Most are also very well trained in anatomy and much else from mainstream medicine, though obviously without as much practical experience of both diagnosed and not-yet diagnosed patients, as they would have if they had been through medical school.

An increasing number of fringe practitioners also now support proper randomized trials. But no single clinical trial can provide complete confirmation (or complete negation) of any theory or belief, and it seems likely that some hold so strongly to their convictions that they will believe only those trials that seem to confirm them. Only a small minority seem to have a reasonably open mind.

Reasons at least not to encourage it

So does yet another wave of enthusiasm for fringe medicine (there have been many previous ones in history) do any real harm? Mainstream medicine has always believed in curing sometimes, relieving often, and 'comforting always'. This basic, traditional teaching cannot be denied merely because some doctors fail to live up to it. And fringe medicine, even if it is 95 percent placebo therapy (compared with mainstream medicine's equivalent figure of perhaps 60 percent in the early part of this century and perhaps 30 percent now), can at least help with the comforting. So why not let people spend their money this way if they wish? Well, here are a few points that at least should make us pause before we do anything that encourages still further the recent huge expansion of fringe medicine:

1. Diagnosis: possible serious delay before the correct diagnosis is made. And a possible failure, due to lack of training in a medical school, to recognize the nature of later changes or complications. Less training of the medical school type also means less ability to give confident reassurance when there are needless fears.
2. Treatment: possible serious delay before the best treatment is given. Perhaps it is never given. Perhaps what is actually done is either worthless or second best.
3. Psychology and morale: whenever patients suffer from some condition whose cause remains unknown, they may at first be comforted by some alleged explanation based on one of the numerous fringe medicine beliefs – and by the treatment or ritual that follows from it. But later, if they

relapse, some of these theories can do harm. For example, the currently popular idea, especially with cancer, of pretending to be 'in control' (rather than calmly and philosophically hoping for the best, which used to be preferred and admired) can sometimes, in the event of relapse, make patients feel that this is due to their own inadequacy or to their failure to follow some regime of dubious value.

4. Money wasted ... often money that can ill be afforded. True, many healers are very sincere in their wish to help people for a reasonable charge – or even for nothing at all. But there is a wide range and it goes all the way to what most people would call gross overcharging. Some innocents are being really ripped off by those who see the rapid expansion of fringe medicine as a chance to make quite a lot of money. And, though those who hate the mainstream drug companies would love to think otherwise, there are obviously commercial vested interests in the manufacture of remedies for both camps.

5. Attitude to mainstream medicine: some healers give patients a false picture of the aims, ideals, and teaching of mainstream medicine. Several examples have been given.

6. The big increase in the popularity of fringe medicine, with its frequent emphasis on 'ancient' or 'natural' remedies is to some extent a step backwards to the superstition, sorcery, and magic of the past. Fringe medicine has not substantially changed. In general, it is stuck where it always was – and in a situation not very different to where mainstream medicine used to be more than a hundred years ago.

7. The language and behaviour of much of fringe medicine is basically that of magic rather than reason. For example, there is little exchange of information or attempt to iron out contradictions or inconsistencies. There is little or no talk of failure or of disappointment after initial hopes. There is very little puzzling over unsolved problems or hope of progress and better results in the future. It's all black or white and you either believe it and think it's marvellous or you don't.

8. Priorities and progress: though life is without question safer and longer than it was a hundred years ago (with far fewer children dying, far fewer young adults dying, and a more active old age) there is still much work to be done and many baffling mysteries to unravel if the incidence of premature death is to be further reduced. In terms of society's priorities – and in terms of public attitudes to science and rational problem-solving – there is a danger that the present big increase in fringe medicine will tend to slow down progress. Avoidable tragedies will be the result. It seems that some of us are more comfortable with mysticism than with progress, no matter how many problems remain unsolved and no matter how many people continue to die before their time.

Motivated Distortion of Personal Memory for Trauma
Mark Pendergrast

The nature of memory is an eternally interesting topic. Speculation about how memory works took a dangerous turn in the 1990s, however, when the notion that the trauma of child abuse might cause victims to forget the abuse entirely until a therapist helped them 'recover' those memories, usually under hypnosis, gained ground. The problem thus created has a name: false memory syndrome. In this talk, given at the Remembering Trauma Conference held in London in September 2003, independent scholar **Mark Pendergrast** *(www.nasw.org/users/markp), author of* **Victims of Memory**, *an investigation of false memory syndrome, describes how people can develop false memories of terrible events.* Appeared in XVII. 4.

People can come to believe in extremely traumatic events that never happened. It is quite clear that this does happen in the case of alien abductees or in the cases of medically verified virgins who remember being raped during their childhood. It is also quite clear to me from my research that this has happened in thousands, if not millions, of cases in North America and the UK, but I cannot prove that assertion. Still, some cases of illusory memories are provable. What follows is an explanation of how this is possible.

Motivation

First, to get someone to remember something horrible that never happened to them in their childhood, they have to be very *motivated*. There is a common misconception that therapists can 'implant' memories. I do not like the word *implant* at all. In order to believe in repressed memories, you have to be very motivated, and your motivation usually involves a quest to solve the puzzle of your life. We all want to have explanations for what has happened to us, and we all tend to seek fairly simple explanations, so it is very appealing to say, 'Well, I have trouble with relationships, I have an eating disorder, I have trouble with my self-esteem, and these are symptoms of sexual abuse, so maybe I was abused and repressed the memory.' During the height of the recovered memory movement, in the late 1980s and early 1990s, this was a common belief system, and many still believe it. So, many people – particularly women seeking therapy – were highly motivated to come up with a solution to their life problems.

Secondary gain

Secondly, there was *secondary gain* involved in almost every case I investigated. What I mean by that is that people, by being victims of sexual abuse, got a lot of attention they would not ordinarily have had. They got a lot of sympathy and, not to be harsh about it, they also could avoid a lot of responsibility for things in their lives at various points. This is not to say that this kind of belief system did not also cause extreme suffering, but there is no question that there was secondary gain.

Belief systems

The third point is, you have to have a *belief* in the theory of massive repression or massive dissociation, and many people did, and many people still do. When I was living in England for two months in the spring of 2003, I did an informal survey of people as I was travelling on trains, or when I was in pubs, or when I was walking up and down the barge canal. I asked people, 'If you were eight years old and you had a terrible, terrible thing happen to you, do you think that you could block that completely out, not have any memory of it, and then remember it later in life?' The vast majority of people said, 'Oh yes, you can do that, that happens.' I then asked, 'Well, how do you know?', and they would answer, 'Well, I just know,' or 'I've seen it on television or in a movie'. So – you have to have a belief that massive repression is something that people can do.

Authority figures

It also helps, although it is not necessary, to have an *authority figure* you go to who says, 'Oh yes, that's true. I know this is true because I have a PhD [*or* I'm a psychiatrist *or* I'm a social worker], and I've seen many people come through my office who had exactly the same symptoms that you do – these troubled relationships, problems with self-esteem and eating disorders – and many of them had these memories come back, that they had not remembered for many years, of being sexually abused, and so I think you may have repressed memories, too.' It really is an encouragement to illusory memories, but I'd like to emphasize that it is not necessary. You don't need an authority figure – illusory memories can be totally self-induced and, in many cases, they are.

Use of hypnosis, dream analysis, body symptoms, and other kinds of theories

A great deal has been said or written about the hazards of *hypnosis*, but I do want to add other things, and this is primarily what you will find in the chapter on 'How to Believe the Unbelievable' in my book *Victims of Memory* (1996). In this chapter, I went through tick, tick, tick; these are the ways that you can come to believe things that did not happen. Certainly hypnosis (or *guided imagery, visualization, meditation,* or *prayer,* which are all forms of hypnosis or auto-hypnosis if used to try to recall 'repressed' memories) is a very good way to do that, particularly if the authority figure who is leading you in the form of hypnosis has a vested interest in this theory of massive repression and believes that you may very well have been abused. I also want to warn about something called 'inadvertent cueing'. Many therapists are told, 'Don't use leading questions with people, don't lead your clients'. I do not think that anybody does intentionally lead their clients, but I interviewed many, many therapists who believed in repressed memories, and they all *did* lead their clients. They told me in the next sentence, after they had told me exactly how they had led their clients – 'but you must be very careful never to lead your clients. I always maintain a totally neutral stance', and so on.

If you believe in this idea that you can forget years of horrible things and then remember them much later, you are likely to convey that belief to your clients. And so I have told therapists – 'Be careful what you believe!' I think that ultimately this whole thing comes down to something I again want to emphasize, a belief system. It does not really matter what modalities you use. As Harvard Professor of Psychology Richard McNally found in his studies, many people have a very firm belief that they are incest survivors without having any actual memory of anything happening to them. They simply believe it, and once you believe it, I think that it is almost a foregone conclusion that you will come up with something.

For instance, recovered memory therapists use *dream analysis*. Frequently we dream about things that we are worried about, and if you are in therapy and you think that maybe your father sexually abused you, or that someone else did, you begin to obsess over it, and that is precisely what you will dream about. Consequently, many of these things become self-fulfilling prophecies. The same thing is true of so-called *body memories* where they tell you that you may have some panic attack or you may have some bodily symptom and then you sort of work yourself up into it, or pay particular attention to it.

Rehearsal

Once you come up with a scenario – and I saw this over and over again in this type of misguided therapy – you come up with a fragmentary image. What would happen would be that the therapists would take these fragmentary images and then they would have people *rehearse* them over and over again. In fact, they would tell them, 'Pretend that you have a movie screen or a television screen in your head and you have to visualize it, and you have to zoom in and freeze frame.' They would literally tell people to do those things – it was all very visual. So people would develop a script, a narrative, and they would have them write the narrative down over and over again, or repeat it in group sessions over and over again. The more you repeat something and the more you rehearse it, the more it becomes true for you.

Many retractors who took back their memory beliefs because they decided that they were incorrect still cannot get rid of the intrusive images. They have post-traumatic stress disorder. That would be an interesting thing to study – these people who have gone through this kind of therapy and developed a false belief system, then disbelieved it, but still cannot get rid of the intrusive memories of something they know rationally did not happen to them, such as, say, being in a Satanic cult.

Cognitive dissonance

This is a theory that was put forward by Leon Festinger quite a few years ago. It is quite an interesting theory and I think it makes sense, but it is just a theory. The idea is that you cannot have two contradictory ideas in your head at the same time. One of them is going to push the other one out like a cuckoo pushing an egg out from the nest. So if you opt for the idea that daddy did this horrible thing to you, you cannot very well have the idea that daddy was also a loving parent who did all these nice things with you, even though you have these very valid memories that he was a nice guy in many ways. So once you plump down on the side of this new belief system it is almost like a see-saw that goes 'whomp', and to 'unwhomp' it is very, very difficult to do. Once somebody opts for a belief system, and invests in it, and goes public with it, it is extremely difficult to undo.

Many, many times, people have said to me, 'Why would anybody make up something so dreadful? Why would anybody want to make up something so horrible about someone as central in their lives as their parents?' But it is not a matter of wanting – it is a matter of having a seed planted in your mind and having it grow almost inevitably. So it is really a belief system, followed by methods that really are quite suggestive to your memory. Memories are always reconstructive, and they can be changed – sometimes permanently. So I can only hope that you can remember some of what I have said here at least fairly accurately.

The Mosaic of Memory
Chris French

*"How far can you trust human memory? This question matters greatly when trying to assess a paranormal claim, because most of the time you are trying to assess someone's report of a personal experience rather than witnessing the event directly yourself. The person recounting the incident may be honest, sincere – and yet still make errors of perception or interpretation. In the case of the Knock apparitions, for example, the description of the figures the villagers saw as two-dimensional and unmoving did not stop some from concluding that they had seen the Blessed Virgin Mary with St Joseph and St John the Evangelist. Two related strands of psychological research are relevant to this issue. First, as discussed by **Mark Pendergrast** in the previous chapter, is the phenomenon of 'memories' that have no basis in fact. Second, with a much longer history within psychology, is the question of the accuracy of eyewitness accounts which over time may become so distorted as to be completely unreliable. Professor Chris French, head of the Anomalistic Psychology Research Unit at Goldsmiths College, University of London, and co-editor of* The Skeptic *(2001–present), explores the workings of human memory. Appeared in XVII.1."*

Textbooks often begin their discussion of memory with the rather obvious observation that memory does not work like a video camera. At first glance, it might strike you that it would be better if it did. Imagine if you could just press the right mental button and be treated to an exact mental replay of events you had witnessed in the past – wouldn't that be fantastic? Well, yes and no. One can think of several situations where it would be advantageous – settling arguments between husbands and wives, for example. But I only have to think about the disorganized state of our video collection at home to realize some obvious problems. How on earth would you ever find the memory that you wanted?

But the problem isn't just one of locating the right bit of mental footage. Unlike, material recorded on videotape, memories can and do change over time. A memory is more like a dynamic mosaic than a series of static unchanging frames recorded by a video camera. The very first time that you try to recall an event, you will engage in a constructive process – you will literally build that memory from different bits and pieces. Some of those bits and pieces will correspond to more or less accurate memory traces laid down at the time you witnessed the event, but even then you may not put them together properly. Furthermore, the mosaic you build will be influenced by things that happened to you before the event in question that led you to have particular expectations and a particular way of viewing the world. It will also be influenced by your current view of the world and of yourself. There will also be a general tendency to fill in any gaps in such a way that the whole 'makes sense'.

In general, we do not remember the surface details of events at all well; we remember the gist. We automatically extract the important essence of events and forget the superficial and transitory packaging. This is both the great strength and the great weakness of the way our memories work. It is a strength because we don't process and store all of the minutiae of life. We pay attention to the important stuff and forget the rest. Why lay down in memory a complete verbatim record of every conversation you ever had or every song you've ever heard? But it is a weakness because sometimes we do need that level of detail and it will probably elude us. Or, worse still, we may confidently believe that a memory we hold is a true reflection of an event when in fact it may be distorted beyond recognition.

There are only a few areas where the accuracy of our memories is so important that we make any attempt to assess it. Examples include forensic psychology – it appears that we are probably far more impressed by eyewitness testimony to crimes than we should be. Another area where it becomes important is anomalistic psychology, the psychology of unusual experiences and beliefs. Just how accurate are eyewitness reports of UFOs, ghosts, and the Loch Ness monster? Or even alien abductions? And of course there's always the settling of marital arguments.

Most of the research on eyewitness testimony has been driven by the need to understand factors affecting the reliability of reports from witnesses to crimes. It is now generally accepted that such reports can often be wildly inaccurate, leading to gross miscarriages of justice. The circumstances surrounding crimes are often precisely those that will lead to poor recall. The event is unexpected, often over in seconds, and sometimes extremely frightening. Or it may be that the police need details of events that preceded a crime – events which no one at the time realized would be that important. One obvious reason that we may fail to remember things accurately is simply that we failed to pay attention to the right details at the time. Typically, we pay attention to the information that is relevant to our goals at the time – and it can sometimes be amazing what we miss!

I can illustrate this with a true story of a visit to an estate agent that I made with my wife when we were looking to move house many years ago. As we left the estate agents, having looked at details of various houses, I said to my wife, who is also a psychologist, 'That was very strange. It reminded me of a psychology experiment.' She was rather confused by this and asked me what I meant. I said 'You mean you didn't see it?' 'See what?' she said. I told her to look through the estate agents' window to see if she could see anything a little bit unusual. She did – and could not believe that she had failed to spot a full-size stuffed bison that for some unknown reason was on display in the office! This nicely illustrates the fact that people may vary in terms of what information they encode at any particular moment. My wife was very focused on house buying – what price, where, how many bedrooms – my mind was perhaps not so fully focused on the important task in hand.

Research into what is known as 'change blindness' provides another illustration of our inattention to aspects of our surroundings. In a typical study, people queuing at a library issue desk are handed a form to fill in by the librarian. At one point in the interaction, the librarian disappears from view, as though retrieving a dropped piece of paper, but another completely different person emerges in their place. Around half of the participants simply do not notice the change.

A huge amount of experimental evidence, in addition to our everyday experience, shows us that our memories are poor if we haven't paid attention in the first place. No big surprise there. But what about those situations where it's really important that we pay attention and get things right? Even here, our memory can play cruel tricks. Donald Thomson, a psychologist in Australia, was arrested by the police and forced to take part in a line-up. He assumed he was being harassed in response to his strong views on the unreliability of such line-ups. Things got very serious, however, when he was identified by a very distraught woman and told that he was being charged with rape. It transpired that the rape had taken place with the television on in the room at the time of the attack. The programme being shown was a live debate on the reliability of identity parades, featuring both Thomson and the Assistant Commissioner of Police. The victim had unintentionally based her description of the rapist on Thomson, who was on television at the time. Fortunately, he had a large number of viewers to provide him with a watertight alibi.

There are, of course, those vivid memories that we just *know* are right. One example is so-called flashbulb memories. We can all remember with perfect accuracy where we were, what we were doing, who we were with, when we heard about the attack of September 11 – can't we? There seems to be something about such moments that burns the details into our very brain cells. I can still remember, for example, hearing the news of John F. Kennedy's assassination. I was only 7 years old at the time, so when I heard the newsflash on TV, it didn't mean that much to me. But I remember ambling into the kitchen to tell my mum and dad about it anyway. It was from their reaction that I realized that this was news of stupendous importance. I used this example of a flashbulb memory in my lectures for years in my adult life and on one occasion happened to mention this to my mother. She told me that it just didn't happen that way at all. We were not at home and it was not me that broke the news. Interestingly, I had been the victim of a false memory that put me right at the heart of the action! Again, experimental evidence has shown that flashbulb memories – often held with great conviction – are often just plain wrong. American students recorded details of how they heard the news of the Challenger disaster the morning after it happened – who they were with, what they were doing, and so on. A couple of years later, many of them had completely different recollections of that event.

It appears that when we try to recall something, the mosaic memory we bring to consciousness consists of memory traces of the original event plus other memory traces, perhaps relating to other similar events or even to daydreams or fantasies. Gaps in memory will sometimes be effortlessly and automatically filled in to produce our recollection – and we will often have no way of knowing which bits we can trust and which we cannot. Sometimes we may be fooled into thinking that something really happened when in fact we only imagined or even dreamt it. Our ability to distinguish between memories for events that really happened and those memories that are internally generated is known as *reality monitoring*. An everyday example is trying to decide whether you really did lock the backdoor or just *thought about* it. At the other extreme is psychotic breakdown in which the sufferer is totally unable to distinguish between mental events and events out there in the real world.

Although psychologists have long recognized that firsthand accounts of witnessed events were unreliable, it is only within the last decade or so that research has been directed at the possibility that people may sometimes have rich and detailed memories for events that they have never actually witnessed at all. The main reason for this explosion of research into false memories was the sudden increase in cases of alleged recovered memories of childhood sexual abuse, especially in the USA. Typically in such cases, adults would enter psychotherapy suffering from a variety of common psychological problems such as depression, low self-esteem, or insomnia. As part of their psychotherapy they would engage in mental exercises such as hypnotic regression and guided visualization, intended to unlock any repressed memories of traumatic childhood events thought to be causing their problems. Many thousands of people who had entered therapy with no conscious memories of being abused as children became convinced that their now-aged parents had indeed inflicted terrible suffering upon them decades earlier. In some cases, these allegations included claims of Satanic ritualized abuse, involving human sacrifice, cannibalism, sexual torture, and forced abortions. Many of these cases went to court and led to convictions even though the cases rested entirely upon verbal testimony. Families were torn apart in the most brutal way imaginable.

Experimental psychologists tended to doubt the accuracy of the memories recovered via hypnosis and related techniques. A huge amount of experimental evidence shows quite convincingly that hypnotic regression does not provide a magic key to unlock the unconscious mind, forcing it to reveal its hidden memories. Instead, the hypnotic regression procedure is such that it provides a context in which individuals often produce an account mixing fantasy with pre-existing knowledge and expectations – and then believe with total conviction that the account reflects events that really took place. Indeed, experimental psychologists have expressed doubts about the very concept of repression itself. The idea that the unconscious mind can somehow automatically take over and hide away memories for traumatic events is not supported by any convincing experimental evidence, although there are many accounts of what appears to be repression occurring outside the laboratory.

In the early days of the controversy, those who believed that recovered memories were largely accurate would sometimes object that, although memory for peripheral details of a witnessed event might be distorted, there was little evidence that people were prone to false memories for episodes that had never actually occurred at all. Things have moved on since then, thanks to the pioneering work of Elizabeth Loftus, amongst others. We now know that it is alarmingly easy to plant false memories in a sizeable minority of the population using well-established experimental techniques. It has been shown, for example, that hypnotic regression is not the only way to induce false memories. Simply getting people to imagine events that did not actually take place is often sufficient to lead people to believe that they did witness or take part in the events in question.

The difficulties of deciding whether a memory reflects a real event or not is illustrated by something that happened to Elizabeth Loftus herself. Loftus's mother had died by committing suicide. She had drowned herself in a swimming pool, but Loftus had never actually seen her mother's body – or so she thought. Many years later, and long after Loftus had established her reputation as the leading psychologist in false memory research and one of the main critics of the concept of repression, she was attending a family get-together when one of her uncles insisted that she had in fact seen her mother's body. He said that Loftus was the person who had found the body floating face down in the pool. An image of her mother's lifeless body immediately filled Loftus's mind. She was flabbergasted – for years, she had questioned the notion that the mind just locks away memories that are too ghastly to face. But it appeared she had done just that. Over the next few days, her memory of that terrible sequence of events become clearer and more detailed as she dwelt upon this horrible revelation. And then she called her brother to tell him – and he said the uncle was wrong, Loftus had not found the body! This was confirmed by other family members. Far from experiencing a recovered memory, Loftus had, in fact, been the victim of a false memory.

5

Faking it

Many paranormal claims and beliefs have their origins in perceptual mistakes on the part of the observers, often fuelled by the desire to believe: recognizing patterns where none exist, preferring the sensational over the mundane, favouring the comforting over the scary. Some, however, are deliberately produced by trickery. Magicians won't reveal how they do their stuff – but skeptics will.

Muddying the Waters
David Langford

In the early 1990s, Whitley Strieber achieved considerable notoriety by following up several horror novels with **Communion,** *an allegedly true, autobiographical account of his interactions with 'visitors' – that is, aliens. David Langford is famous in science fiction circles for winning more Hugo awards for his witty, compact fanzine* **Ansible** *than anyone in the history of the genre. He is also author of a number of books including* **The End of Harry Potter?** *and* **The Leaky Establishment.** *His experience in perpetrating a UFO hoax is an example of why skeptics need to be very careful about such things; over time and repeated tellings, they become true ... or at least, true enough to be picked up by other people's bestsellers. As Mark Twain might have written, a lie can cycle infinitely around the internet while the truth is still lying in bed at home. Appeared in IV.3.*

Towards the end of 1989 I heard the rumours. In 1990, confirmation came in the form of a big, fat, and much-hyped hardback. Yes: I, humble and obscure Langford, had been selected from millions of other SF authors as an influence on that god amongst men, Whitley Strieber. It is a proud and lonely thing ...

It is time for a flashback to 1978. The original daft suggestion came from Paul Barnett, now better known as the author John Grant, but then my editor at David & Charles Ltd and struggling to break free of this publisher's relentless specialization in trains and canals. Constantly editing things called *201 Interesting Stretches of Canal Visible from Norfolk Railway Lines* can make you yearn for new horizons.

His brief to me was: write a spoof book about a nineteenth-century UFO encounter. 'Examine' the 'evidence' as a physicist would. Lambast modern UFOlogy for its lack of scientific rigour. Make the Victorian UFO sufficiently over the top that no close reader could believe it. What larks, what larks! More than one skeptic has been tempted in this way to exert the happy irresponsibility of the SF writer, only to find the resulting satire embedded (like a fly in ointment) in the pseudoscience which was supposed to be satirized ...

For the antique UFO report, Paul lent me a period stylebook in the form of Thackeray's *Adventures of Philip*. My wife searched her family tree for an impeccably documented ancestor: William Robert Loosley, undertaker and craftsman of High Wycombe in Buckinghamshire, and provider of posh confirmation of something-or-other furniture to Disraeli. Unearthed from the dusty recesses of my typewriter, Loosley's first-person narrative (in tone oddly reminiscent of Thackeray, with a random larding of biblical phrases) had, it seemed, been miraculously preserved for more than a century, just handy for publication in 1979.

A surrounding commentary by that little-known savant David Langford proved quite inconclusively that during his carefully recorded encounter in the Buckinghamshire woods, Loosley was exposed to advanced knowledge of nuclear physics, quantum mechanics, general relativity, black holes, and indeed everything else I could remember from an Oxford physics course.

No, this isn't a plug for the book, long out of print despite its snappy title of *An Account of a Meeting with Denizens of Another World, 1871* (David & Charles, 1979; St Martin's Press, 1980). I come to bury it, not to praise it, and as usual my publishers had the same idea. There was an abrupt change of editors, and the new chap combined integrity with economy by omitting two key elements of the original plan – simulated pages from 'Loosley's manuscript', and a non-zero publicity budget. Instead, he wondered whether the book could make its own way as a jolly good SF novel. In the face of this rampant indecision about how and whether to promote it, my squib passed away quietly to that remainder shelf from whence no traveller returns.

Nevertheless, *An Account* had made its mark. The grottier sort of newspapers and magazines ran Amazing UFO Proof stories, their devotion to investigative journalism being amply shown by the fact that not one asked the obvious question, 'How about giving us a look at this 108-year-old manuscript, then?' Enshrined in many a footnote, plus two pages of the doubtless deeply scholarly *The World's Greatest UFO Mysteries*, Loosley has passed into history – at least, that peculiar alternative history beloved of so many UFOlogists. My finest hour came when I was attacked for the excessive caution and skepticism of my own commentary on Loosley's narrative.

Later I found that I wasn't the only SF writer to have gleefully muddied the waters of research. John Sladek, as 'James Vogh', had gone to the extent of inventing the lost thirteenth sign of the zodiac. His books on the sign Arachne, he told me, 'were conceived as jokes, but very quickly turned into moneymaking enterprises. Only they didn't make a lot of money, either. So finally they turn out to have been a gigantic waste of time.' I probably picked a slightly better market. Astrology already has its fact-proof theories and doesn't require more, while UFOlogy seems prepared to assimilate any odd incident whatever, declaring it to be further conclusive confirmation of something or other.

(And as we all know, an explained or exploded incident never attracts the same attention as the original enigma. Even *Skeptical Inquirer* displayed no interest in an offer to confess my own folly in their pages – though they did condescend to report the revelation when, instead, I published it as an essay in *New Scientist*.)

The moral seemed to be that SF authors writing with tongue in cheek should stick with SF. In off-trail phenomena as in bodice-ripping romance, the book market sniffs at jokesters but rewards sincerity, even misguided, self-deluding, and totally barmy sincerity. (I do not, at this juncture, mention Whitley Strieber and *Communion*.) It felt vaguely depressing to have contributed another snippet of disinformation to the already over-large folklore, without even the compensation of getting rich. I ended my first confession with apologies to all, most especially my bank manager.

Now, the sequel.

Personally I still incline to the opinion that any true first contact with alien thingies will be as clear and unequivocal as the message beamed Earthwards in my and John Grant's disaster novel, *Earthdoom*: 'YOU EARTHLING SCUM ARE THE DREGS OF THE UNIVERSE. WE COME TO ANNIHILATE YOU PAINFULLY AND RAPE YOUR PLANET.' However, I do admit that there are UFOlogists of integrity ... which according to me means a readiness to entertain the wild supposition that UFO does not *necessarily* stand for Alien Space Vehicle Piloted By Little Putty Men With Enormous Eyes.

One such researcher, Jenny Randles, contacted Paul Barnett with the glad news that the story of *An Account* had been incorporated – without any visible criticism of its content – into the latest work by no less than Whitley Strieber.

(Later, still rocking with laughter, she passed this on to the even more noted UFOlogist Jacques Vallee, who is supposed to have slowly said: 'Oh. God. You mean that *An Account's* a spoof, then?')

For the first time in my life I became frantic to get hold of a book by Strieber. Luckily, before I could do anything terminally rash such as part with money, his British publishers sent me a copy of *Majestic* (London: Macdonald, 1990; £12.95 hbk; 318pp.). This I skimmed avidly until I found the good bit, which is on pages 46 and 47.

In what some might call a dramatic break with his former practice, Strieber presents this as a novel, though one very closely based on truth. This allows him to tinker a little with his source material, and indeed to omit source references which might be checked. Although his two good pages are a direct condensation from *An Account*, there's no mention of the book itself, or of its being copyrighted in my name. Perhaps being a major bestseller puts you above things like literary ethics.

Again, because Strieber is going on about the purported UFO crash in New Mexico in 1947, he carefully backdates the discovery of William Robert Loosley's fabulous manuscript from the 1970s to 1941. (The 1979 edition of *An Account* says that it was found 'only a few years ago', which by no stretch of imagination includes 1941. Internal evidence is arranged to indicate a date later than 1975. Of course it had been, as it were, found in 1978.)

Even in this book's brief summary, Strieber's keen critical intelligence can be shown by his rendering of a rather carefully phrased comment about this hard-to-locate MS:

> *I can only declare that the manuscript has so far withstood every test of authenticity to which it has been subjected. (An Account, 1979)*

> *The ms. has been authenticated by British antiquarians. (Majestic, 1989)*

Exercise for the beginning student: which of these sentences admits the possibility that the number of 'tests of authenticity' might have been less than one?

Exercise for the advanced student: how closely based on a 'true incident' can be a book whose reconstruction of 1947 US Intelligence documents incorporates a text which I didn't draft until 1978? Come to think of it, why wasn't the Loosley story publicly expunged from UFO legend after the appearance of my 1988 *New Scientist* article?

Exercise for a weary reviewer: do I really have to struggle on to page 318 and its plea for me to rush in a letter telling Strieber about all the occasions on which I've been abducted and/or offered little yellow flowers by passing aliens?

Exercise for you all: if someone reproduces a story and believes it to be factual, does he perhaps have a responsibility not to tamper with the facts? Conversely, if someone does so while believing it to be fiction, might the word 'plagiarism' not conceivably apply?

I suppose that I should at least be cheered by the prospect of reaching, for the very first time, a readership numbered in the millions. Surely this is every pure-souled author's dream. Before long I will learn not to chafe at anonymity, and to stop making the obsessive calculations which begin: 'two pages out of 318, that's ... that's ... I wonder how much 0.63% of Whitley Strieber's royalties would be?'

Postscript

As it turned out, many of this article's queries and speculations were more or less answered when (after bitching to his publishers) I heard indirectly from the great man himself. Apparently he never even saw my book. Apparently Whitley Streiber, the most famous UFO pundit in the entire universe, does his research in such quick-buck compilations as *The World's Strangest Mysteries*. This instant remainder from Octopus includes the exact same text and typography as the earlier rip-off of my book in *The World's Greatest UFO Mysteries*, complete with a misquote about the manuscript's 'authentication'. (Nigel Blundell, compiler of both books, believes in recycling his own as well as others' writing.) And therefore, the US publishers' lawyers triumphantly concluded, I have absolutely nothing to complain about.

... Except that even this debased text says quite clearly that the Loosley MS was hidden for 'nearly one hundred years' since 1871 and gives enough information for even a feebly conscientious researcher to get in touch with me. Dear old Whitley just wrote to Octopus and, getting no reply, went right ahead and used the story anyway.

However, it does look as though future editions of *Majestic* will carry, on the copyright page, a proper acknowledgement to my book. That leaves me happier, if no richer.

Knock: Some New Evidence
David Berman

The Skeptic began in Ireland in the 1980s, where even then, the 1879 Knock apparitions were still a cause of much speculation; the site was being built up as a world pilgrimage site. In this case, the Blessed Virgin Mary and several other figures appeared to fifteen villagers, who described the figures as two-dimensional and unmoving.

*The leading theory, that they were created deliberately by a magic lantern placed under the eaves of the church, was demonstrated effectively in the 1987 television programme **Is There Anybody There?**, produced by Karl Sabbagh for Channel 4. This theory had been mooted in 1979 by **David Berman**, an associate professor in philosophy at Trinity College Dublin. After his article was reprinted in **The Skeptic**'s very first issue, some contentious debate followed in the letters column. Leslie Shepard (1917–2004), editor of the **Encyclopaedia of Occultism and Parapsychology** and founder of the Bram Stoker Society, argued insistently that a village priest lacked the opportunity, the motive and the dishonesty necessary to carry out the deception. **Berman**, however, found evidence that seems to be conclusive. Appeared in II.1.*

In an article published in *The Freethinker* (October 1979) and *The Skeptic* (I.1), I argued that the 1879 apparition at Knock, Co. Mayo was most probably brought about by a magic lantern. This conclusion was reached largely by an analysis of the depositions of the witnesses, and particularly of the variants in the two printed versions of these depositions in the *Weekly News* of 21 and 28 February 1880 and *The Apparition and Miracles at Knock* by John Macphilpin (Dublin, 1880). Since that article, new evidence has come from two sources, which corroborates the lantern hypothesis. First, those familiar with optical equipment have tried to show that a magic lantern of the time could, given the physical conditions, have produced an effect similar to that described by the witnesses (in particular, see the television documentary on the paranormal *Is There Anybody There?*, Channel 4, 31 October 1987).

But why, it has often been asked, would someone have perpetrated such a bizarre hoax? Where is the motive? Who is the culprit? Clearly, one needs to find someone who would have (1) benefited from the hoax, (2) had access to the church or schoolhouse, (3) had an insider's intimacy with the village of Knock, and (4) had the ability to have acquired the magic lantern and engineer the hoax.

The person who best meets conditions two to four was the parish priest of Knock, Archdeacon Bartholomew Cavanagh. And it is clear from the new evidence that I present here that he also meets condition one. For he needed just such an event to bolster his authority in the parish, authority which had been dramatically undermined only two months before the apparition. This comes out in a confidential intelligence report to the Irish Chief Secretary of a meeting at Knock on 1 June 1879. The document is among the State Papers in Dublin Castle; it is headed 'confidential' and dated '3rd June 1879'. As it has never (as far as I am aware) been quoted or even mentioned, I reproduce it here nearly in full:

> *All the men, about 300 who marched to Knock on that day, assembled at a place called Baring-Carol and proceeded thence in fours.*
>
> *They were profusely decorated with green sashes, rosettes, ribbons and laurel branches and leaves. They were commanded by JW Nally, suspect, Balia, John O'Kanee, suspect, of this town, and P.J. Gordon, Bootmaker who lives here also. Another man who was introduced as a W. Jones of Dublin had a command, but he was actually a person named Sheridan, who is a native of Bohold in this district. All these men addressed the people assembled on the occasion who numbered about 1500. Sheridan was the first who delivered a speech. He said: Father Cavanagh (P.P.) had endeavoured to stamp them as blackguards, he had done everything to brand them (cries down with him – cut off his supplies). He should not trample on the people who hoped to benefit their Country. He had referred to one man by name (Shame, and nine cheers for O'Kane) and said that he was actually drawing money and purchasing arms. The only motive is the common benefit of our Country, that, by banding themselves together against the tyrant Landlords. There were police present: let them hear a sample of their ideas. Let them openly declare their determination to stand and die together. They were threatened with setters (the Constabulary. in allusion to the formation of a barrack at Knock) but they should be no longer lukewarm or cowardly, but proclaim in daylight what was required.*
>
> *O'Kane next spoke: Father Cavanagh had made a wanton attack upon him who wished to see his Country free. It was said they were fenians – if that means haters of British Rule they were all fenians. Did Father Cavanagh wish to be reconciled to British Rule? Who made the Country a desert? Would they be reconciled? (three cheers for the Zulus) They should wait for their opportunity. England was as hostile as of old, the fair fields of Ireland are converted into bullock pastures. He had promises from America – if they work together they would work out the freedom of their Country. When England would be engaged by Russia it would then be the time. He did not want to conceal that when the opportunity offered it would be embraced.*
>
> *No police station was required at Knock; it would be an outrage to bring those ruffians – the police – amongst the people, it would not deter them to do their*

duty. They should resist the invaders and drive them into the Atlantic. His line was chalked and he'd not depart from it. Gordon directed the people to pay no rent without getting an abatement.

If the landlords resisted they'd make the tenants not pay.

A Resolution was then put forward by Sheridan in which it was proposed that Nolan Farrell's Tenants (in this district) should hold out against their tyrant landlord, the scoundrel who would crowd the workhouses of their saxon enemies and their Gaols – that they should stand together.

Having had to wait to receive the notes taken at the meeting by the Kiltemagh Constabulary, I was unable to report until today.

J.C. Carter

(Dublin Castle State Papers Office C.S.O.R.P. – 1879-9632)

Plainly, Archdeacon Cavanagh had endangered his prestige in the area by championing the landlords and attacking the local Fenian or Land League leaders. He would surely have been alarmed by the 'cries down with him – cut off his supplies'. And I should point out that this report was taken very seriously in Dublin Castle; for an official, probably the Attorney General, has annotated it with words: 'Very bad, I assume the words can be proved. E.G., 20/6/79'. County Mayo was, it would seem, in the grips of a 'conspiracy against all landed property which widely exists there'. These are the words of Lord Mayo, the Lieutenant for the County, in a letter (also unnoticed) to the Chief Secretary, dated 26 September 1879. Speaking of the 'alarming state' of Mayo, he continues:

I have no hesitation in saying that as soon as agents are instituted or allowed by their employers 'to insist upon the payment of rents – whether in the whole or in part – many districts will be violently disturbed, and not only property, but life will be seriously endangered.

Threatening notices are posted everywhere, and on all estates however moderately rented and where all rights of property are most leniently exercised, the tenantry are, through fear of assassination, prevented paying their rents when ready and willing to do so ...

... it is to communism alone the present state of things in that country is to be attributed, and this communism is the consequence of the violent agitation raised and maintained for their own political purposes by a few

demagogues – of whom one is a Justice of the Peace – who are constantly inciting the tenantry to resistance of all authority, and all rights of property ...

I find it impossible to understand why there is such a total absence of the military, not alone in Mayo but in the whole of the province of Connaught; surely there is no part of Ireland where at this moment a military force is as necessary as it is in Mayo...

(Dublin Castle, State Papers Office, C.S.O.R.P. – 1880-580)

Property and authority were under fire in Mayo in 1879. Hence it seems plausible that Archdeacon Cavanagh, whose own authority and livelihood were especially threatened in June of that year, should look for a way to re-establish his position, which would also strike a blow for the forces of law and property and against the subversive Fenians and Land Leaguers, There is a long tradition, possibly going back to Plato, of deceiving the vulgar in the interest of some (supposed) higher good. And I should point out that in the 1870s apparitions were featured in the Irish Catholic periodicals – for example, various numbers of the *Illustrated Monitor*, Dublin, for the year 1875. It is surely plausible, then, that the recently denounced Archdeacon Cavanagh should consider engineering an apparition by means of a magic lantern for certain higher goods. But was it likely? That is, was Archdeacon Cavanagh capable of subordinating truth to some other ideal?

Consider the following account of Sister M. F. Cusack, a nun who worked in Knock in the early 1880s. Initially, as she tells us in *The Story of My Life* (London, 1891), she was 'full of enthusiasm' for the apparition; but she 'soon found cause to cool down':

While I was in the church one day I saw a bright light above the altar, and all the people were exclaiming, 'There it is! there it is! Now we have seen it for ourselves.' I was somewhat impressed myself, and hoped that at last I had seen a supernatural sight, even if it was only a bright light. I was kneeling when I first saw the light, but when I rose up from my knees the light disappeared. I at once knelt down again, and lo, the light shone once more as bright as ever. I tried this experiment several times, and was then convinced that it was some reflection. I had made up my mind to investigate everything thoroughly when I came to Knock, though my prejudices were in favour of believing everything. I now went near the altar, and at once found out the cause of what seemed supernatural. It was simply a very large glass stone, which had caught the reflection of the setting sun.

I dared not touch anything about the shrine, so I went at once to Father Cavanagh, whose house was quite near, and asked him to come and remove the vision, for I thought it was dreadful to have the people deceived, But to my amazement – and I must admit also to my indignation – he would not remove it. This made me very skeptical as far as he was concerned. (pp. 268–91)

From this circumstantial account I take it that Archdeacon Cavanagh was capable of deceiving the people for what he probably considered some higher good – whether guarding private property and public order, or increasing religious devotion. I should also mention that the question of such deception is still a matter of debate; for consider those who sanction deceiving terminally ill patients about their illnesses, or governments falsifying information in the interests of national security, or parents telling white lies to children about Santa Claus.

Although I have claimed that Cavanagh engineered the apparition, I am not claiming that he actually operated the magic lantern. I take it that he hired the lantern, but it may have been operated by someone else in Knock, under Cavanagh's supervision. There is a letter in the Tuam diocesan archive from a Michael McConnell, from Belfast, who says that a friend of his called Constable McDermott, who had been stationed at Knock, had told him that the apparition had been produced by a magic lantern operated by a Protestant policeman stationed at Knock. (See Catherine Rynne's *Knock: 1879–1979*, Dublin, 1979, pp. 67–70.) This, of course, is hearsay, as is the statement I heard nearly eight years ago from a senior member of the Irish judiciary, to the effect that a solicitor of his acquaintance told him that his grandfather hired a magic lantern to Archdeacon Cavanagh during the week in question.

Such oral information is unlikely to persuade believers, but it is worth preserving, if only because it may lead to the discovery of hard evidence in, for example, a letter or diary.

There is some hard evidence (long known) that makes sense within the case I am making, namely, the striking fact that, although Cavanagh was within five minutes' walking distance of the apparition, he refused to see it when asked by his housekeeper, Mary McLoughlin, the first to observe the apparition. Later, Cavanagh is reported to have consoled himself that: 'If I had seen it, many things would have been said that cannot now be advanced with any fair show of reason or probability on their side' (*Weekly News*, 14 Feb. 1880). I take Cavanagh's absence from the apparition to be nearly as striking (and suspicious) as the disappearance of the original manuscript depositions. My explanation for his absence is that he *was* implicated, and that his *post factum* statement suggests his implication. The pattern is not unfamiliar to psychologists: in short, the original cause is transformed into an excuse or consolation.

A similar reversal of cause and effect is also evident, I think, in 'a vivid local memory, passed down in the family of [Patrick Walsh] one of the ... eyewitnesses to the apparition', according to which there was a meeting of Whiteboys, to which young Walsh came:

Later, Patrick Walsh apologised to Archdeacon Cavanagh for hearing him denounced at this meeting which he attended. The people felt that the priest was so devoted to Our Lady that she protected him from the Whiteboys and those like them. (Knock: 1879–1979, p 83)

In William Coyne's *Venerable Archdeacon Cavanagh* (Roscommon, 1953), there is an even more dramatic story (again unsubstantiated) about a secret society that had determined to punish Cavanagh for 'preaching caution and restraint to his flock'.

At length it was resolved ... to have his ears cut off... However, before the date fixed for the sacreligious act the extraordinary events of the 21 August 1879 (the apparition) had occurred at Knock. There was a complete change ... even the hardest of hearts ... regarded it as a direct sign through Our Lady that a crime of the kind contemplated was a desecration ... (pp. 82–4)

Here again we have, I think, a reversal of cause and effect; that is, we are able to see what Archdeacon Cavanagh originally intended to achieve by his hoax. He wanted the appearance of the Virgin Mary to 'bring about a complete change ... even in the hardest of hearts' just as he wished to make his flock ashamed at having heard and supported his denunciation at the 1 June 1879 meeting.

Acknowledgements
I am grateful to Dr William Vaughan for drawing my attention to the June 1879 item in the State Papers Office, Dublin Castle, and to Professor William Lyons for commenting on an earlier version of this paper.

A Case of Spirits
Chris Willis

Chris Willis (1960–2004), a scholar of Victorian literature who taught at Birkbeck College, was a frequent contributor to **The Skeptic** *on a wide variety of topics, including Harry Potter, Mrs Gaskell's elephant, and spontaneous human combustion. Here she explores the history of spirit photography, the success of which relied largely on the general public's lack of familiarity with what was then a very new technology. Now, of course, Photoshop has made convincing photographic fakery easily achievable by almost anyone. But of course we're too sophisticated these days to be fooled. Aren't we? Appeared in XV.2.*

The camera cannot lie – or can it? From the mid-Victorian era to the 1920s, thousands of people were hoaxed by photos which supposedly proved the existence of ghosts. A fascinating selection of such photographs has now been put online by the American Museum of Photography (www.photographymuseum. com/seance.html).

Unscrupulous photographers made large sums of money by producing photographs of sitters accompanied by other-worldly 'spirits'. These spirits were usually supposed to be the ghosts of the sitter's recently deceased friends or relatives. Desperate for some reassurance of life after death, the bereaved sitters were unlikely to question the result.

The first spirit photographer was American William H. Mumler of Boston, who produced hundreds of photos during the 1860s. Many of his victims had lost sons, fathers, brothers, or husbands in the American Civil War and were desperate for consolation. One of Mumler's most vocal opponents was circus impresario P. T. Barnum. He condemned Mumler as a fraud, and pointed out that the unscrupulous photographer was exploiting the vulnerability of people whose judgement was clouded by grief. Barnum gave evidence at Mumler's trial for fraud in May 1869. Mumler was charged with having 'swindled many credulous persons, leading them to believe it is possible to photograph the immaterial forms of their departed friends'. To show how easy it was to fake a spirit photo, Barnum and a photographer friend, Abraham Bogardus, produced a photo which appeared to show Barnum with the ghost of Abraham Lincoln.

Spirit photos were easy to fake. Popular knowledge of photography was limited at this time, and most people did not know that such pictures could be produced by a simple double exposure. Another method was even simpler. In Barnum's era, exposures of up to a minute were needed for photographs. So, while the subject was sitting still and gazing at the camera, the photographer's assistant, dressed in suitably ghostly robes, would step into the picture and stand behind them, moving gently so as to create a 'ghostly' blur which would render his or her features less recognizable. Alternatively, a dummy could be put into place behind them, and revealed by pulling back a curtain. Other methods involved tampering with the photographic plate during processing.

Mumler narrowly escaped conviction when the judge reluctantly decided that there was insufficient evidence against him. Others were not so fortunate. In Paris, Édouard Buguet and his associate M. Leymarie were imprisoned in 1875 after investigators discovered the dummies and cardboard cut-outs which they used to create 'spirits' for their photographs.

Spirit photography enjoyed a revival in Britain after the First World War. One of the best-known spirit photographers, William Hope, took over 2,500 spirit photographs before being exposed as a fraud by Harry Price of the University of London Council for Psychical Investigation. Sir Arthur Conan Doyle tried to rescue Hope's reputation in his 1922 publication, *The Case for Spirit Photography*. This book is lavishly illustrated with spirit photographs which Doyle felt proved his case. To the modern reader, these appear to be simple double exposures, but knowledge of the technical aspects of photography was less common in the 1920s, and many people appear to have been convinced by Hope and others of his kind. Magicians such as Harry Houdini were indefatigable in their quest to expose such frauds. In 1922, the popular press gleefully reported the exposure of two fraudulent 'spirit photographers' by a body of professional magicians: the Occult Committee of the Magic Circle. This body specialized in investigating the claims of self-styled mediums and psychics, many of whom used magicians' tricks to fool people into thinking they had supernatural powers.

One of the most notorious post-war cases was that of spirit photographer Ada Emma Deane. On Armistice Day 1924 she produced a remarkable photograph which appeared to show the spirits of dead soldiers hovering over the Cenotaph in Whitehall. The photo was published in the *Daily Sketch*, which asked whether any of its readers recognized the faces in the photo. Unfortunately for Deane, many of them did. The 'spirits' were not dead soldiers but living footballers and boxers, copied from other photographs. The furious *Sketch* condemned Deane's 'clear intention ... to play upon the feelings of unhappy people who had lost sons in the war'. It challenged her to produce a genuine photo under test conditions, offering her a reward of £1,000 if she was successful. Deane refused the challenge, giving the *Sketch* ample justification to proclaim her 'a Charlatan and a Fraud'.

Spirit photography continued well into the late twentieth century. One incredible photo (reproduced to accompany an article by Matthew Sweet in the *Independent on Sunday* in 2001) shows Conan Doyle's face apparently materializing in the middle of a blob of repulsive ectoplasm which is emerging from a medium's nose. As Sweet comments, such 'supernatural elements now telegraph their paste-and-paper fraudulence'. But to many people at the time they appeared to be proof of what they desperately wished to believe – that their loved ones had some kind of life after death.

Modern writers are rightly skeptical about spirit photographs. But spirit photography still exists, albeit in a slightly different form. Not long ago I visited a New Age fair where an enterprising photographer offered to take a photo of my aura for an extortionate fee. She seemed surprised when I declined the kind offer. But maybe spirit photography will soon be superseded by more modern technology. A recent UK television documentary featured a medium who claimed to be able to contact the dead via the internet. Now there's a terrifying thought. Imagine being bombarded with junk email from beyond the grave!

The Amazing Dummy Pill
Edzard Ernst

When is fakery a good thing? If the placebo effect – the phenomenon in which patients given inert pills or potions report improvement – helps practitioners of quack therapies make patients believe they're being helped, what can it do for medical science? **Edzard Ernst**, *Director of the Centre for Complementary Health Studies at the University of Exeter, asked this question years before 2003, when Dylan Evans' book,* **Placebo: The Belief Effect** *(www.dylan.org.uk) kicked off a new round of study of this fascinating mystery of mind over matter. Appeared in IX.6.*

Physicians use it more than any other therapy, yet they are barely aware of it, feel uncomfortable about discussing the issue, and rarely conduct focused research on the subject. We are, of course, speaking about placebo. Before powerful and effective drugs began to emerge some hundred years ago, doctors relied almost entirely on the amazing effects of placebos, and at all times they falsely attributed any therapeutic success thus achieved to the specific actions of their prescriptions. The fact that placebo effects are part of the response to (almost) any treatment was pushed aside; to knowingly give placebos to the ill was often equated with quackery. For a long time this attitude barred the systematic investigation of the phenomenon.

So what is a placebo? It used to be described simply as 'make-believe medicine' or 'medicine of convenience'. Today there are numerous elaborate definitions but, to keep it simple, it can be described as the *form* of a therapy without its *content*. The term 'placebo effect' is often used as a synonym for non-specific effects of therapy. Yet placebo effects don't require placebos or any therapy at all; the mere intention to treat a patient, to talk to him or her, or to attempt a diagnosis will usually result in some effect, even without the prescription of a dummy pill.

Most physicians have amusing stories about placebo effects. Mine dates back to the days when I was still at medical school. I had been taught to wire up patients for electrocardiograms (ECGs), diagnostic tests to monitor the electrical activity of the heart. After I had finished the ECG of one of my first patients, an elderly lady, she gave me a tip (the first money I ever earned in medicine!) and said with a smile, 'Thank you, that was great. I feel much better, all my pain has gone.'

It would be fascinating to define why placebo effects are sometimes powerful and on other occasions almost totally absent. This seems to depend on the *type of treatment*; an invasive or in other ways impressive procedure is likely to induce stronger effects than a pill. My patient was obviously impressed with the 'high tech' atmosphere of being wired up to a sophisticated piece of equipment. There are studies showing that sham surgery (opening the skin without doing the actual operation) can bring relief to 100 percent of patients. Surgeons won't like this, but surgery invariably comes with a complementary powerful placebo response. Acupuncture is another example: it is invasive in that it entails puncturing the skin, and some trials show that close to 100 percent of pain sufferers benefit from sham acupuncture, where needles are stuck into non-acupuncture points. Other studies show that the size and colour of a dummy pill will influence the effect it has on volunteers.

Furthermore, the response will depend *on the patient*: the higher the expectation, the stronger the effect. Obviously, the elderly lady in my story was full of expectation. Involving the patient in the therapy will also enhance the placebo effect. In a controlled study of patients with varicose veins, our team has demonstrated that a placebo pill is less beneficial than a placebo cream: the cream has to be rubbed onto the skin and the patient therefore gets actively involved in the treatment, which in turn seems to yield a better outcome.

The expectation of the *doctor or therapist* is also crucial. It will determine the interaction with the patient which conceivably influences the therapeutic success. When I did the ECG I certainly tried to make up with kindness and understanding what I lacked in experience. Some studies show that doctors who believe in a given remedy have more success with it than those who are more skeptical about it. Similarly, a positive encounter with the patient has been shown to increase the success rate by as much as 100 percent compared to a negative one.

The *nature of the condition* being treated is another potential factor. It is often believed that placebos affect only subjective parameters like pain, anxiety, or well-being. This is not quite true. Numerous studies show that objective variables like blood tests, postoperative tissue swelling, body temperature, or the healing of wounds are also placebo-prone. Certain conditions tend to respond better than others – pre-menstrual tension, depression, sleeplessness, and migraine or other types of pain are complaints that usually respond well – but there is hardly any disease or symptom that yields no response at all.

At present we do not fully understand all the influences on the placebo response or their possible complex interactions. There are simply too many unknowns. One large multi-centre study, aimed at pinpointing them more closely, showed that the most important determinant was 'the centre'. In other words, even within one single study there are remarkable variations from site to site and we cannot define exactly why there are differences from one setting to another.

In the early 1950s, Henry K Beecher analysed several placebo-controlled trials in a paper that became most influential, and concluded that, on average, one-third of all patients responded to placebo therapy. This led to the misunderstanding that placebo effects contribute about one-third to the total therapeutic response. Again, this is not true. Beecher's figure was an average, but the range can be virtually from zero to 100 percent.

Some researchers also postulated that there is a certain type of personality which can be called a 'placebo-responder'. False again! Research over the last decades has failed to identify psychological traits characterizing responders as opposed to non-responders. The individual who shows a reaction to placebo today may, under different (or even the same) circumstances, not respond tomorrow, and vice versa. A French researcher recently demonstrated this in a trial aimed at testing whether homoeopathy was more than a placebo. In the first phase of this study all patients with pre-menstrual tension were treated with placebo: 22 percent responded positively; they were excluded from the second, placebo-controlled part of the trial in an attempt to exclude 'placebo responders'. Yet no less than 75 percent of those included in phase two and treated with placebo responded positively. It is therefore not possible to identify placebo responders as a distinct species.

A further misunderstanding claims that 'it is all in the mind'. This notion is made unlikely by a number of facts. Pharmacologically, placebos behave much like drugs: they elicit dose- and time-dependent effects, and placebo reactions can accumulate just as one would expect after administering 'real' drugs. Moreover, as mentioned above, placebo also affects objective signs – anything from cholesterol levels to hair loss.

Having established that placebos are potentially powerful, we might ask whether they can also cause side effects. Adverse reactions to placebo, often termed 'nocebo effects', are well known. On average some 20 percent of healthy volunteers and 35 percent of patients report side effects after placebo pills: the variation is large again, probably ranging from zero to 100 percent. Many placebo-controlled drug trials show that the nocebo effects, seen in placebo-treated patients, behave in parallel with the side effects of those receiving the experimental treatment. If, in one trial, a drug is tested that caused headache, the placebo group too will frequently report headache. If, in another trial, the experimental drug causes loss of appetite the same symptom will be prevalent in the placebo group. We cannot be sure at present why this is so; possibly there is some (non-verbal?) communication between these groups, but other factors may be involved as well. The notion that nocebo effects are always mild and therefore not really important is refuted by those who see voodoo deaths as a strong nocebo reaction and proof to the contrary.

Psychologists, physicians, and other professions have repeatedly tried to identify the mechanism by which placebos work. Several theories have been developed; they range from alterations of the endorphin levels in our brain to the theory of cognitive dissonance. Interestingly, the endorphin theory finds some support from rare cases of 'placebo addiction' that have been described.

When there was previous exposure or experience, like in most cases (who has never been medically treated?), classical conditioning may also come into it. To date, these theories remain unproven and we cannot really tell what exactly happens. Common sense tells us, however, that expectations and suggestions play a prominent role, and so does a certain degree of anxiety associated with almost any medical treatment.

After a flurry of interest in the 1950s, research into placebos became almost an exotic sideline of medical research. Most researchers saw the placebo effect as the 'background noise' in a clinical experiment, a nuisance that was not to be researched but accounted for through adequate study designs and controls. This attitude is presently changing. Some physicians now remember just how beneficial placebos can be in their daily practice and aim at optimizing rather than suppressing their effect. If a doctor doesn't elicit a powerful placebo response, they say, he or she has chosen the wrong profession. Others still have conceptual problems with this notion and fear that knowingly prescribing placebos means 'cheating' the patient. Yet surveys show that placebos are popular: around 80 percent of nurses, for instance, state that they have used them at some time or other.

The totality of the evidence available today leaves no doubt that placebo effects help many patients every day. They are complementary with virtually every medical treatment we may receive. Instead of ignoring this, taking it for granted, or feeling embarrassed about 'placebo quackery', physicians and scientists might consider finding out more about the phenomenon in order to better serve the patient – after all, 'placebo' means 'I shall please'.

Radio Ga-Ga
Tony Youens

One of the reasons psychic claimants can seem so persuasively insightful is the technique known as 'cold reading', in which they feed back to you information you've already given them. Despite psychics' denials that they use such tactics, **Tony Youens** *(www.tonyyouens.com), one of the founders of the Association for Skeptical Enquiry (ASKE) and an experienced cold reader himself (in TV appearances as an astrologer and a Tarot reader he has been accepted by sitters as genuine) had no trouble finding these techniques in use. Appeared in XII.3–4.*

Skeptics have long said that psychic readers achieve their results, either consciously or unconsciously, by the technique known as 'cold reading'. This term refers to a reading given without any prior knowledge of the sitter.

When I debate psychics and mediums they flatly deny using any such technique and some have claimed that they have never heard of the phrase. Of course, very few then offer to have their claims tested and visiting them as a client is likely to be costly. However, such psychics now make frequent radio appearances that allow us to carry out at least some analysis of how they operate.

Some years ago, I can remember reading in *Psychic News* about mediums who appeared on radio phone-in programmes and provided callers with startlingly accurate information that they couldn't possibly have known about by any normal means. They would describe the listener's wallpaper, health problems, recent bereavements, and provide numerous other titbits and trivia. What was going on? Did they have friends phone up, was it a series of lucky guesses, or were they, in fact, really psychic?

A few months after Talk Radio UK started I turned on the radio one evening when a 'spiritualist medium' was doing a turn. The show's host was 'Caesar the Geezer' and his spiritualist guest was one Kevin Wade. I listened to Kevin with great interest as he had a very curious way of talking. To start with, virtually all his 'statements' sounded like questions. This was because he usually said 'please' at the end of every sentence. An example might be, 'Your Father's passed into spirit, please.' Was this a question or not? He also said things like, 'Can I say to you, please, that you're not always appreciated, please?' These are not actual examples but they are typical of the curious way he used, or maybe abused, the English language.

I tried to speak to Kevin, but getting though was impossible. He was only on for about an hour, and such was his popularity that I constantly got the engaged tone. In fact, since then it has been confirmed to me by various presenters that psychic phone-ins routinely generate a massive response from the listeners. Then one evening Caesar suddenly said he wanted to hear from skeptics. He wanted to put Kevin to the test. This time I got through and eventually spoke to Kevin. What follows is most of our conversation. I do not pretend I was at my most eloquent but this was the first time I had spoken to a radio station.

Fortunately however, as I had tried to get through on previous occasions I had already compiled a list of test questions. Caesar himself had suggested we should ask specific questions in order to test Kevin's talents. Kevin claimed to be able to talk to the spirits. He had spirit guides to help him (I can't remember but I'm sure one or both were 'American Indians') and he had certainly been on form that evening with no apparent communication problems.

The following extract is taken from a tape recording that I made at the time and although I cannot remember the actual date when it took place, it would certainly have been 1997 or earlier. I began by saying that I wanted to ask some precise questions of Kevin and emphasized that I did not want a 'cold reading'. I also said that, if Kevin was not given the answers from the 'spirit world' he should just say that he couldn't answer that particular question and not be tempted to guess.

Question one

Tony Youens (TY): Are either of my parents dead?

Kevin Wade (KW): I feel that one of them is please.

TY: Which one?

KW: Can I say I want a mother link please?

TY: Right, neither of them are dead. So you are wrong.

KW: Right, carry on.

A few comments at this point. Why, for goodness sake, didn't Kevin just give me a simple answer? 'I feel that one of them is, please' is vague enough but what about 'Can I have a mother link, please'? Normally when Kevin was trying to determine a dead member of the family, rather than say, 'Your mother' he would use the phrase 'mother link'. If it then turned out that Mum was alive and well he would remind the caller that he only said 'mother link' and was therefore referring in general terms to the mother's side of the family. A rather pointless tactic in this instance, as I had specifically asked about my parents. Of course Kevin never said which parent until pressed, and when he committed himself he only compounded the error.

Question two

TY: All my grandparents are dead, can you give me any of their names?

KW: Can I have Albert, please?

TY: You can have him but he wouldn't be my grandparents.

KW: You understand why I want Albert?

TY: No, we're slipping into cold reading.

KW: Carry on, carry on.

TY: Right, so that was wrong.

KW: Carry on.

Whether deliberate or not, this is certainly cold reading. Look at the way Kevin answers a perfectly reasonable question, 'Can I have Albert, please?' I asked a direct question, so why didn't I get a straight answer such as, 'Albert'? Even 'I believe your grandfather's name was Albert' is at least normal speech. His claim is that he can communicate with the dead, and normally he can come up with names quite happily. Of course, when standard cold reading techniques are used it is on the lines of, 'I'm being given the name Albert' to which the caller might obligingly respond by saying, 'I had a grandfather called Albert'. The word 'had' would indicate that he is now dead (that's passed into spirit if you prefer) and a suitable response might be, 'That was on your mother's side?' The fact that this is phrased as a question is almost undetectable. If a positive response is given, it's a hit. On the other hand, if the caller says, 'No, he was on my father's side', this is just ignored and dealt with by saying, 'Only, I'm also getting a man who says he's from your mother's side'. With any luck they will help the medium out with 'Oh, that might be Cyril'. Rather than be so obvious as to actually say 'Yes, I know', the cold reader might instead imply that he or she knew it all along it by adding something trivial like 'Did he have a dog?' Once again, ready to adapt to either a positive or negative response, and so the fishing expedition continues.

Kevin tries to salvage something by asking if I understand 'Why he wants Albert', thus getting me to do his job for him. Albert is a common enough name for a male grandparent, of which there are two, but there are also uncles, friends, brothers, and so on, and as far as Kevin is concerned it seems any Albert will do. Intentional or not, this smacks of cold reading. As it turns out, I am completely unaware of any 'Albert' in my family, and even if there were one it's not the answer to my question.

Straight questions deserve straight answers; imagine on *Mastermind*:

Magnus: What was the name of the British engineer who built the Clifton Suspension Bridge?

Kevin: Can I have William, please?

Magnus: No it was Brunel.

Kevin: Do you understand why I'm getting William?

Magnus: Well ... no ... ?

Question three

TY: A friend of mine died tragically twenty years ago in a car accident ...

Caesar [interrupting]: *You shouldn't have told him that.*

[I explain that I told Kevin because he might say something vague about 'them dying tragically', etc.]

TY: They died in an accident, OK. They died near Oxford and were buried near Oxford. I won't tell you where they were buried, although I don't expect you to come up with that, but could you give me their name?

KW: No I can't.

TY: Right so that's another one ... that we've missed on.

I imagine Kevin did not try a name is because I gave no indication of my friend's gender. It would be embarrassing to ask for 'a Nigel, please' and be told her name was Wendy. Wisely Kevin decides not to risk it, or perhaps his spirit helpers are beginning to tire.

Question four

TY: My wife's maternal grandparents, are either of those alive?

KW: Your wife's grandparents?

TY: Her maternal grandparents.

KW [slightly hesitating]: *Yes, I feel that they, one of ... yes I do, yes I feel they are alive.*

TY: Right, they're both dead.

I had of course already mentioned that my grandparents were dead so it would seem likely that I had a reason to specifically mention my wife's maternal grandparents; surely one or both were probably alive. Kevin plumps for 'both living' only to find his normally accurate spirit guides have let him down once again. I did tell him not to guess.

Question five

TY: And could you tell me their surname?

KW: No I can't do that at all.

But why not? Their surname was Gregory. We know that Kevin can be given names, although these are always first names and fairly common first names at that. Gregory can be a first name; therefore I can only conclude that surnames are never given because they are too difficult to guess. There is an exception to this, though. If a psychic or spiritualist is talking to a large audience it's possible to have a try at a few surnames. For example, 'Robinson' would be acceptable. It's common enough without being obvious like 'Smith' or 'Jones'. Chances of success are fairly good if you also consider that someone might simply know of a Robinson. This can still appear to be a 'hit' to the faithful.

I summarize for Kevin his lack of success and refer to his earlier comparative accuracy.

TY: So those were my questions and you failed on all of them. I mean [slight chuckle] *in that respect ... I mean I'm sure you could go on now to tell me that I'm having trouble with the cat or something. Many of those things you said to people, that Caesar said weren't generalizations; they certainly applied to me. I could think of somebody who died of cancer. I know people who have died tragically as I mentioned there.*

Anyway, the questions are now over and Kevin has scored a duck. He needs to salvage something quickly, hence:

KW: You know someone who lost a limb as well ... Tony.

TY: You see, we're slipping into cold reading now.

KW: Just say yes or no.

TY: No I don't.

KW: Who lost a leg?

This is another cold reading tactic. Having told me just to say 'yes or no', he then refuses to accept my answer. It can appear that it's me who cannot remember rather than Kevin who has made a bad guess. This can be dealt with in a variety of ways. The medium can shift the problem onto the caller by using phrases and methods like the following: 'Do something for me. Go and ask someone in your family if they remember someone who lost a leg.' As they are never going to come back they can afford to be a little bolder and offer more details: 'He was fairly young when it happened and I'm being shown someone with dark hair. The name James or maybe it's Jim is connected with him. Promise me you'll check.' What can the caller do but agree to check? Of course they come up with nothing but hey, the show's over.

Continuing with the 'missing limb' conversation:

TY: Well, I just said I don't know so if we keep pursuing it now until I think of someone ... I said I don't know anybody that's lost ... I mean, you know it depends what you mean ... Long John Silver did, I believe, and I've read about him. [Caesar laughs in the background.] But otherwise, if you're saying anybody in my immediate family ...

KW: I'm not talking about Long John Silver.

TY: Are you saying anybody that I've known in my entire life?

KW: No. All I'm getting is someone that lost a limb ... a leg.

TY [laughing]: Well I don't know anybody that's lost a leg ... at all.

I think we can finish there. I remember that following my call Kevin had a more sympathetic listener, even though he was supposed to have stopped by then. It obviously takes more than scoring a big fat zero to deter the faithful.

More recent examples

Talk radio psychics have moved on a bit now. They seem to have a much easier time these days. Obliging callers start by clearly stating their question, such as 'Can you see any change of career for me?' With this as a starting point the psychic can prattle on with confidence. The conversation proceeds something like this:

Psychic: Well, I can't see anything in the next couple of months. What is it you're thinking of doing?

Caller: I was thinking about a job in sales.

Psychic: In that case I think you should hear something by about the end of this year. It may be a bit sooner but I don't think so.

The conversation can take various turns but the sequence is pretty much consistent throughout. First, a question from the caller, followed by a response from the psychic that refers to a future event. That's nice and safe as it can't be challenged. The rest is the psychic asking questions and, depending on the response, churning out more possible future events. The questioning is quite bare-faced. It's done in the same manner that a phone-in solicitor might use, simply to allow the problem to be homed in on. One positive change since the early days is that talk radio does not allow any questions about health and potential callers with medical queries are told to see a doctor.

A while back *BBC Late Night North* asked me to take part in a debate with a spiritualist medium named Jean Duncan. I had never heard her before and did not really get much opportunity to listen to her work beforehand. I asked the researcher if Jean would be prepared to undergo a brief test (I had in mind the questions I had asked Kevin Wade). She refused. Since then, I have had the chance to listen to her and analyse her particular style.

In one show earlier this year I noted the number of callers and the number of questions Jean asked them. The average was between twelve and thirteen questions per caller, the range being between five and twenty-nine and the total number of questions a staggering one hundred and sixty-two. (This question counting is not so easy as it seems and there is some subjectivity in assessing what should be regarded as a question. I took as my working definition is anything that was said by the medium that was likely to provoke the caller into providing more information. Even then it was difficult. To allow for disputes I missed out some questions that didn't get any worthwhile information and those that were simply restated. So if anything my figure is fairly conservative.)

I also made a note of the names Jean uses. They are all fairly common. The 'hits' were: Hilda, Margaret, John, Bob, David, Michael, and James. The misses were: Ann, Thomas, William (when this missed she changed to Bill or Billy – still no luck), Robert (Bob was accepted), Ron, Rodney, Alan, and Alec. These names are just thrown out, as in 'Who's Michael?' or 'Why am I getting the name Margaret?' If the name means anything to the caller then it's a hit. With these names, some hits are virtually guaranteed. James, for example, was the name of a caller's boss. In my own family I have noted at least seventeen different, but fairly common names. If I extend possible connections to friends and work colleagues the figure easily doubles.

Jean usually begins with a general question such as 'How are you?' Simple and polite but she seems to use this as a springboard for the start of the reading. The caller may respond with 'Not too bad.' Or 'Fine.' Either way Jean seems to use this as her starting point.

She sometimes asks a trivial question such as 'Who's seeing a doctor?' or 'Who's got a bad leg?' If there is a positive response she builds on it, but if it's a miss she tries to modify it by referring to the spirit she is talking to with something like, 'Only, I'm being shown a man in a white coat'. If this can be reinterpreted by the caller then there is still the chance of a hit. As always, the caller is the one who has to do the matching. Another trivial question with almost guaranteed success is 'Who's got a bad back?' My answer? About two-thirds of the population.

Jean avoids jumping in with, 'Your dead husband's here and wants to say something.' Instead, she tends to prefer the much safer 'There's a gentleman beside me ...'

As is usually the case, her questions often sound like statements. For example, she might say something like, 'You're not planning to move, are you?' The way it is said makes the meaning imprecise. She could either be telling the caller she is not moving or asking if she is. Curiously, sometimes the spirit is talking to Jean ('He's telling me ... ') and at others it uses pictures or objects ('I'm being shown ... '). The reason for this is unclear. I cannot understand why this leads to such confusion. If she can hear him, why not ask him who he is instead of the caller. If she can only see him, then why doesn't he hold up a placard saying, 'It's me, Monty, and I'm her husband'? The whole thing works because we assume (rightly) that communication with the dead is going to be difficult and a certain amount of clarification will be needed by the medium to make sure they are on the right track. But why do they know someone is called 'Thomas' but not that it's in the spirit world until it's confirmed by the caller? If a name can be picked up, which after all is only a word, why not the word 'brother', 'father', or 'uncle'? Why does communication become so much easier after the facts have been established?

How about a test?

How is a psychic chosen to appear on radio? Do they undergo testing prior to giving readings on air? Or, as is more likely, are they simply judged on their popularity? Cold reading is known to work and the technique has been widely written about in mentalist literature. So how does a radio station know that this technique is not being used unless a proper test has been carried out? It would appear that as long as those who phone in are impressed then this is test enough.

In devising a test the only way to decide on the psychic's ability is on the accuracy of the information provided. But not any information. Mediums and psychics always fall down on the detail, or, more precisely, the verifiable detail. An obvious exception to this, of course, is if they manage to obtain information prior to the reading. Any test will obviously have to be adapted depending on what powers the psychic claims to have. But in the case of a medium, five people could be chosen at random from a list of thirty volunteers and the psychic has to provide specific information on each of them such as: the volunteer's name (would just the first name do?) Are they married? Do they have any children? (If yes, how many?) Is their partner still alive? Names of dead or living relatives (parents, grandparents, children, brothers, and sisters). Both the name of the relative and the relationship is required, for example: grandfather, he's dead, and his name was Ferdinand.

The candidate is allowed only one answer per question and the sitter is not permitted to respond until after the test. No questioning by the medium should be allowed. If they get around 70 percent accuracy then they get to go on air; otherwise they need to return to psychic development classes. Before even this test can begin it would need to be established whether or not the medium needs to hear the voice of the sitter or perhaps know their gender. If they do require this information then I think some kind of explanation is required as to why this is needed. Perhaps the hit rate could to be moved to 80 or 90 percent in such cases. Once the voice has been heard the sex of the sitter is then known along with approximate age and maybe even some indication of education and social background.

Sadly no such testing is likely ever to take place. If it were, and were done properly, then there would be little chance of any psychic making an appearance and that would not help the ratings, would it?

6

Science and anti-science

Science – bless it – provides an almost endless supply of esoteric terms that can make any theory, no matter how off-the-wall, sound respectable. The survival of consciousness after death? 'Quantum coherence in the microtubules.' ESP or telepathy? The Heisenberg Uncertainty Principle – or maybe quantum mechanics. Creationism and Intelligent Design? 'Evolution is just a theory.' The jargon factor, plus the fact that scientists themselves do not like to speak in certainties but hedge what they say with caveats and statistics, make it hard to explain why one statement is science and another anything but.

Skepticism is inquiry; science is a process. It is religions and belief systems that claim to provide answers. Science claims only to provide the best self-correcting method we have for establishing the best approximation to the truth at any given time. Anti-science sounds like science, but mangles it: quotes are taken out of context, concepts are wilfully or ignorantly misrepresented, and any new evidence that doesn't bolster the hypothesis under consideration is promptly discarded. Confirming evidence is, of course, accepted immediately; the television producer and science writer Karl Sabbagh has called this the 'ratchet effect'. This section compares and contrasts the workings of science and anti-science.

Death and the Microtubules
Susan Blackmore

TV seems like it ought to be an unparalleled opportunity to present a skeptical point of view. The problem is that, more often, skeptical voices are used as counterweights to the more obviously sensationalist stuff that producers think is more entertaining. Here, Susan Blackmore, herself an experienced broadcaster, shows that even experienced interviewees can be hoodwinked. She also sets the record straight on why the BBC's The Day I Died *(2003) was wrong about microtubules and near-death experiences. Appeared in XVII.1.*

I never should have said yes. I'd promised myself I wouldn't do any more 'rent-a-skeptic' slots, and here I was appearing on one of the worst-ever TV shows on near-death experiences (NDEs). So how did it happen?

The producer, Kate Broome, told me that *The Day I Died* would take the science seriously, that there would be a searching exploration of the whole topic of consciousness, and that this programme would be entirely different from its predecessors. So I believed her. She and her BBC team came to my house and we did a very interesting and enjoyable interview. We covered not only the physiology of NDEs, but theories of consciousness, the reasons why quantum theories of consciousness fail, the nature of self, and why NDEs might be genuinely mystical experiences without being evidence for life after death.

Then I saw the advance advertising: 'NDEs used to be the domain of parapsychology, but now research by some scientists and medics is daring to suggest the impossible – that NDEs are evidence that the mind can live on after the brain has stopped functioning ... ' Different from its predecessors? Hardly. Popular? Of course. This is what every previous NDE programme has claimed, and this is what most people already believe.

In the end, as anyone who watched the programme will know, *The Day I Died* was just an updated version of all the myriad shows that have gone before. Some of the new cases were excellent, and the interviews with people who had experienced NDEs were fascinating, but the science was not. Peter Fenwick and Sam Parnia described their recent research and their belief that it proves the independence of mind. Rent-a-skeptic said her usual pieces about tunnels, lights, and how they are constructed in the dying brain (they could have cut them from interviews I did ten years ago instead of carefully extricating them from what I wanted to say this time).

Finally they got to consciousness. With clever computer graphics and '*Horizon*esque' hype they explained that brave scientists, going against the reductionist grain, can now explain the power of the mind to transcend death. It all comes down to quantum coherence in the microtubules. And to make sure the viewer knows that this is 'real science', the ponderous voiceover declared, 'Their theory is based on a well-established field of science: the laws of general relativity, as discovered by Einstein.'

This was where my fury erupted. As I wrote to the producer afterwards,

> *It is dishonest to present a completely unworkable and mysterious theory as though it were real science, and to dress it up in the trappings of real science, as you did with Hameroff's theory. It may be true that you 'were very clear to point out it that is not proven', but pointing out that it is not proven is not the same as pointing out that it (a) does not make sense, (b) does not fit with lots of reliable evidence about the brain, and (c) is rejected utterly by most scientists and philosophers who know about it.*

And there is no way they could claim ignorance as I had explained, in the interview, the many problems with the theory.

So, in case you are wondering, why can't quantum coherence in the microtubules explain consciousness and the NDE?

The theory first appeared in 1989 in *The Emperor's New Mind* by mathematician Sir Roger Penrose. Penrose argues that when mathematicians have conscious insights they are not doing ordinary computations such as might be carried out by a computer or a neural network. Instead, they must be capable of handling non-computable functions. He accepts that our brains are completely controlled by physics of some kind but, he claims, it needs to be an entirely new kind of physics.

Penrose explains that there are two levels of explanation in physics: the familiar classical level used to describe large-scale objects, and the quantum level used to describe very small things. The trouble starts when you move from one to the other. At the quantum level superposed states are possible; that is, two possibilities can exist at the same time. But at the classical level either one or the other must be the case. So when we make an observation at the classical level, the superposed states have to collapse into one or other possibility, a process known as the collapse of the wave function. Penrose argues that all conventional interpretations of the collapse of the wave function are only approximations, and instead proposes his own theory of 'Objective Reduction'. This new process is gravitational but non-local in nature. This means that it can potentially link things in widely separated areas, making large-scale 'quantum coherence' possible. Although this can only happen when the system is isolated from the rest of the environment, Penrose suggests that this might happen inside the brain – but where?

It was the American anaesthesiologist Stuart Hameroff who suggested that the answer might lie in structures called microtubules. He had come across evidence (subsequently found to be invalid) linking microtubules to the abolition of consciousness in anaesthesia. He reasoned that microtubules might therefore be necessary for consciousness. This was the idea that gave rise to the Penrose–Hameroff theory explained so enthusiastically in *The Day I Died*.

Microtubules are, as their name suggests, tiny, tube-like proteins. Hameroff and Penrose proposed that their shape and the spiral structure of their walls might mean that quantum effects within them could be kept reasonably isolated from the outside, making quantum coherence possible. But why is this relevant to consciousness? Hameroff argues that the real problems for understanding consciousness include the unitary sense of self, free will, and the effects of anaesthesia, as well as non-algorithmic, intuitive processing. All these, he claims, can be explained by quantum coherence in the microtubules. Non-locality can bring about the unity of consciousness, quantum indeterminacy accounts for free will (see Daniel Dennett's *Freedom Evolves*, for reasons why it cannot), and non-algorithmic processing, or quantum computing, is done by quantum superposition. As for NDEs, on *The Day I Died*, Hameroff explains that when the brain stops functioning, the information in the microtubules is not lost. Rather it leaks out into the universe at large and then continues to hang together by quantum coherence. This, he claims, can explain how the conscious self can be experienced as hovering above the body.

So how good is this explanation? We can begin with consciousness itself, which is conventionally equated with subjective experience. The 'Hard Problem' of consciousness (see David Chalmers' 1996 *A Conscious Mind*) is to explain how *subjective* experience can arise from (or perhaps *be*) the *objective* activity of brain cells. Penrose and Hameroff's theory has nothing whatever to say about this. If quantum computing does occur in the brain this would be very important, but it only adds another layer of complexity to the way the brain works. So we must still ask, 'How does subjective experience arise from objective reduction in the microtubules?' The strange effects entailed in quantum processes do not, of themselves, have anything to say about the *experience* of light or space or pain or colour or time.

One of the strengths of the theory is supposed to be that it accounts for the unitary sense of self, but nothing in the theory explains how to get from interacting quantum effects to the feeling that 'I' am a continuing self who makes decisions and lives my life. Also, as we have seen, the theory requires that the quantum process be isolated from the rest of the environment, but a hovering self during an NDE would not be.

Several commentators have pointed out these and many other problems. Many conclude that the theory just replaces one mystery (subjective experience) with another (quantum coherence in the microtubules?). Even people renowned for their unconventional thinking have rejected it outright, such as computer engineer and futurist Ray Kurzweil. But the most devastating critique is made by philosophers Rick Grush and Patricia Churchland. They take Penrose's arguments step by step, and demolish each one.

An obvious problem is that microtubules are not specialized structures confined to brains: they occur in almost all cells of the body, in both animals and plants, and are involved in supporting the cell's structure in cell division and in transporting organelles within the cell. It is true that some anaesthetics affect microtubules, but many others do not, even though they obliterate consciousness. Also, drugs are known that damage the structure of microtubules but appear to have no effect on consciousness, and there is no evidence that microtubules are implicated in other major changes in consciousness, such as sleep–wake cycles.

Concerning the physics, Grush and Churchland argue that microtubules cannot provide the conditions of purity and isolation required by Penrose's theory, nor could effects be transmitted from one microtubule to another, as is required for explaining the unity of consciousness in the way Penrose requires. In addition the theory provides no explanation of how the quantum effects could interact with effects at the level of neurons, neurotransmitters, and neuromodulators, when the microtubules are supposed to be isolated from their environment.

Grush and Churchland concluded in 1995 that, 'the argument consists of merest possibility piled upon merest possibility teetering upon a tippy foundation of 'might-be-for-all-we-know's ... we judge it to be completely unconvincing and probably false' (p. 12). In 1998, Churchland put it even more strongly: 'Quantum coherence in the microtubules is about as explanatorily powerful as pixie dust in the synapses.'

They also ask why such a flimsy theory has proved so popular. Perhaps, they suggest, it is because some people find the idea of explaining consciousness by neuronal activity somehow degrading or scary, whereas 'explaining' it by quantum effects retains some of the mystery.

Whatever the reason, the TV show proved equally palatable, and if the producers' aim was popularity, then they certainly succeeded. Most viewers want to believe in life after death and they like to see 'evidence' that confirms their traditional dualism. I accused the producers of making a dishonest programme and misleading viewers, accusations they strongly denied. Kate Broome replied that, 'I think we tried to at least suggest that there are other ways of looking at this subject other than in a reductionist way.' Yes, they did. It's just that every previous programme on NDEs has done exactly the same, giving viewers the answers they want rather than trying to find out the truth. Although we may never get to see it on TV, the real science of NDEs is much more exciting than quantum coherence in the microtubules.

A Look at Probability and Coincidence
Chip Denman

Nothing contributes as much to confusion about paranormal claims as innumeracy. At least some understanding of statistics ought to be – and isn't – a professional requirement for journalists. **Chip Denman**, *a statistician at the University of Maryland College Park, explains the basics. Appeared in IX.4. This article originally appeared in* **Skeptical Eye**, *the newsletter of the National Capital Area Skeptics.*

> *When you can measure what you are speaking about, and express it in numbers, you know something about it; but when you cannot measure it, when you cannot express it in numbers, your knowledge is of a meagre and unsatisfactory kind. (William Thomson, Lord Kelvin, 1824–1907)*

Measurement is not enough. Scientific understanding lies in comparing measurements and understanding their uncertainty. Statistics is the discipline which not only tolerates uncertainty, but embraces it. Virtually every field of scientific inquiry has contributed to the language, variations, and styles of presentation which make up the body of statistics.

Statistics: a word which has struck fear into many a student. Graduate students from Agronomy to Zoology have been left clueless by introductory statistics and research methods courses everywhere. Undergraduates have despaired over chi-square formulae and F-tests. Those who never had such a course may feel even less comfortable with the 'correlations', 'margins of error', and other terms slung around in the morning paper. Sometimes, I suspect, being more self-consciously ignorant may be better than being blissfully half-smart, statistics being merely the example that I know best.

The language of probability and statistics is everywhere. All of these are from the same edition of a newspaper:

> *At least in the near future, state and local government is probably not going to generate a lot of jobs.*

> *Witch Doctor in the 8th race, odds: 9-2.*

> *The likelihood of developing severe symptoms was 20 percent in patients receiving the highest dose of AZT.*

> *Cancer: You'll have luck in matters of finance, romance.*

> *Gemini: Because Mercury, your ruler, now joins the sun and Mars in that area of your solar chart which governs work and career matters, you should be quietly confident about the future.*

Most of these examples convey a straightforward, everyday meaning (well, maybe if you are a Gemini). Sometimes this everyday meaning is not the same as the precise mathematical meaning that underlies the original intention.

The very term 'statistics' has many connotations. I once spent an hour on the phone with an attorney who called to find out if a certain product was safe. 'Give me the data', I suggested, 'and I can develop the risk estimates.'

'Data? You are a statistician; you are supposed to *know* these things!' A good librarian might have helped; I could not.

Let me be clear: My role as a statistician is that of a professional skeptic. My training is in mathematical tools for looking at data and evaluating hypotheses. My obligation is to ask tough questions about the data and its source.

The classic statistical paradigm (brushing aside the differences between the philosophies of Fisher, Neyman-Pearson, and Bayesian statistics) is a mirror of the mythic scientific method as promulgated in textbooks:

1. Formulate hypotheses (in terms which relate to probabilities).
2. Use data to derive a quantitative summary which relates directly to the probability statement above.
3. Reject (or not) hypotheses based on an evaluation of probabilities.
4. Repeat as necessary.

Of course, real-life data analysis rarely follows such a recipe exactly. But, hey, if you've seen me in the kitchen, you know that I rarely cook exactly by the book either. In the last twenty years graphical methods, especially those suited to exploratory data analysis, have expanded the statistical menu. Computer-intensive methods based in part on (pseudo) random numbers and repetitive enumeration were unthinkable even a few years ago.

All of these statistical methods have one fundamental theme: human intuition is very fallible at evaluating likelihoods and coincidence. Even the very meaning of 'random' is far from obvious. We can give a precise definition of probability in terms of abstract mathematical properties (for example, measure theory), but the mathematics *per se* do not define everyday experience. What is this probability thing anyway?

The so-called classical approach to probability provides a convenient way to calculate, at least for simple, finite situations. According to this approach, derived from gambling problems and formalized philosophically by Pierre Simon de Laplace (1749–1827), probability represents the ratio:

$$\frac{\text{number of (equally likely) ways something can happen}}{\text{total number of (equally likely) possible outcomes}}$$

This works fine for things like lotteries and other gambling games, but it's a bit of a reach to apply it to complex events.

To call this the classical approach is misleading. Other ways of thinking about probability have been with us for just as long. The relative frequency interpretation is common among modern statisticians, but this same kind of thinking can be found in the mortality tables published in 1662 by John Graunt of London. In slightly more modern terms (proposed by John Venn in 1886 and developed mathematically in the 1920s by Richard von Mises), imagine an experiment in which we observe whether event E happens or not. If we repeat the experiment many, many, many times, the ratio:

$$\frac{\text{number of times E happens}}{\text{total number of repeats}}$$

will get closer and closer to some fixed number from 0 and 1. If we could imagine repeating the experiment forever, the limiting value of the relative frequency would be the 'probability of E'.

This makes sense in a large number of practical problems. We can easily imagine people playing the lottery time and time again. We can imagine, at least in principle, running a horse in race after race. We can even imagine interviewing a large number of 'Cancers' and asking them about their love life. With a little more imagination we can make this work for, say, weather predictions. 'A 30 percent chance of showers' could mean that if we could somehow observe a really large number of days with conditions just like today, 30 percent of the time our picnics would be cancelled.

A third (and by no means, final) way to interpret probabilities is as a degree of belief, also known as the subjective interpretation. Only a mental contortionist could devise a frequency interpretation of the statement 'Lee Harvey Oswald probably acted alone'. In this way of thinking, probability represents a measure of your strength of belief. Variations on this idea are useful in trying to represent the degree to which evidence may confirm or disconfirm, say, 'the single bullet theory'. It is also a natural way of talking about the 'prior distributions' in Bayesian analysis. The mathematical niceties of this idea are recent (F. P. Ramsey in 1926 and L. J. Savage in 1954). However, the concepts can be traced to sixteenth- and seventeenth-century jurisprudence in which 'probability' was apportioned to evidence according to its certainty.

In practice, it rarely matters which interpretation is chosen. The numbers remain the same.

Even simple problems can knock intuition sideways. I just tossed a penny in the air. What's the probability that heads is showing? One-half, of course. One equally likely chance out of two. But now I have tossed a penny and a nickel together, and I tell you that one of them, and maybe both, heads. What's the probability that *both* are heads? Surely one coin has no effect upon the other, so is it one-half again? The correct answer is one-third. Huh?

	Penny	Nickel
Case 1:	HEADS	HEADS
Case 2:	HEADS	TAILS
Case 3:	TAILS	HEADS
Case 4:	TAILS	TAILS

Figure 4 The four possible outcomes of tossing two coins.

Looking at the four possible outcomes of tossing the two coins shows why (Figure 4).

There are four equally likely scenarios when we toss both coins. Although the nickel and the penny are certainly independent, we know that they are not both tails up, leaving three possibilities. Double heads is one out of three. The key here is that I did not tell you which of the two coins I was talking about when I said that one of them was heads. If I had let on that it was the nickel, then we'd be left with only two scenarios, which *does* yield the answer of one-half. Something as seemingly trivial as naming or not naming a coin makes all the difference.

If this still seems a bit weird, try the experiment. Toss two coins on the carpet. If both are tails, forget it. Pick them up and toss again. But if at least one head is showing, record the result. Repeat the process until you have a good number of recorded data. What percentage of the record shows double heads? (This same problem is sometimes given in terms of a person with two children, at least one of whom is a boy. For some reason this seems to confuse intuition even more effectively than coins. Try it on someone.)

Another simple problem makes a great classroom demonstration. It is rather unlikely that you and I share the same birthday (day and month, ignore the year). Obviously the more people that we pull into the party, the more likely it is that at least two people will match. How many people do we need in order that a match is more likely than not?

Wishing away the pesky matter of leap years, it's pretty clear that if we invite 366 people, at least two of them *must* share a birthday. So how many before the chances are fifty-fifty? (When I've posed this problem in large gatherings, I sometimes get answers like 'One thousand'. Go figure.)

If you've never heard the answer before, it just doesn't feel right: twenty-three. Figure 5 shows the calculation.

Probability of *no match* with two people:
1st birthday can be any day out of the year: 365/365
2nd birthday can be any of the other days: 364/365
So chance of *no match* is (365/365) × (364/365) ≈ .9973
So, probability of a *match* ≈ 1 – .9973 = .0027

For three people the chance of no matching birthdays is:
(365/365) × (364/365) × (363/365) ≈ .9918

For 23 people the probability of no matching birthdays is:
(365/365) × (364/365) ... (343/365) ≈ .4927

So the probability of getting *at least one* match with 23 people is:
1 – .4927 = .5073, which is just a little better than 50%. Voila!

Figure 5 The 'Birthday Problem' Solved.

The key again is that we did not specify which birthday had to match. We did not specify 25 June, nor did we require that James and Shirley had to match. We are merely looking for some coincidence, somewhere, anywhere.

Simple puzzles like these do more than point out the weakness of intuition. They also can give us a start toward quantifying more real-life coincidences. Persi Diaconis and Frederick Mosteller have presented extensions to the birthday puzzle that show how easy it is to get near-misses like birthdays one or two days apart. But what about the 'psychic' puzzlers like we've all encountered, at least second-hand? Is Aunt Martha's dream that came true beyond the reach of probability and statistics?

Here's a way of thinking about such events that I first saw sketched out in *Innumeracy* by John Allen Paulos. If there are absolutely no psychic powers whatsoever, it's pretty unlikely that a dream of yours will predict the future. How unlikely? I don't know ... let's start with the guess of one chance out of ten thousand. What constitutes a hit? It doesn't really matter; be your own judge. Since this is just an approximation, let's also pretend that you remember one dream a night and that each dream is independent of the rest. Just like in the birthday calculation, start by looking at the probability that a dream *does not* match with the future. Probability of one non-matching dream:

$$\frac{9,999}{10,000} = .9999$$

Probability of non-matching dreams for two nights in a row (note for non-mathematical readers: the symbol '≈' means 'approximately equal to'):

$$.9999 \times .9999 \approx .9998$$

Probability of a whole year of non-matching dreams:

$$(.9999)^{365} \approx .9642$$

In terms of the relative frequency interpretation of probability, we should expect that about 96.4 percent of us will not have any matching dreams over the course of a year of dreaming, waking, and remembering.

But this means that we should also expect those other 3.6 percent to have *at least* one dream each which seems to predict the future. And remember, we are talking about what would happen *without* psychic powers, just relying on pure blind luck. The population of the United States is about 250 million, so we should expect about 9 million people in the US alone to have 'precognitive' dreams just by chance!

An individual who dreams for 19 years will have almost exactly an even chance of having at least one such spooky dream $(1 - .9999)^{365 \times 19} \approx .5002$. It's no surprise to me that many of my students at the university tell me it's happened to them.

Even if you think that our original guess of 1/10,000 was too high, this kind of analysis is still revealing. What if we try one chance out of 100,000? We still should expect 900,000 people to have the illusion of a psychic flash. Even if we try a ridiculously low chance of only one out of a billion, we should expect enough 'precognitive' dreams for *Unsolved Mysteries* to re-enact one a week and have plenty left over as fodder for *The X-Files*.

These kinds of tentative analyses are not proof. The numbers are guesses – your mileage may vary. But they are educated guesses. They show how even elementary arithmetic can go a long way towards slowing the jump to hasty conclusions.

Astute readers will have noticed that I said that I would talk about statistics, but in fact I have talked mostly about probability. I lied.

Abduction Theory
Nick Rose

*About ten years ago, I was on two TV shows in the same week. One was about ghosts; the author of a new book described waking up at night, cold, with a heavy weight pressing on his chest, knowing there was a presence nearby. One was on alien visitations: the author of a new book described waking up at night, cold, with a heavy weight pressing on his chest, knowing there was a presence nearby. The first said he'd been visited by a ghost, the second by an alien. My rather obvious conclusion: both were describing a common phenomenon that they interpreted individually according to their pre-existing beliefs. There was indeed such a phenomenon: **sleep paralysis**. Here, **Nick Rose**, now a science teacher but then a research assistant in Susan Blackmore's lab at the University of the West of England, explains the connection in the case of alien abductions. Appeared in X.4.*

In October I was asked to take part in a radio interview commenting on a report in the tabloid press that a man from Dagenham had paid £100 to insure himself against being abducted by aliens.

Whether or not the original story was true, which is highly doubtful given its source, it does represent something of a continuing trend in UFO mania. If the story were true then it would raise some interesting questions. How would an insurance company define an alien abduction? How would the company evaluate the risk of Dagenham 'Dave' being abducted? What proof could satisfy a skeptical claims assessor that an abduction had taken place?

In 1992, Budd Hopkins, David Michael Jacobs, and Ron Westrum commissioned a Roper Poll survey of unusual experiences which they believed were associated with UFO abductions. Over the period of three months, and at considerable cost, this carefully sampled survey was carried out on nearly 6,000 adult Americans. Might they have the answers to any of these questions? From Hopkins' and his co-authors' interpretation of the poll it appears that we can define an abductee as anyone who has had, at any time in their lives, four out of five 'symptoms' of an alien abduction. At the risk of being accused of attacking a 'straw man', I'd like to examine these 'symptoms' a little closer. Just what do they tell us, if anything, about the apparent phenomenon of alien abduction?

It is interesting to note that the item which yielded the highest number of 'yes' responses is the experience of waking up paralysed with a sense of a strange person or presence or something else in the room. Something like 18 percent of their poll had experienced this at least once, which they equated with about 33.3 million Americans. This item in the poll is actually a combination of two separate experiences: an experience of waking up paralysed, and sensing a strange presence.

Sleep paralysis is the phenomenon of feeling that your body is paralysed, and usually manifests when you are in a half-awake/half-asleep state. From our own research this appears to be a common experience. About 34 percent of children and 46 percent of adults reported an experience of sleep paralysis. This compares well with a Japanese survey which found an incidence of around 40 percent.

The paralysis itself may be due to the body being locked up from having been in, or entering, dreaming (it is known that the body is paralysed so that you don't act out your dreams). Sometimes sleep paralysis occurs with hypnagogic or hypnopompic hallucinations, often accompanied with the feeling of a presence in the room. Hypnagogic hallucinations are the period of hallucination that everyone gets once in a while when falling asleep; hypnopompic hallucinations occur just as you start to wake up. Hallucinations of this sort can include hearing strange humming noises or voices, feeling apparent changes in size, shape, or position of one's body, seeing faces (sometimes malformed or horrific), seeing lights and patterns, and an array of quite bizarre, but perfectly normal, effects. A combination of hallucination and sleep paralysis can be understandably terrifying.

Sleep paralysis is not a recent discovery, and nor are sleep paralysis myths. In his 1982 book, *The Terror That Comes in the Night*, DJ Hufford examined the folklore surrounding the legends and traditions of the 'old hag' among the people of Newfoundland in Canada. The Vietnamese have long had stories of a 'grey ghost' that enters their rooms at night. In medieval times demonic incubi and succubi came to their victims at night to seduce them. Is alien abduction our modern equivalent of a sleep paralysis myth? It seems that many people interpret sleep paralysis as some external force or agent, restraining their movements or crushing the breath from their chest. If the paralysis feels like an external force then many people, in their search for an explanation for the experience, will assume that it is. What form that external force takes will depend much upon that person's cultural information. In this country, for the moment at least, the interpretation of the force as an extraterrestrial one is still relatively rare. Ghosts and spirits still enjoy a relatively strong position in popular belief compared with extraterrestrials.

Of the Roper Poll's other symptoms, two were experiences that could be associated with sleep states: a 'feeling that you were actually flying through the air although you didn't know why or how' and having 'seen unusual lights or balls of light in a room without knowing what was causing them, or where they came from'. The first of these 'symptoms' is basically a description of an out-of-body experience (OBE).

Many people who regularly have OBEs describe a period of paralysis shortly before the experience begins, traditionally known as 'astral catalepsy'. A number of OBE-ers might believe that this experience stems from something actually leaving the body and flying around, although a more convincing explanation has been offered by Susan Blackmore in her books *Beyond the Body* and *Dying to Live*. Within our research, however, none of the OBE-ers have interpreted their experiences as extraterrestrial in origin, usually preferring a psychic or spiritual interpretation. As for the 'balls of light' we, too, found a number of respondents who claimed to have had such an experience. The Roper Poll found that 8 percent of Americans reported lights. In our surveys the figure was higher: 17 percent of adults and 28 percent of children. Strange lights and patterns of lights are common forms of hypnagogic or hypnopompic hallucination, so it is unsurprising that the incidences are so high. What is surprising is the suggestion that such natural, common experiences are indicative of alien abduction.

I have little to say about the final two 'symptoms'. They were: losing track of time for an hour or so (more ominously called 'time-loss'), and the finding of 'puzzling scars' the origin of which the respondent could not recall. Suffice it to say that human memory is not a video tape recorder and absences and inaccuracies in our memories are neither uncommon or evidence of extraterrestrial activity.

None of these individual 'symptoms' is exclusively 'caused' by alien abduction, and to be fair Hopkins *et al.* do not suggest that they are. To come under their definition of an abductee, you have to have experienced at least four of the five symptoms. This roughly comes out as 3.7 million Americans (about 2 percent). On that basis, I'm surprised that the insurance premium was not higher, as the chances of getting snatched (if we can assume that abduction rates are the same across the Atlantic) seem pretty high!

Even Hopkins, Jacobs, and Westrum accept that individually any of the symptoms can arise naturally, independently and without the intervention of ETs, so why should we accept that any combination of the experiences be evidence of abduction? If a person suffered four out of the five symptoms within a single episode that might be more impressive (but hardly inexplicable), but the poll gives no indication of whether these symptoms occurred together or separately over a space of many years.

From having delivered similar types of questionnaires myself, I suspect that the latter is more likely and that the respondents to the Roper Poll were remembering: that time in 1988 when they had an attack of sleep paralysis, an occasion when they were little when they thought they saw a light in their room, an occasion last week when they discovered a small cut on their hand but didn't remember how they did it, and so on.

For the past year Dr Susan Blackmore and I have been collecting reports and conducting surveys of sleep paralysis and other unusual experiences for a research project funded by the Perrot-Warwick fellowship. From our research it appears that, rather than 'symptoms' like sleep paralysis and hypnagogic hallucinations being caused by alien abduction, it is rather the other way around.

Alien abduction, in many cases, is an interpretation of sleep paralysis and hypnagogic hallucination. Experiences of abduction that follow this form will be entirely subjective experiences, so there will be no physical proof that the person has been 'snatched'.

Any skeptical claims assessor would require more than reports of non-specific 'symptoms akin to post-traumatic stress' or accounts elicited while a person is under hypnosis before handing over the cheque. I doubt very much that the story of Dagenham Dave has any basis in fact, but if it were true the insurance clerk who sold the policy would be laughing up his or her sleeve.

7

Skeptics speak

A few years ago, a friend of mine went to a selective event where the participants included former presidents, important thinkers and business people, and intellectually gifted celebrities. His problem: finding a conversation that didn't wind up with someone expressing a belief in some bit of pseudoscience. His experience is not uncommon, and it's why one of the first things I learned when *The Skeptic* began was that many people of a skeptical bent feel isolated. But more than that, although believers often talk about the ridicule they face for their beliefs, the general public seems to think being a skeptic is pretty weird, too. Present yourself as a skeptic, and you'll find you get asked a lot of questions as if you were some sort of exotic bug to be studied and probed. 'Haven't you ever seen anything you couldn't explain?' is a common question. Well, yes: what characterizes skeptics in fact is the willingness to accept that we don't know the answer. What is it like to approach life with a skeptical frame of mind? In this section, you'll find examples of how a few people have answered that question.

Proper Criticism
Ray Hyman

*Skepticism is a habit of mind: it means inquiry. But for some of us it's also a cause. Where should skeptics draw the line in attacking pseudoscience? How do you measure a response carefully when you're under pressure to produce instant reactions and clever sound bites for the media, especially when the person you're countering is seemingly kind and sympathetic, driven only by the desire to help people? How can skeptics produce credible yet effective criticism that promotes, rather than damages, the cause of critical thinking? In its early days, even the Committee for Skeptical Inquiry got this balance wrong. Based on those experiences, **Ray Hyman**, professor emeritus in psychology at the University of Oregon at Eugene and a Founding Fellow of CSI (formerly the Committee for Scientific Claims of the Paranormal, or CSICOP), wrote this cogent mini-manual. Appeared in I.4. Reprinted from CSICOP's in-house newsletter, **Skeptical Briefs**.*

Since the founding of CSICOP in 1976, and with the growing numbers of localized skeptical groups, the skeptic finds more ways to state his or her case. The broadcast and print media, along with other forums, provide more opportunities for us to be heard. For some of these occasions, we have the luxury of carefully planning and crafting our response. But most of the time we have to formulate our response on the spot. But, regardless of the circumstance, the critic's task, if it is to be carried out properly, is both challenging and loaded with unanticipated hazards.

Many well-intentioned critics have jumped into the fray without carefully thinking through the various implications of their statements. They have sometimes displayed more emotion than logic, made sweeping charges beyond what they reasonably support, failed to adequately document their assertions, and, in general, have failed to do the homework necessary to make their challenges credible.

Such ill-considered criticism can be counterproductive for the cause of serious skepticism. The author of such criticism may fail to achieve the desired effect, may lose credibility, and may even become vulnerable to lawsuits. But the unfavourable effects have consequences beyond the individual critic, and the entire cause of skepticism suffers as a result. Even when the individual critic takes pains to assert that he or she is expressing his or her own personal opinion, the public associates the assertions with all critics.

During CSICOP's first decade of existence, members of the Executive Council often found themselves devoting most of their available time to damage control – precipitated by the careless remarks of a fellow skeptic – instead of toward the common cause of explaining the skeptical agenda.

Unfortunately, at this time, there are no courses on the proper way to criticize paranormal claims. So far as I know, no manuals or books of rules are currently available to guide us. Until such courses and guide books come into being, what can we do to ensure that our criticisms are both effective and responsible?

I would be irresponsible if I told you I had an easy solution. The problem is complicated and there are no quick fixes. But I do believe we all could improve our contributions to responsible criticism by keeping a few principles always in mind.

We can make enormous improvements in our collective and individual efforts by simply trying to adhere to those standards that we profess to admire and that we believe that many peddlers of the paranormal violate. If we envision ourselves as the champions of rationality, science, and objectivity, then we ought to display these very same qualities in our criticism. Just by trying to speak and write in the spirit of precision, science, logic, and rationality – those attributes we supposedly admire – we would raise the quality of our critiques by at least one order of magnitude.

The failure to consistently live up to these standards exposes us to a number of hazards. We can find ourselves going beyond the facts at hand. We may fail to communicate exactly what we intended. We can confuse the public as to what skeptics are trying to achieve. We can unwittingly put the paranormal proponents in the position of the underdogs and create sympathy for them. And, as I already mentioned, we can make the task much more difficult for other skeptics.

What, then, can skeptics do to upgrade the quality of their criticism? What follow are just a few suggestions. Hopefully, they will stimulate further thought and discussion.

1. Be prepared

Good criticism is a skill that requires practice, work, and level-headedness. Your response to a sudden challenge is much more likely to be appropriate if you have already anticipated similar challenges. Try to prepare in advance effective and short answers to those questions you are most likely to be asked. Be ready to answer why skeptical activity is important, why people should listen to your views, why false beliefs can be harmful, and the many similar questions that invariably are raised. A useful project would be to compile a list of the most frequently occurring questions along with possible answers.

Whenever possible try your ideas out on friends and 'enemies' before offering them in the public arena. An effective exercise is to rehearse your arguments with fellow skeptics. Some of you can take the role of the psychic claimants while others play the role of critics. And, for more general preparation, read books on critical thinking, effective writing, and argumentation.

2. Clarify your objectives

Before you try to cope with a paranormal claim, ask yourself what you are trying to accomplish. Are you trying to release pent-up resentment? Are you trying to belittle your opponent? Are you trying to gain publicity for your viewpoint? Do you want to demonstrate that the claim lacks reasonable justification? Do you hope to educate the public about what constitutes adequate evidence? Often our objectives, upon examination, turn out to be mixed. And, especially when we act impulsively, some of our objectives conflict with one another.

The difference between short-term and long-term objectives can be especially important. Most skeptics, I believe, would agree that our long-term goal is to educate the public so that it can more effectively cope with various claims. Sometimes this long-range goal is sacrificed because of the desire to expose or debunk a current claim.

Part of clarifying our objectives is to decide who our audience is. Hard-nosed, strident attacks on paranormal claims rarely change opinions, but they do stroke the egos of those who are already skeptics.

Arguments that may persuade the readers of the *National Enquirer* may offend academics and important opinion-makers.

Try to make it clear that you are attacking the claim and not the claimant. Avoid, at all costs, creating the impression that you are trying to interfere with someone's civil liberties. Do not try to get someone fired from his or her job. Do not try to have courses dropped or otherwise be put in the position of advocating censorship. Being for rationality and reason should not force us into the position of seeming to be against academic freedom and civil liberties.

3. Do your homework

Again, this goes hand in hand with the advice about being prepared. Whenever possible, you should not try to counter a specific paranormal claim without getting as many of the relevant facts as possible. Along the way, you should carefully document your sources. Do not depend upon a report in the media either for what is being claimed or for facts relevant to that claim. Try to get the specifics of the claim directly from the claimant.

4. Do not go beyond your level of competence

No one, especially in our times, can credibly claim to be an expert on all subjects. Whenever possible, you should consult appropriate experts. We, understandably, are highly critical of paranormal claimants who make assertions that are obviously beyond their competence. We should be just as demanding on ourselves. A critic's worst sin is to go beyond the facts and the available evidence.

In this regard, always ask yourself if you really have something to say. Sometimes it is better to remain silent than to jump into an argument that involves aspects that are beyond your present competence. When it is appropriate, do not be afraid to say, 'I don't know.'

5. Let the facts speak for themselves

If you have done your homework and have collected an adequate supply of facts, the audience rarely will need your help in reaching an appropriate conclusion. Indeed, your case is made much stronger if the audience is allowed to draw its own conclusions from the facts. Say that Madame X claims to have psychically located Mrs A's missing daughter and you have obtained a statement from the police to the effect that her contributions did not help. Under these circumstances it can be counterproductive to assert that Madame X lied about her contribution or that her claim was 'fraudulent'. For one thing, Madame X may sincerely, if mistakenly, believe that her contributions did in fact help. In addition, some listeners may be offended by the tone of the criticism and become sympathetic to Madame X. However, if you simply report what Madame X claimed along with the response of the police, you not only are sticking to the facts, but your listeners will more likely come to the appropriate conclusion.

6. Be precise

Good criticism requires precision and care in the use of language. Because, in challenging psychic claims, we are appealing to objectivity and fairness, we have a special obligation to be as honest and accurate in our own statements as possible. We should take special pains to avoid making assertions about paranormal claims that cannot be backed up with hard evidence. We should be especially careful, in this regard, when being interviewed by the media. Every effort should be made to ensure that the media understand precisely what we are and are not saying.

7. Use the principle of charity

I know that many of my fellow critics will find this principle to be unpalatable. To some, the paranormalists are the 'enemy', and it seems inconsistent to lean over backward to give them the benefit of the doubt. But being charitable to paranormal claims is simply the other side of being honest and fair. The principle of charity implies that, whenever there is doubt or ambiguity about a paranormal claim, we should try to resolve the ambiguity in favour of the claimant until we acquire strong reasons for not doing so. In this respect, we should carefully distinguish between being wrong and being dishonest. We often can challenge the accuracy or the validity of a given paranormal claim. But rarely are we in a position to know if the claimant is deliberately lying or is self-deceived. Furthermore, we often have a choice in how to interpret or represent an opponent's arguments. The principle tells us to convey the opponent's position in a fair, objective, and non-emotional manner.

8. Avoid loaded words and sensationalism

All these principles are interrelated. The ones previously stated imply that we should avoid using loaded and prejudicial words in our criticisms. We should also try to avoid sensationalism. If the proponents happen to resort to emotionally laden terms and sensationalism, we should avoid stooping to their level. We should not respond in kind.

This is not a matter of simply turning the other cheek. We want to gain credibility for our cause. In the short run, emotional charges and sensationalistic challenges might garner quick publicity. But, most of us see our mission as a long-run effort. We would like to persuade the media and the public that we have a serious and important message to get across. And we would like to earn their trust as a credible and reliable resource. Such a task requires always keeping in mind the scientific principles and standards of rationality and integrity that we would like to make universal.

A Panoply of Paranormal Piffle: Stephen Fry
Steve Donnelly

*Actors and other show business personalities are famously credulous: name a wacky idea and you can usually find a celebrity who promotes it. A significant exception is **Stephen Fry**, known for his comedy work with Hugh Laurie as well as his many other stage, movie, and television roles, including a recent turn as a psychiatrist on the series **Bones**. Spotted as a skeptic by **Steve Donnelly**, former editor of **The Skeptic** (1989–98), Fry agreed to be interviewed. Appeared IV.5.*

For anyone possessing a television, a radio or, for that matter, the Friday edition of the *Daily Telegraph*, it is difficult to avoid Stephen Fry's pugilist's nose, mellifluous tones, and dry wit. The actor's art does not give much scope for personal opinion but in his writings Fry's irreverence for the irrational, his antipathy for the antiscientific, and his intense disdain for daftness become apparent. In *The Listener* in December 1988, for instance, he wrote, 'It's extremely unlucky to be superstitious for the simple reason that it is always unlucky to be colossally stupid.' It was in the context of this skepticism, unusual in actors, who are generally regarded as a superstitious lot, that Stephen Fry agreed to be interviewed by *The Skeptic*.

It was perhaps appropriate that our conversation began with an unintentional spot of comedy. This resulted from the fact that I could not initially persuade the reels on my (borrowed) cassette recorder to turn round. The first recorded phrase of the interview was thus '… and you are an electrical engineer and you don't quite know how to operate a cassette recorder … '

But then (I suspect unusually for actors) Fry is quite at home with technology and is a keen user and programmer of Apple Macintosh computers. It would be tempting to think that this was perhaps natural for someone whose father is a physicist and a computer buff but in fact his father's scientific, mathematical, and musical abilities had the effect of initially pushing Fry away from these areas.

From an early age – and without wanting to be too psychoanalytic about myself – I think I probably gave up on things that I thought I could never compete with my father on. So I became far more interested in the arts and gave up piano lessons as soon as I possibly could – at the age of about eight – and went round claiming I had a maths block. But after I'd left Cambridge when I was a bit more grown up I became very interested in computers – I got an early BBC Micro and then bought a Macintosh the year they came out and began programming and discovered I didn't have a maths block at all.

Although he was a student at Cambridge at the end of the 1970s (1978 to 1981), this was a few years after the student community's infatuation with

Eastern religions. And although his mother's family was religiously Jewish and his father's family Quaker, Western religion did not feature greatly in his upbringing either:

> *I had a sort of vague yen to go into the church when I was about fifteen or sixteen – I rather fancied myself in a cassock – but I think, generally speaking, I have always inclined towards what is loosely called liberal humanism. I've never really been strongly drawn to anything religious. This is not to say that I can't be drawn towards anything spiritual. which is not the same thing at all. But I've always, for as long as I can remember, had an irritation with things superstitious. I have a great belief in reason – the world is so remarkable and extraordinary anyway that to try and find things that are subject to no testing, no logic and no reason is ugly. The world is far too mysterious a place in its own right to try to add mysteries.*

Although he read English at Cambridge and took no science courses, Fry nonetheless has a sympathy for science which is unusual in arts graduates, and does not feel that a scientific understanding of the world reduces our appreciation of it.

> *Just as there is nothing intrinsically dry and unspiritual about science, similarly there is nothing intrinsically mystical and irrational about the study of literature. Indeed, when I was at Cambridge we were going through the great structuralist debate and a lot of people were saying that the trouble with structuralism is that it is a rather scientific method, so that at linguistic levels you actually have complex formulas for the description of phonemes and so on. They felt that English should be about your response to a text, and there is of course room for that, but my view has always been that you don't find the Lake District less beautiful just because you happen to know about the rock structure underneath it. If anything, geologists may even find it more beautiful because they see what Eliot might call the skull beneath the skin, which gives them a greater sense of the beauty of it. Similarly, I have no patience for people who say that Shakespeare was ruined for them by having to study it at school; a further understanding of something never ruins its beauty.*

At this point Fry paused to blow his nose and remarked on the fact that for many years he had felt that he was immune to colds as he never seemed to catch them. Unfortunately, a few days previously, the Cosmos had responded to this false confidence by giving him the granddaddy of all colds – and in the acting world having a cold brings its own problems.

> *I would say the worst thing about being in a play is the moment you get a sniffle like I've got now, and you're in your dressing room, suddenly there is a knock on the door and you hear: 'Stephen, hello it's Lucy here. I heard your cough and*

there's a wonderful little man in Camden Passage who does Bach wild flower remedies. Here's his card.'

'Yes thank you'

And then there's another knock: 'Would you like to borrow my crystals?' somebody else says.

And it continues: 'Knock, knock' – 'I've got four piles of vitamins. Here's a bottle of vitamin C, there's one of vitamin B, one of vitamin D, and one of vitamin K, which not many people know about.'

'Get out!' I cry. 'I've got a cold, for God's sake leave me alone, I don't want your crystals, I don't want your homoeopathy, I don't want your little weird spongy trace element pills that melt on your tongue. I don't want any of this drivel, I just want a handkerchief!'

But he does proffer an explanation for this type of almost superstitious belief in unproven, quack remedies or formulae for self-improvement that seem so popular amongst actors and perhaps more particularly amongst actresses: 'One of the explanations is that actresses' careers are very difficult. They have to rely so much on their personal appearance, on their health, and on their skin quality, that they're desperate for anything that they think might even have a 0.01% chance of making them fitter, or look better or glossier.'

Fry, himself, however, did not avail himself of a unique opportunity for self-improvement which he had seen on a TV programme: 'I was so staggered when I saw some television programme about an American who is genuinely producing jeans with crystals sewn into a special gusset because he believes the crotch is the centre of consciousness and that the crystals resonate with some cosmic frequency. He's making a fortune out of people buying jeans with bits of mineral in them.'

As a lone skeptic in the midst of a generally credulous community of actors and actresses, an easy course of action might be to keep one's views on homoeopathy, astrology, and psychic powers to oneself. Stephen Fry, on the contrary, expresses his views and expresses them forcefully. Andrew Lloyd Webber has a long-weekend party at his house in Newbury every year and often organizes a debate in the evenings. One year Fry was asked to propose the motion, 'Sydmonton (the name of Lloyd Webber's house) Believes that Astrology is Bumf', and was seconded by John Selwyn Gummer (famous for feeding his four-year-old daughter a hamburger on camera in 1989 to oppose a beef ban at the height of concern over mad cow disease). The motion was opposed by no less a personage than Russell Grant, who was seconded by the woman who taught TV's cuddliest astrologer his mystical arts.

Fry began his speech in blunt terms: 'I said that not only does Sydmonton believe that astrology is bumf, it believes that it is crap, it's a crock of horseshit, that it's bullshit.' But this rhetoric was followed up with some good skeptical entertainment, as Fry had asked his agent to obtain 'serious' astrological readings based on information given to a number of astrologers about him, Hitler, and various other persons. He proceeded to amuse the gathering by reading these totally inaccurate personality profiles, thereby somewhat weakening the opposition's argument.

Astrology is clearly a subject about which Fry has strong feelings (to be expected in a Sagittarius):

> *The constellations are all based on the parallax from which we view them, so that it is totally arbitrary when we say that a particular constellation looks like, say, a pair of scales. Then to say, given that from this particular point of view this particular constellation looks slightly like some scales, someone born under it therefore is balanced is just the most insane thing you've ever heard. Or to say that someone born under Gemini, the twins, displays some kind of split personality; it seems so clear that this is just nonsense. And then people say 'It stands to reason you know … ' It stands to all kinds of things, but reason is certainly not one of them.*

He recently participated in a television programme on Channel 4 called *Star Test* in which celebrities are interviewed by a computer. The interviewee is alone in a studio with the cameras operated remotely and is asked by an electronic voice to select a topic and then to select a number from one to five. So far so good – but the next question asked of him was, 'What is your star sign?' – not a good question to ask the man who once said, in an interview with the *Independent,* that the length of his penis was likely to reveal as much about his personality as his star sign (and no Freudian will disagree with that!).

'And so I refused to say anything and just stood up – you're supposed to sit down – with the cameras following me, and spoke angrily about astrology for about two minutes. I expect they'll cut this bit because I went on and on and on and on … '

Fry, when confronted with the there-are-more-things-in-heaven-than-are-dreamt-of-in-your-philosophy school of logic, stresses the word 'dreamt' and insists that he also dreams of heffalumps, unicorns, and tolerable estate agents. However, he does accept that it is possible for people to have a significantly greater sensitivity to certain stimuli than most of us and that this can lead to, for instance, an apparent ability to dowse for water.

> *I was in the South of France recently where a friend of mine who is a great skeptic, Douglas Adams (author of* The Hitchhiker's Guide to the Galaxy), *has a*

house. Now, all of Provence is desperately short of water, it's the worst crisis they have ever had. If you want water you have to ring up for the water lorry and pay a vast amount of money to have your tank filled. It really is very, very bad. And he was talking to a chap who looks after a lot of houses belonging to English people in that area who was saying, 'Well, you either pay for the lorry each time it comes or you can have someone to come and dowse.' And indeed there are dowsers in Provence who make a fat living out of finding water for people.

Now, goodness knows I certainly don't believe that a mystic power comes out of the earth but I do believe in hyperaesthesia and I know of a great many people who are able to read signs in a semiotic way; who are able, for instance, to see someone talking and know that he is lying simply because they are so good at reading signs that most of us don't notice. Similarly, someone who is experienced in the kinds of places where water is likely to be, may well see patterns in the plants or geology of the area that indicate the presence of water – perhaps at a subconscious level. But he may genuinely believe that the water is influencing his dowsing twig. So I won't dismiss dowsing because, in my view, anybody who can make a decent living by dowsing, amongst people as naturally cynical as the French, in an area where water is so rare, must have some talent for finding water. But I don't for a moment believe that there is any outside agency which is making the twig move.

Another esoteric art for which Fry has a certain respect – but without believing that there are any mystical elements to it – is the use of randomness to help gain insights into oneself or into problems:

I think the use of the aleatory in life is rather good. The I Ching for instance – which I don't actually think any Chinaman believes to be particularly mystic – is a rather useful way of confronting anything. But the thing that you must do is think of the question you want to ask, ultimately, yourself. In fact, you can use any random event. For instance, you may have an important decision to make and what you can do is concentrate on the first thing you see out of the window – which could be a sparrow. You look at this sparrow with the question in your mind and anything the sparrow now does – via the natural patterning and metaphorical symbolizing abilities of the mind – will help you to come to grips with the problem. Essentially, you have the answer yourself but you just want to be shown an authority for it. Everyone needs a sense of some authority behind what they're doing it; no one wants to think of himself as being entirely alone and self-determining. In reality, of course, the real authority comes from oneself but we search for something to sanction what we're doing and rather reasonable things like the I Ching, ultimately, turn the authority back to oneself by the way in which one is obliged to frame the question.

Tolerant of oracles and dowsers, vociferous in his opposition to astrology and quackery – but what is Stephen Fry's particular *bête noire* amongst the mindless, mystical menagerie?

> *I suppose the one that really gets me going probably more than most is what the Greeks used to call* metempsychosis – *what we now call reincarnation. It doesn't take much to realize that even at the rate at which we are increasing as a population, there are still many more dead people around than there are living ones. Therefore there is a surplus of dead people so that they can't all be reincarnated – except as wasps perhaps, rather than WASPs. So I would love to hear one of these fatuous people who claim they've been around in previous lives just for once having lived in a period of time or as a person that wasn't dramatically interesting. Why must they all have been a serving maid to Cleopatra or caught up in the persecution of the Jews in York or something that is so easily researchable, so pointlessly predictable?*
>
> *And the other thing that really annoys me is the people who claim to have seen ghosts. They nearly always – because they think it's going to impress you more – tell you about it in a rather matter-of-fact tone of voice. Whereas, if I was going to even vaguely begin to believe that someone had seen a ghost, I would expect them to be absolutely staggered because it turns upside-down one's whole preconception about what the physical universe is.*

He leaned forward and gesticulated with his cup of cappuccino.

> *If I dropped this and it went upwards, I would be talking about it for the rest of my life. I wouldn't just dismissively say, 'Yeah, it's interesting – I let go of this cup and it fell upwards – would you like another cup of coffee?' And similarly with ghosts. Seeing a ghost would overturn everything you understand about the universe around you. You would have to be excited about it. Yet the person who recounts his experience pretends he's bored with it. How can you take it seriously? The whole paranormal panoply gets me going. It's all such ineffable piffle, isn't it?*

I couldn't have put it better myself.

Women are NOT from Gullibull
Lucy Sherriff

*When **Lucy Sherriff**, holder of a degree in physics and former science correspondent for **The Register**, was working in PR in the early 2000s, she had to read women's magazines as part of her job. Cruel and unusual punishment, perhaps. Why, she asks, are they so full of credulity about the paranormal? Appeared in XIV.3.*

Women's magazines are increasingly a source of real information – decent articles that provide us with details about recent breakthroughs in medicine, safety, health and fitness, and so on. For example, in one recently launched fashion magazine, there was a four-page article about the very real dangers of sexually transmitted infections. As the AIDS awareness campaigns fade into history, apparently people aren't using condoms any more and cases of chlamydia and gonorrhoea are on the increase. Certainly a topic that should be covered.

And yet, at the same time, nearly all women's publications carry horoscopes. Most of us really do only read them for a laugh, and let's face it, the horoscope debunking has been so thorough that the people who actually take it seriously are few and far between. So, why are they still there?

But more worrying, for me at least, is the number of articles about utterly spurious psychics, auras, and similar psychobabble nestling in between real news and discussion of serious issues.

Take an article that appeared in a popular health and fitness magazine not too long ago. It was a profile of a prominent 'psychic' who was telling the readers all about 'How to see your Aura!' She was given several hundred words to do this. (This is in a magazine that also carries regular features about the importance of self-screening in the prevention of breast cancer.)

After explaining, at length, how important one's aura was, and how it could be a really useful barometer of our physical and spiritual well being, she explained how we, too, could learn to see auras. The trick – and you'll love this – is to look at your reflection in the shiny side of a CD. No, really. Apparently the colour you see dominating the area around your head is your aura.

In the interests of scientific experiment, and trying really hard to keep an open mind, I had a go. After a bit of twisting and spinning around, I concluded that I had many different auras. Which one seemed to depend on the angle between me and the light in the middle of the room. What could the explanation possibly be?

The same magazine that wrote about the importance of safe sex featured an article in which readers contributed spooky stories of strange happenings that had no rational explanation. Among the tales were the usual suspects: predictive dreams, hauntings by dead friends, and bizarre coincidences that even the most hardened skeptic would still notice as odd. Explicable, but odd nonetheless.

Try this one for sheer brazenness. though: 'We used to keep small change in a glass bowl in our flat,' says Laura, 26. 'One day I saw it was full and suggested to my boyfriend that we take it to the bank. The next day, when no one but us had been in the flat, we found the bowl was completely empty.'

The 'paranormal psychologist' who was analysing the readers' experiences had this explanation: 'This is most unusual, and only a paranormal explanation, transference – objects moving by themselves – can explain it.'

The only possible explanation was transference? Perhaps sock gremlins had branched out into small change? Maybe it was *The Borrowers*, and she'll have her cash back sometime next year?

Back in the real world, maybe her boyfriend had taken it to the bank. Or, what about theft? I mean, let's be sensible about this. If no one but Laura and her boyfriend were in the flat and she knew she hadn't taken it, he is the prime suspect for having nicked it. More worryingly, the flat could have been broken into.

At least with spontaneously shattering candlesticks it is sufficiently out of the ordinary that you can (with a little grimace) understand why people resort to paranormal explanations.

My real gripe, though, is not that this was a particularly lame attempt at invoking the paranormal, but that the paranormal is still considered a proper topic for discussion in women's press. It doesn't get coverage in the comparable men's magazines unless it is being mocked.

I find it insulting to have equal coverage given to breast cancer and aura tutorials. And if the people who put together these publications keep filling them with this kind of junk, how am I to take them seriously when I read articles about Rohypnol or slave labour on the cocoa farms of the Ivory Coast?

It isn't harmless fun any more. It is trivial rubbish and women everywhere should be as irate as I am that it is considered worthy of our attention.

Paul Daniels
Michael Hutchinson

Magicians have a special place in skepticism: their carefully acquired skills at misdirection make them perfectly placed to spot attempts at deception. Middlesbrough-born **Paul Daniels** *(www.pauldaniels.co.uk) is one of Britain's best-known magicians; at the time of this interview the twelfth series of* **The Paul Daniels Magic Show** *was being broadcast on the BBC (it ran from 1979 to 1994). Daniels's views about the paranormal are not as well-known as he is; he spelled them out clearly to* **Michael Hutchinson**, *probably Britain's longest-serving skeptic. A portion of this interview appears verbatim in the FAQ on Daniels' Web site. Appeared in V.1.*

'That's a fiddle. It's sleight of hand' was Paul Daniels' reaction when, in the early 1970s, Granada television showed him their film about psychic surgery in the Philippines. Their response was to say that they had watched the surgeon. 'But I watched the assistant,' he said. Standing next to Daniels was a leading spiritualist who wasn't convinced.

'No, it isn't a cheat,' he asserted. 'But you can see it,' Daniels insisted, but to no avail. The man just couldn't be persuaded.

With eleven television series and numerous specials behind him, Paul Daniels is a well-established household name. When I went to interview him for *The Skeptic*, I knew from previous interviews I had read that he is very outspoken about religion and morality (in its widest sense). However, what I wanted to discover were his opinions about psychics and psychical research, and whether he had originally been a believer in the paranormal. He answered my questions with great enthusiasm.

Yes, as a growing lad in the North, I believed that it was probable that people could transmit thought waves to one another. I believed in religious mysticism and I thought therefore, that as an extension of transmitting thought waves, telekinesis might be possible. I used to sit for hours trying to move a ping-pong ball across a table. It was only when I could afford a wider range of books that I became a lot more logical, and a lot more observant.

This wider range of books included books about magicians of the past and the history of magic itself. 'Magic meaning conjuring,' he clarified.

It was Robert Houdin in the last century who said that a conjuror is an actor playing the part of a magician, magic being a thing of fable, fairy stories, and dreams. I realized that religion was a set of rules for society to live by that was operated by a set of guys doing magic tricks. It was an Egyptian guide who explained to me that Tutankhamen was a sentence: 'King Tut, son of the sun god'. At that time in history kings, pharaohs, and religious leaders were frequently called 'son of god', and frequently given a virgin birth. I thought: Why wasn't I told this at school? Within a primitive society you may need a mystical fear to control children, but I believe that now you can educate them as to why those rules are good to live by and that if you break them there's a pyramid effect of people who are going to get hurt by your action. I really would like to see all schools have religion removed from them. It's time for the world to grow up. If people want religion they should give it to their children at the weekend.

These are strong statements, and come – surprisingly – from a man who was once a Methodist lay preacher.

Equally surprising, perhaps, is that Paul Daniels is very sympathetic towards Uri Geller. *Humanist News* once reported him as saying that he doesn't mind Uri and that he goes up and does his act, adding that Uri 'is a nice guy'. Daniels told me:

Uri is interesting. On the next series of The Best of Magic *he comes out of the closet and does a magic trick – a trick similar to one we did a few years ago in which you set a clock up and do certain things while the clock is ticking, and then you take the clock back the amount of time you've been busy. We boiled water, for example, and although the water has boiled you pour it over your hand and it's cold again. Oddly enough, rumour has it that despite his paranormal powers the whole thing didn't work anyway and it had to be reset behind a screen. But he is a great showman. I don't know where you draw the line. I mean if people say he's a con-artist to what extent is he a con-artist? Who has he conned? He is entertainment value, but, in my view, he has no psychic powers whatsoever. I don't believe that he can bend metal by thought waves – or do anything else by thought waves. He's a good entertainer if you leave it at that. In fact, he goes to a few magic conventions now and David Berglas (President of the Magic Circle) is a close friend.*

Daniels once got a typist to retype the star sign information from an astrology book, but switched the headings around. 'Several times at parties people asked me, "What star sign are you?" and I'd say "It's funny you should ask. I'm doing a book on that" and show them the piece marked with their star sign. They'd say "Yes, this is me".' He laughed. 'When I told them what I'd done I lost so many friends … '

But why do so many people seem to need to believe in the paranormal?

I think that because of bad education – capital B-A-D – people have a need for mysticism; they're missing out on the simple fact that what you are is amazing;

what you are is wonderful. What you are. No extraneous influences. What you are, inside you, is just fantastic. It really is, and yet they sit in front of the TV and watch David Attenborough going on about some mysterious animal that has developed its eyes so that it can see in the dark and they say, 'Isn't that wonderful?' And they miss out on the fact that the thing that's watching the programme is the most developed animal of all in terms of thinking, and movement, and sense – and yet they look for mysticism, and that just drives me up the wall.

Nobody's promoting the human animal as being it, as being the be-all and end-all. Only humanists to an extent. But humanists aren't really promoting it, are they? They're not getting out there, writing articles, and getting on television programmes. Maybe the answer to the paranormal is an awful lot of practical proof of what you are, what you can do. What we as a group can do without invoking paranormal powers.

Although it's not difficult to find skeptical books, people are not made aware by the media that they exist. It's sad that the people who have written these books which say 'Oh, come on! This is nonsense' don't get much publicity. When you do, you're the bad guy. When Doris Stokes died, I got a phone call from the press, and I told them it was nonsense before, and it's nonsense now. I got quite viciously attacked in the press because they said I didn't pick up on her while she was alive. Well, I did – at every opportunity. So I became the bad guy, although I was telling the truth. And I think that's the real oddity in human nature. An oddity, but understandable. It's a truth, isn't it, that the mass of the people will always be poor, comparatively, and it's the poor people that need mysticism. The mass press will therefore always promote it.

TV people doing skeptical programmes do it in the wrong order. People flip channels and there is research to show how soon after the start of a programme they do so. [This research shows that viewers flip from The Paul Daniels Show later than most programmes.] What they should do right at the start of a debunking programme is say, 'What you are about to see is a programme that will show you how these people cheat, how they play on emotions. The people are fakes.' They should say that right up front, but they don't. Inevitably, they do the programme as if it's for real and then they do the debunking. It's at the wrong end of the programme because by then you've convinced a major proportion of viewers who have changed over. 'Oh well, yes it's another psychic and we know about psychics don't we?

He picked up a copy of *The Skeptic*. 'This word, "skeptic", is going to drive away the people you're trying to get to. Might I suggest a change of title to *The Paranormal?* with a question mark?'

In the last few years, Daniels has spent two days a week developing and promoting a high-speed language learning system which uses an ancient Greek memory technique. Already there are courses in French, German, Italian, and Spanish. Using the system, Daniels learned enough Spanish in a week to perform his act before a Spanish-speaking audience. Portuguese has just been recorded and Japanese is next in line for the treatment.

'Japanese is proving very interesting. It is different, not because of the sound, but for the way they speak. But it's marvellous. Very difficult for the Japanese to explain it to me.'

Daniels strongly approves of James Randi's work. 'It's something that really needed to be done. I think in his life he must have done more than anyone has ever done to raise public awareness – certainly in America – among thinking people. The saddest part is that Randi isn't young, and that he isn't on every day doing this, as the audience is changing all the time. It should be taught in school. To me, the works of Randi should be taught alongside the works of Shakespeare because it's as necessary for your quality of life as art or literature.'

For several years in addition to his series and Christmas special Daniels also made a special Halloween show which he enjoyed doing. The BBC would only allow a 1990 show if it was made in the middle of his new magic series. This would have meant putting up with the enormous physical and mental strain of doing two different shows in two days.

But what I find odd is, here's an organization that's got, arguably, a pretty good magician, and Halloween is a mystical kind of an evening, and they don't use it as part of an annual celebration of entertainment. I think it's a mistake. Well, come on, it's hard enough as it is to fill the schedules, and here's a free gift, almost. Funnily enough, a BBC radio producer phoned my manager and wanted me to go on his show and perform a miracle on Halloween. Mervyn said I wasn't available that particular night, but would be the following week. 'Oh, no!' said the man. 'You don't understand. It's on Halloween. That's the day their powers are greater isn't it?' This is a BBC producer in 1989. But come on! In this day and age he believes my powers are greater on a particular day of the year!

Some psychics maintain that I have a negative attitude. But I am a professional magician who has been in love with magic since the age of 11. The one thing I would love to encounter is somebody who could really do it. This is my hobby, my life. I wouldn't be offended at all. If I could find somebody who could really do magic, really bend metal, I'd put him on my programme. On the other hand, if you really had that power, would you want to spend your life bending spoons? To say I'm negative is a joke. I want to meet a real psychic; I want to see a ghost. And I would be prepared to pay. Even now, with all the knowledge and the reading that's in my head, I'd really like to meet one. Wouldn't you?

8

State of the art

At first glance, it may not be clear what an investigation of a near-death experience, a complaint that feminism has failed to embrace science, the speed of alien spacecraft, and perpetual motion machines have in common. The link is that each is, in its way, a story about the interaction between human beliefs and the technology of modern times.

I would love to believe that 'progress' means increasingly widespread acceptance and understanding of science, but it clearly means nothing of the kind. If science is a process, so is skepticism.

Perpetuum Mobile: The Perpetual Search for Perpetual Motion
Anthony Garrett

Wouldn't it be great if we could solve all our energy problems by coming up with a perpetual motion machine? About once a decade or so, someone comes up with a new version of this physics-defying idea: Joseph Newman's energy machine (www.josephnewman.com), the water-powered car (www.water poweredcar.com). But the US Patent Office typically rejects all applications to patent anything that smacks of perpetual motion. Explaining why this blanket dismissal is not just prejudice is **Dr Anthony Garrett**, *a former member of the Australian Skeptics and the Manchester Skeptics. Garrett studied physics at Cambridge and Glasgow; he is now founder and managing editor of SCITEXT Cambridge (www.scitext.com). Appeared in III.2*

The promise of a machine which runs forever, a perpetual motion machine, is irresistible. Perpetual motion was a hot topic in the nineteenth century, because the age of the engineer was at its height and the demand for new energy sources great. It is no coincidence that the science involved was worked out at this time; yet even today, over a century later, people continue to propose machines which don't work.

The reason for the enduring popularity of perpetual motion is of course the dream of conjuring energy from nothing. Were this feasible, all coal-fired power stations, with their carbon dioxide and sulphurous emissions, could be closed; likewise, nuclear fission power plants with their radioactive waste and the need to disfigure the landscape with arrays of solar cells or windmills would vanish. The enormous sums spent on energy research could be redeployed, and cheap energy made readily available to developing countries. The inventor of a free energy source would be fêted throughout the world.

Perpetual motion proposals are of two types, and the distinction is crucial. A perpetual motion machine of the first kind actually creates energy. Some of this is inevitably rendered inaccessible through friction losses in bearings, or air drag on moving parts, or the like; but the rest is available to the world as free energy. By contrast, a perpetual motion machine of the second kind neither creates nor destroys energy. It runs forever by completely eliminating friction in the bearings, air drag, and such; but any attempt to extract energy from it causes it to slow down.

These two types of machine respectively contravene the first and second laws of thermodynamics. The first law states that energy is conserved, and the second that entropy increases. More on these in a moment.

Most publicity attaches to perpetual motion proposals of the first kind. Their proponents generally agree with scientists as to the laws of force and torque operating within their machines. The law of force was first elucidated by

Isaac Newton three centuries ago, and states that *Force = Mass × Acceleration*. Similarly, angular acceleration is proportional to the applied torque.

Once it is accepted that undisturbed motion is a body's natural state, that it alters its velocity (that is, accelerates) only when a force is acting on it, and that slowing down is not the natural state but the result of frictional forces, the path to Newton's laws is easy and intuitive. It nevertheless took a genius of Newton's magnitude to overthrow the Aristotelian dogma of the day, and comprehend this for the first time.

But, crucially, the perpetual motion proponents do not accept that the force and torque laws also imply conservation of energy. This makes good sense: no force, no velocity change, no energy change. But in a complicated machine the same principle is one step further removed from the forces and torques which people can feel, and so is often beyond untutored intuition. I am told, with a don't-blind-me-with-science look, 'Maybe, but what is wrong with my machine?' Perpetual motion advocates, having once got into a physicist's office, are reluctant to leave until a lengthy impasse is reached.

One catch occurs so often it is worth singling out. Perpetual motion machines, in common with many others, are almost invariably cyclic: after sufficient operation, called a cycle, the machine returns to its initial configuration. A wheel making one complete turn is the simplest example. (Cyclicity is a matter of convenience, since a non-cyclic machine would be difficult to exploit.) In evaluating cyclic machines it is essential to consider the energy balance over a complete cycle. Cyclic machines with an obvious acceleration mechanism in one part of the cycle, but a subtle deceleration process in another, are particular favourites.

Even more subtle are those machines which interchange energy between its various forms: motion, heat, latent heat of evaporation (the 'drinking bird', a popular toy), electromagnetism, and so on. Some of the subtleties are quite ingenious, but if physics is operating as it has been understood for three centuries, the catch is inevitably there somewhere.

Perpetual motion machines of the second kind, though less commercially attractive, are no less interesting. Moreover, they exist! From Newton's laws it follows that an isolated system in motion, with no forces or torques acting on it, exhibits precisely perpetual motion of the second kind. How can this be reconciled with the running down of a top due to friction at its tip? The answer is that the energy has not been destroyed, but converted into heat at the tip. Since heat is motional energy of the atoms in the tip, we could still see continuing motion if our eyesight were good enough. The motion is therefore perpetual – though on an atomic scale rather than an everyday one. We say the energy of the top has degraded into heat, and this process translates into physics through the second law of thermodynamics. It is a consequence of our inability to see things on the atomic scale, rather than a fundamental property of nature like the first law.

A further example of the second kind is electrons orbiting the atomic nucleus. Obviously there is no air resistance! Because of the peculiarities of the quantum theory of atomic processes, we can no longer picture the process simply. Nevertheless, the criterion for perpetual motion of the second kind is still satisfied: verifiable predictions are not altered unless the system is disturbed. In other words, the electron does not 'run down'. Energy conservation still holds good in quantum mechanics.

A large-scale example is the earth orbiting the sun. Meteorite strikes and other external influences, which affect the motion, are separate issues. Clearly, perpetual motion of the second kind is common on celestial and atomic scales, but rare on Earth. However, we now know how to set up a simple quantum state as large as we like. The secret is to cool the system sufficiently near to absolute zero. The most famous example is superconductivity, currently in vogue, in which an electric current circulates in a wire loop with zero resistance, needing no battery to drive it. Although the current itself is still invisible, its effects are observable. Another example is superfluidity, in which a liquid flows up the inside of a tube immersed in it, and back down the outside, indefinitely.

How do these systems beat the second law? This law is ultimately only probabilistic reasoning, used in the absence of detailed information about each atom. Since we normally ask questions only about large-scale quantities, the enormous number of atoms being averaged over guarantees our answers accurate with almost total certainty. (Entropy relates to the amount of information needed to specify the system at the atomic level.) In the examples just given, we are dealing not with millions of particles, but with one electron, one planet, one known quantum state. Our reasoning then is exact; the second law is a different form of reasoning used in different circumstances. Proposals which violate the second law, all ultimately equivalent to impossible heat engines, tend to be more subtle than proposals of the first kind.

Finally for theory, conservation of energy still holds in Einstein's theory of relativity, provided that mass m is seen as a further form of energy E, related by the famous equation $E = mc^2$ where c is the speed of light. Because this is so large, mass is a very concentrated form of energy: we can do three hundred million times better by converting the mass of a tank of petrol than by burning it! The complexity of nuclear reactors indicates the difficulty of transforming mass into accessible energy. But if, conversely, we invest energy in making antimatter, we have the perfect fuel, for antimatter spontaneously converts to readily accessible energy when mixed with matter. Just one tenth of a gram of antimatter, safely confined, would propel a car for life!

We now turn to the entertaining history of perpetual motion. Arthur Ord-Hume's book, *Perpetual Motion: The History of an Obsession* (Allen & Unwin, 1977), gives a modern survey.

Today it is difficult to imagine a time when energy conservation was not firmly established, and the equivalence of different forms of energy, particularly heat, was fiercely debated. Yet that was the situation up to the middle of the nineteenth century; and earlier still, before Mayer, Joule, and Helmholtz settled the first law, and Carnot and Clausius the second. Perpetual motion proponents should be judged by their own times.

A Sanskrit manuscript from the first half of the fifth century refers to a wheel, free to rotate about a horizontal axis, with sealed holes drilled in radially from the circumference, part filled with mercury. Once started, the wheel was supposed to maintain its rotation. Presumably its inventor fell for the 'cyclic' fallacy, believing that the extra momentum, due to the mercury on the descending side of the wheel moving under centrifugal force to the circumferential end of the tube, provides sufficient impetus to keep the whole thing going.

This is the earliest known coherent suggestion for perpetual motion. It is also the prototype of many proposed in Europe, in which weights attached to the circumference of the wheel dispose themselves further from the axis on the descending side of the wheel than the ascending.

Some of these were marvellously intricate, and the Marquis of Worcester, who is believed to have constructed the first practical steam engine, claimed success for one in 1655. (Worcester's biographer, Henry Dircks, published in 1861 a comprehensive survey of the preceding three centuries of perpetual motion.)

This was pre-dated by the Italian philosopher Zimara, who in 1518 proposed a crank (inoperable, incidentally) for linking a windmill to a set of bellows aimed at it. Interconversion between forms of energy, here wind and mechanical energy, is a characteristic concept of perpetual motion.

Perpetual motion was eminently respectable during the Renaissance: contemporary with Zimara, Leonardo da Vinci was involved in drafting sketches for six designs. By far the most common proposals concerned self-propelling water wheels. The water mill was the dominant mechanical device in Europe; what could be more natural than to harness its power to raise the water once more? The aptly named Robert Fludd (1574–1637), an English physician, and Georg Bockler, of Nurnberg, were two leading visionaries of this kind. It mattered little that John Wilkins, Cromwell's brother-in-law and later Bishop of Chester, tested a similar scheme unsuccessfully during the Civil War, and pronounced his skepticism in 1643. Perpetual motion was in the air of the time. Wilkins, in fact, continued to be fascinated by perpetual motion to the end of his life.

The decline of a great many superstitions in the Age of Reason left perpetual motion untouched, for it could still be phrased as a scientific hypothesis. Indeed, proposals proliferated from the 1720s onwards. The eighteenth century also saw the first clock to be powered by changes in atmospheric pressure, giving an illusion of perpetual motion, by the London clock-maker James Cox. It now rests in the Victoria & Albert Museum.

In the nineteenth century, while the laws of thermodynamics were being established, the harnessing of electromagnetism led to a new series of proposals. These all essentially coupled motors back to generators. In fact, the earliest coherent magnetic proposal goes as far back as 1570, when a Jesuit priest suggested that an iron ball, rolling down a ramp under gravity, could be drawn back along a different path by a magnet. We now know that any magnet strong enough to do this would keep the ball from rolling in the first place.

The combination, in that century, of the mechanical explosion and popular ignorance led to exploitation and fraud. E. P. Willis, a machinist of Connecticut, charged admission to view an asymmetrical-wheel machine, which he set up in New Haven and subsequently New York. It was maintained in a glass case, and was actually powered by compressed air passed up a strut and over one of the gears. Willis simply challenged viewers to state how the machine could run, rather than claimed perpetual motion.

No such constraints attached to Charles Redheffer, who in 1812 set up a machine in Philadelphia which ran unceasingly. Needless to. say, viewing was not free of charge. A team of experts sent to examine it in connection with Redheffer's application for funding detected that the wear on two connected gears was on the wrong side, and were satisfied that fraud was involved. They did not detect its nature, but instead built a similar machine with concealed clockwork, and a winder disguised as an ornamental knob. Redheffer privately offered its owner, Sellers, a large sum to reveal his secret. Instead, Sellers denounced Redheffer. Worse was to come in New York, where Redheffer, undaunted, built a further machine. The submarine pioneer, Robert Fulton, recognized its uneven speed through one cycle as characteristic of a crank (appropriately), and denounced it on the spot. He then dismantled a suspicious-looking support strut to reveal a catgut-belted drive run by a man turning a wheel in a nearby room. The crowd, which had paid $5 a man, then a large sum (ladies free, for some reason), demolished the remainder, and Redheffer fled.

Perhaps the finest fraud was perpetrated by John Keely, again of Philadelphia. In 1875 he unveiled a complicated variant on the steam engine, into which he would blow for half a minute and then pour in five gallons of water. After a whizz-bang show of manipulating various valves and taps, he would then announce that the apparatus was charged with a mysterious vapour, at a pressure of 107,000 pounds to the square inch. Keely claimed that the power source was the disintegration of water. Latter-day enthusiasts prefer, like Keely, to tap 'new forms of energy', rather than deny its conservation. This is theoretically possible, but it is highly unlikely that easily exploitable new forms will be found.

The main reason for Keely's success – he raised over a million dollars to set up the Keely Motor Company – was showmanship. Keely was an imposing figure with an air of honesty, who was given to baffling the uninitiated with phrases like 'hydro pneumatic pulsing vacu engine', 'sympathetic equilibrium', and 'quadruple negative harmonics'. Such pseudoscientific terms are often used by today's charlatans: *plus ça change*! With men of science Keely was more guarded, and took pains to ensure none could examine his machines closely.

In the 1880s the Keely Motor Company, discouraged by his failure to produce a commercial motor, cut off his funding. He found an alternative source in a wealthy widow, and promptly unveiled a new idea: vibrating energy in the aether, which underlay the disintegration of water. The Motor Company sued him for reimbursement, but he claimed his latest idea was unrelated to earlier ones and refused to pay. After a spell in prison, he succeeded in satisfying the courts of this. Keely was forced to tread warily when his benefactress attempted to have leading scientific figures validate his device. Tesla and Edison declined, but a visit in 1905 led the engineers involved to suspect compressed air sources. They were right. After Keely's death three years later, the son of one of his backers promptly rented the house, and found it was comprehensively 'wired' to a three-ton air tank in the basement.

The first patent on a perpetual motion proposal was granted in Britain in 1635, only twelve years after patenting was introduced. By 1775, the Parisian Academy of Sciences was refusing to accept schemes. Since this was long before the establishment of energy conservation, the gentlemen of Paris can only have been disillusioned by the repeated failure of all such devices in practice. Nearly a hundred years later, the US Patent Office decreed that a working model should be submitted within one year of the initial application; but enthusiasts still gummed up the works, and finally, in 1911, a working model was demanded from the start.

This rule has, inevitably, been challenged in the courts, with inventor Howard Johnson finally winning US patent 4151431 on his 'magnetic motor'. Nevertheless, the world hardly waits with bated breath. The furore in the 1980s over Joseph Newman's motor, which supposedly tapped into unknown gyroscopic fields associated with subatomic particles, further demonstrated that perpetual motion will never die away entirely. (Present-day physics successfully predicts the spin properties of elementary particles to a staggering one part in a hundred million, which is as far as experiments have gone.) However Newman's device ran, it proved subtle enough to confound several scientists. The story of perpetual motion exemplifies the entire human endeavour: an upward crawl to enlightenment, with theory and practice advancing side by side; momentous discoveries by pioneers, which become the bedrock on which the next advances are built; gradual diffusion of the new ideas into general awareness; and ever the self-deluded, and the charlatans preying on ignorance.

The story has been presented here as a case history rather than a warning, but if any lesson is to be drawn it is that the best insurance against nonsense is a scientifically educated public. It is faintly credible that the US Navy came close to backing one machine in 1881; but astounding that as recently as 1986 a jury acquitted a perpetual motionist of fraudulently raising $685,000, because (the attorney later found) it believed perpetual motion and energy creation possible. The sooner that cannot happen, anywhere, the better.

Pearce 2: (clockwise starting upper left):
"Have a look now. It's ten miles closer." (Appeared 16.4 - "Mars is frowning on us.")
"Well, if you made more of an effort they wouldn't have had to fake it!" (Appeared 19.1)
Actually no caption. (Appeared 19.2 - "Psychic scam warning")
Also no caption (Appeared 16.3 "Split decision")

Women and the New Age
Lucy Fisher

*In the 1970s, feminism aimed at two things: equality for women in workplaces, at home, and in public policy, and destroying the prejudice inherent in 'feminine' stereotypes. Both are valid goals. But from a skeptical point of view, one of the most significant failures of feminism, an accelerating trend in the 1990s, has been its failure to embrace science and reason and push for an end to the mindset that holds that men are good at logic and science and women are intuitive and emotional. In other words, a different twist on the worst attitudes of the women's magazines that Lucy Sherriff complained about in a previous chapter. London-based journalist **Lucy Fisher** examined this mindset and asked whether New Age ideas are damaging the feminist viewpoint. Unfortunately, it's not clear that things have changed much since then; witness the noticeable drop in numbers of women entering technical fields such as computer science. Appeared in VI.3.*

For centuries women were oppressed, and their supposed irrationality was one of the excuses. Many women are now taking pride in irrationality as an ancient female power. Is it a substitute for the political power they lack? Or are they compensating for feelings of inferiority by emphasizing powers they have always (supposedly) had? Ought we to persecute them for trying to raise their self-esteem?

In her book *The Skeptical Feminist* Janet Radcliffe Richards deplored the fact that some feminists rejected logic and reason on the grounds that men had used them for bad ends. This branch of feminism, instead of withering away, has burgeoned and now seems the most healthy part of the plant.

Is this perception correct? Feminist academic Janet Montefiore agreed that feminists still reject reason: 'But academic feminists put it rather differently. They reject the contamination of so-called masculine rationality.' In the eighteenth-century Enlightenment philosophers said that women were irrational. When academic feminists discard rationality in response to this they are 'deconstructing the rhetoric'. They think reason has been contaminated by rationalization, 'but, according to Montefiore, they don't use words like that. They're more likely to say it's "phallologocentric". Ten years ago we were discovering our true female nature – "We reason with our bodies, we feel it in our wombs etc." The academic version of this is, "We are decentred subjects and we have dethroned King Phallus (King Reason)".'

How does this get translated to the woman in the street? 'There is a popular version of the academics' polysyllabic arguments ("We don't want male logic")', but, said Montefiore, it's not fair to criticize what people say in pubs, as it's not the same as what they say in academic discourse. She concluded that it was an unresolved argument in feminism.

However, even if feminists claim to have rejected reason, it doesn't mean they actually have. It's possible to declare you have rejected reason without knowing what it is. Women may fear its name because men invoke it (this is not the same as using it) as a weapon to keep them in their place. The feminist magazine *Spare Rib* may put 'proof' in quotes, but the decline in the Bristol Cancer Centre's attendance after the 1990 report claiming that its complementary therapies were dangerous shows that people do want proof (or 'proof'). (The unfavourable Bristol study was later discredited.)

The women's movement has certainly become less pragmatic. Instead of working on issues such as abortion, day care, and equal opportunities, women are worshipping the goddess. Instead of campaigning against unnecessary episiotomies, they are applying Bach flower remedies. According to Freya Aswynn (www.aswynn.co.uk), a Netherlands-born Odinist, former witch, and author of *Leaves of Yggdrasil*, feminism since its 1960s incarnation ('women's rights and all that') has developed into 'lesbian feminism on the one side and the development of worship of the goddess, also a great awareness of the earth, animals, plants, trees on the other'. Feminism has taken on many of the characteristics of the New Age.

The 'New Age' is about as new as the New Forest. Superstition has always existed side by side with official religions and learning, adapting to suit the time and the place. All you have to do is change the trappings. Superstition has moved upmarket, shedding its image of elderly ladies with badly dyed hair making a poor living reading tea leaves in a seedy backstreet. Out go the crystal ball and the chenille table cloth with bobbled fringe, in come the Arts and Crafts-designed Tarot cards and the stripped pine furniture. The New Age has gone for the people with most spare cash, and repackaged superstition for the middle classes.

There's supposed to be something particularly female about all things New Age. The right side of the brain (the 'good' side) is associated with 'feminine' qualities such as spirituality, intuition, and aesthetics. This sounds familiar – isn't it the little woman whose brain can't cope with science but can throw together a pleasing colour scheme for her sitting room? The early 1970s feminists fought against such stereotyping.

According to Aswynn, occultism is divided into separate realms:

> *There are basically two branches. One is the celestial branch, usually tied up with intellectual people who study astrology, or hermeticism, or runes. And then there are the people who work with the earth: herbalism, healing, seasonal energies, festivals. And the two are complementary. And it is in the latter category that you find most feminists. Women are more interested in the earth, which of course is only natural.*

In the past, women were always pegged as the superstitious sex, but it was hard for them to know better because they were barred from education. And some of their 'superstitions', such as herbal medicine, may have been quite effective. One shouldn't throw the baby out with the bathwater, but on the other hand one shouldn't have to take the chaff along with the wheat. Formerly, magic was one of the few routes to money and power open to women. Why are so many intelligent, well-heeled, educated women turning to it now, when it's so much easier for women to get their hands on money, power, learning, and liberty (though the battle is by no means won)?

We should be worried – it is frightening that what seems to be sheer silliness can acquire a sinister power. An uncritical attitude can result in thralldom to those who take money from the vulnerable in the name of spirituality. Though to an outsider she might seem typical of the genre, Aswynn thought her opinion of many features of New Age was 'perhaps not printable'. She thought the recent popularity of the occult was due to fashion as well as cynical marketing exercises. She continued: 'It focuses incredibly much on self-development. It doesn't actually espouse a philosophy of helping people out and trying to alter social conditions. It's a heavy ego-trip: "Oh aren't I wonderful, aren't I liberated". Everybody's really into themselves.'

The goddess

What is the goddess? Leaving aside the question of how a bodiless entity without genitalia or chromosomes can be either male or female, is the goddess a superstition, a genuine religion, or an enabling metaphor? Or is 'enabling metaphor' a respectable term for superstition? 'It all originates from the human mind, though energy exists "out there" that corresponds,' said Aswynn. 'All we do is personalize them into the form of a god or goddess and use that image as a mediator to express ourselves in forms of religion or magic. I know I ought to worship a goddess. There are literally dozens about, but for some peculiar reason Odin it is.' She said that she didn't mean 'worship' in the Christian sense.

> We haven't got that self-abasement. We argue with our gods. We negotiate and drive hard bargains, and we take the piss out of them. It can be a personal idea of a goddess, or god, but it doesn't have to be. Lots of people are into the earth, or into animal liberation, or healing. Most people believe in a spiritual dimension more in terms of the earth. There are people in the occult world who look to the universe as a spiritual dimension of growth, and then there are those who work with the Gaia principle – the earth is an organism, the great mother from which we come and to which we go.

Publishers such as Thorsons and Arkana (a Penguin imprint) are flourishing in the present climate. My local bookshop's health section, as well as a *Nurse's Dictionary* and *Pears Medical Encyclopaedia*, contains: *The Detox*

Diet, Food Combining for Health, Beyond Codependency, Smile Therapy, The Silva Mind Control Method of Mental Dynamics, Aromatherapy, Massage, The Family Guide to Homeopathy, Norman Vincent Peale's *Art of Positive Living, The Greening of Medicine* (foreword by HRH the Prince of Wales), *Peace, Love and Healing: The Path to Self Healing* ('I wish that someone had told me when I was in medical school that over fifty years ago Carl Jung had interpreted a dream and made a physical diagnosis'). Under 'miscellaneous' can be found *The Way of Energy, The Dowser's Workbook, Natural Magic,* James Berlitz (and Isaac Asimov), Fritjof Capra (and James Randi), Carlos Castaneda, Linda Goodman's *Sun Signs,* Nostradamus, Lobsang Rampa, and Robert Pirsig. The shop is owned and run entirely by women, but a spokeswoman denied that it was a feminist outfit. 'We are fulfilling our brief as a general bookshop. It's market forces. A lot of our customers are women with children. There's a large population in the area of, er, literate women.'

Cherry Gilchrist's *The Circle of Nine* (Arkana) is a description of feminine archetypes. It could be seen as a worthy attempt to counteract centuries of the effect of such as the Catholic Church on women's self-esteem, but sadly she has accepted old-style images of femininity and given them a new respectability. Aswynn, on the other hand, rejects the conventional image: 'I work with mainly the female archetype of the valkyrie. Christianity has always kept women suppressed, and Islam, of course.' Gilchrist presents what are not so much archetypes as stereotypes. They are like the character descriptions in an astrological handbook, or from one of those articles women's magazines used to carry about what colours to wear to suit your particular skin type.

Gilchrist's book is well and entertainingly written – no nasty neologisms like Mary Daly's 'gyn/ecology'. And she's not entirely uncritical: she describes an astrology workshop run by women that was left to 'flow' into chaos while the men administered the crèche with military precision. But generally she doesn't bring evidence or support her assertions ('The boundaries between "self" and "other" are less marked in the female'), and a critical attitude is lacking.

So why should we want to know about female archetypes? Gilchrist rehearses the Joseph Campbell/John F. Schumaker argument that myths can be created and that you can alter people's behaviour in socially useful ways by giving them the *right* kind of myths. This sounds unpleasantly *dirigiste* – is propaganda acceptable as long as it is good?

'We have become aware of the need to retrieve symbolic insights into life …' says Gilchrist. What practical purpose has symbolism? Simone de Beauvoir in *The Second Sex* said that the trouble with women was that they mistook symbolic gesture for effective action. The Greenham Common women used the word 'action' to mean gesture ('We did an action at Blue Gate'), though they still managed to have an effect.

And if you aspire to be deep and intelligent without too much hard work, metaphors and symbols represent profundity. They make an impressive sound. However, once Gilchrist gets away from 'the circle is a symbol of receptivity' there are nuggets of practical information and illuminating insights, again like women's magazines. In fact, when she says that everything and everybody is beautiful, and even ugliness has a beauty of its own, and that true beauty (as if you hadn't guessed) can be achieved without fashions and make-up, one cries out 'Come back, Patience Strong, all is forgiven!' (The poems of Patience Strong, a women's magazine staple for many years, aimed to help people – women – accept appalling situations rather than trying to change them.)

Unlike astrology (where the character write-up is chosen for you) you can choose your own archetype from a list including the Queen of Beauty, The Weaving Mother, the Lady of Light, the Queen of the Night, the Great Mother, the Lady of the Hearth, the Lady of the Dance, and the Just Mother. I come out as a cross between the Great Weaving Mother and the Queen of the Night (better than being a Metal Rabbit). The Queen, whose attributes are anger, wit, fierceness, and cunning, is the only archetype which isn't paralysingly *nice*. She has the ability to see through pretence, but unfortunately this is bundled with 'gifts' such as clairvoyance and telepathy. Gilchrist equates handicrafts with astrology, and adds that part of the Weaving Mother's character is a love of intrigue. (I deny this.) According to Angela Carter women have a private, imprecise language – 'a bit of cheese, a knob of butter' – which alienates them from (male) scientific discourse with its language of precise measurements. What about *k1 sl1 psso k2tog*? Woe betide the Weaving Mother if she's imprecise enough to get one stitch wrong.

What's dangerous is Gilchrist's implication that you don't need to think straight, perform double-blind controlled tests, or use your brain to try and understand the world. She moves seamlessly from telling stories around the hearth to divining the future. 'Where such ability exists, [it] is not solely of the feminine province, but is probably more readily acceptable to women. To be divine requires a willingness to let go of "rational" [her quotes] concepts, and to allow intuition and imagination to be the communicators of information.' There is no 'because' between these two sentences, but she implies that it follows that women are more *au fait* with divination because they are, not less rational, but more willing to let go of rationality and turn to intuition. But what does 'intuition' mean exactly?

Montefiore referred to 'worthy articles in the *Independent*' which explain women's intuition in terms of a different style of thought, the ability to listen, and skill at making connections, but 'intuition' in Gilchrist's paragraph refers to magical powers. Aswynn also used the word in this context: 'I am mainly involved in the intellectual side. However I am intuitive myself in that I can do readings for people.' There's a great difference between the two meanings. Magic is said to be irrational, because it's irrational to believe it, but if there was such a thing as magic it would not be irrational in itself. But since it's thought to be irrational to believe in it, those who believe in it claim that you have to be deliberately irrational in order to use it. It might be worth sacrificing reason if you gained magic powers as a result. Though if magic existed, it wouldn't be irrational to believe in it; in fact you wouldn't need to 'believe' it because you'd have enough evidence to know it existed.

Another reason why many women claim irrationality to be a valuable female quality is that they feel that male culture is cold, logical, and scientific. Adversarial argument is seen as aggressive (and aggression is bad and unfeminine). Gilchrist refers to 'cool reason' and 'harsh logic'. Female culture on the other hand is seen as warm, nurturing, magical, poetic, sensitive, caring, and healing. Sarah Miles was recently quoted in the *Independent* as saying: 'Corn circles are giving us an opportunity to rekindle our reverence for the unknown, that in itself is enough.'

'Men can play with ideas; women become them,' asserts Gilchrist. She says that women's reluctance to put forward their beliefs in mixed company is due to a lack of courage:

'We want to put forward our beliefs only when we are reasonably sure that everyone else will assent to them, or at least pretend to.' She says that 'cleverness is a vital feminine weapon', but she means it's a vital weapon for getting your own way, not something to be valued for its own sake. The 'cut and thrust method [of argument] doesn't suit women well,' she continues. 'To men, a verbal battle is enjoyable ... to women it is not.' (There's nothing I like better.) This is the closest she gets to talking about intellectual activity. There is nothing about wanting to find out about things. The three archetypal mothers 'understand the laws of time and space', but not in the same way as Einstein. Her images of women don't include brain surgeons, professors, computer programmers, or managing directors.

Despite the overlay of goddess talk in *The Circle of Nine,* the resemblance to old-style women's magazines is too strong to ignore. The new feminism is depressingly like the old femininity. Superstition was always part of the *Woman's Own weltanschauung.* Gilchrist has taken the image lock, stock, barrel, astrology column, and knitting patterns into the New Age and hence into middle-class respectability. The final impression is of soppiness: the same romanticism and sentimentality that women are fed from 'My Little Pony' to Wordsworth, the vein of tweeness that saps the strength of English society.

Conclusion

I'd like to make several unsupported assertions of my own. In my opinion it's partly a problem of self-image. The image women have of themselves is affected by the feel-good factor. They pride themselves on being warm, caring, intuitive, spiritual: unlike cold, unloving, logical, material men.

These bundles of qualities are supposedly indivisible and mutually exclusive. Women don't want to alienate men, or each other, by being 'aggressive': being logical and arguing about intellectual subjects. But this is a survival tactic – women have got to attract a man (an early 1970s feminist would shriek at the suggestion). Women claim spurious powers because they lack real power, and fear competing with men on what's perceived to be their own ground. Lack of confidence and lack of education lead to alternative methods of boasting, and the adoption of spurious ideas as a substitute for genuine intellectual activity. But logic is not men's ground, it's anybody's. Logic is not a sex-linked characteristic. (Male logic? Don't make me laugh.) Women may think that logic can only be used as a weapon, but it is neutral.

The danger is that the sleep of reason produces monsters. If you can't (or won't) think logically you won't be able to tell the false from the true. We need logic to establish the truth. An illogical statement can't be true, and if it isn't true it can't be of any use. 'The truth shall set you free,' said Jesus – but then he was a man.

An Anaesthesiologist Examines the Pam Reynolds Story
Gerald Woerlee

The Pam Reynolds story is considered to be one of the most compelling near-death experiences – and hence the best proof that there might be life after death. For this reason, practising anaesthesiologist Gerald Woerlee, born and raised in Western Australia but a long-time resident in the Netherlands, thought it worth expert scrutiny. Appeared XVIII.1–2.

Ever since it was first reported by the cardiologist Michael Sabom, the near-death experience of Pam Reynolds has been held by many to be definitive proof of the paranormal and the reality of a life after death. Her story has been told and retold, assuming almost mythic proportions. Finally, here was a person who returned from 'clinical death' to tell of the reality of an existence beyond the veil of this earthly life. Proof at last, according to many!

It is true that the report of Pam Reynolds is a story of a wonderful experience which must have had a profound effect upon her. What Pam Reynolds experienced was not just an ordinary hallucination. She really did 'see', feel, and undergo all she described. She really did undergo a wondrous, seemingly inexplicable, life-changing experience – an experience possibly giving her much spiritual comfort by confirming deeply rooted socio-cultural expectations about a life after death, as well as the nature of the universe. And it was certainly an experience whose details seemingly prove the reality of a life after death. But is this true? I decided to examine the reality of the proof offered by this experience.

Background

Pam Reynolds is the pseudonym of a woman who was 35 years old in 1991, when a diagnosis of a large aneurysm of one of the arteries of her brainstem was made. An aneurysm is a balloon-like weakening of an artery, and in the case of Pam Reynolds, this was a large aneurysm of the main artery providing her brainstem with blood. A large aneurysm of a brain artery is like a time-bomb. It can burst at any moment, causing enormous bleeding within the head, depriving the parts of the brain normally fed by that artery of blood. Pam Reynolds' aneurysm was very likely to burst, so depriving her brainstem of blood. Sudden bursting of this aneurysm would suddenly stop the blood supply to her brainstem, causing her to die immediately, because the brainstem is that part of the brain generating consciousness, and controlling breathing and many other vital body functions. So an operation was planned to remove this aneurysm.

The planned operation technique was complex. Pam Reynolds was brought under general anaesthesia. Her skull was opened and the aneurysm exposed. This was too large to treat safely, so her doctors connected blood vessels in her left groin to a heart bypass machine to cool her body down to 15° Celsius

(60° Fahrenheit). Her heartbeat was then stopped, the blood drained from her head, and the aneurysm carefully removed. Subsequently, her body was warmed up again, normal heartbeat and blood circulation restored, the head, and all other wounds closed, after which she was allowed to awaken slowly in the recovery room. After recovering the ability to speak, she told of a truly amazing experience undergone while apparently unconscious under general anaesthesia and low-temperature cardiac arrest.

She told of awakening and undergoing an out-of-body experience during the initial phase of the operation. She found herself in a position from which she observed the neurosurgeon at work, and where she could 'see' and describe the pneumatic saw used to open her skull. She heard the cardiac surgeon say that the blood vessels in her right groin were too small. Subsequently, she passed through a black vortex to arrive in a world of light where she met with her deceased grandmother and uncle, as well as other deceased relatives. They helped her, 'fed' her, and finally returned her to her body, after which she finally awoke in the recovery room.

This is a fantastic story. Wondrous even. Superficially it appears to be definitive proof of an afterlife. But this is not the case. As an anaesthesiologist hardened and scarred by more than twenty years' busy clinical experience, combined with a personal fascination in the ways the functioning of the body can generate apparently paranormal experiences, I know this experience to be a product of the way the body and mind of Pam Reynolds reacted to her situation and anaesthesia.

The experience

I will begin with the effects of anaesthesia on the body of Pam Reynolds. She underwent a major neurosurgical procedure. I have considerable experience of neurosurgical anaesthesia, and the technique of anaesthesia in all Western countries at this time was very standard. Pam would have undergone a standardized form of balanced anaesthesia with three different types of drugs – a technique that is still in use today.

Sleep-inducing and sleep-maintaining drugs

These may be the same or different drugs. After injecting a short-acting drug to induce unconsciousness, other drugs are administered to keep the patient asleep, or a continuous infusion of the same sleep-inducing drug could be used.

Powerful painkilling drugs

Sleep does not mean a person does not feel or react to pain - so powerful painkilling drugs are administered to reduce involuntary nervous system responses to pain.

Muscle-paralysing drugs similar to curare (deadly Amazon Indian arrow poison)

Persons who have been rendered unconscious and administered powerful painkilling drugs at dosages sufficient to prevent bodily nervous system responses to pain, are in a particular medical condition; they do not breathe because of the combined effects of the sleep-inducing and the painkilling drugs. Painkilling drugs cause their muscles to stiffen, rendering even the remaining breathing insufficient. Furthermore, this combination of drugs still does not prevent bothersome reflex movements in response to pain. All these effects can be eliminated by paralysing every body muscle of these patients with curare-like drugs. This makes the work of the surgeon easier, and in some situations even possible when it would otherwise not be.

There is only one problem with such a combination of drugs: breathing stops totally. So the standard technique is to pass a 1 to 2 centimetre diameter tube through the mouth, through the vocal cords into the trachea (windpipe). An inflatable cuff around the tube within the windpipe ensures an airtight fit, and this tube is connected to a machine called a ventilator which performs the act of breathing for the patient. This is a perfectly normal and standard anaesthetic technique employed for many millions of operations all over the world each year. A person undergoing such a technique of anaesthesia does not breathe, does not move, looks and feels 'absent' – such a person at that moment is no more than a biological mechanism undergoing repair by a surgeon. It is the task of the anaesthesiologist to induce and maintain this situation until the surgeon is ready, as well as to keep the patient alive in spite of all the effects of the operation performed by the surgeon.

Sometimes the concentration of sleep-inducing drugs within the bodies of patients undergoing such a form of anaesthesia is insufficient to maintain unconsciousness. So these people are awake – they hear what is going on around them, they feel the touch of the surgeon and others, and if their eyes are open, they actually see what is happening. But because of the powerful painkilling drugs they feel no pain, and because of the muscle-paralysing drugs they cannot move, speak, or breathe. They lie still and unmoving while observing all that happens to them and around them. Subsequently, after recovering the ability to speak, they can give very detailed reports of what happened to their bodies and about their bodies during their periods of awareness.

This may sound amazing to some people, but everyone can test for themselves the quality of observations made by a person lying still with their eyes shut. Lie blindfolded on a bed. In such a situation you can quite clearly visualize what people are doing and saying in your immediate surroundings, as well as clearly visualize what is happening to your body. This is the situation in which Pam Reynolds found herself when she awoke at the beginning of her operation.

There is another fact that all students of the experience of Pam Reynolds should realize and understand with great clarity. Pam Reynolds could tell no one about her experience until after the tube was removed from her windpipe after she awoke in the recovery room subsequent to the successful completion of her operation. During the period of anaesthesia and operation, until after the tube was removed from her windpipe, she could not speak. So her report of her experiences was a report of remembered experiences. This does not mean she did not undergo these experiences, simply that she had time to process and associate her sensations and experiences with her existing knowledge and expectations. An experience reported at the time it is undergone is sometimes quite different from a remembered report of the same experience. Furthermore, the mental processes of Pam Reynolds were certainly affected by the painkilling and sleep-inducing drugs when she underwent these experiences. After all, she was conscious during her experience, but felt calm, and felt no pain due to the operation – facts proving that her mental processes were affected by anaesthetic drugs during her experience. So an examination of the details of her experience reveals observational facts mixed together with the effects of the anaesthetic drugs, her own expectations, and extrapolations, all welded together into a coherent and wonderful story. Knowing these things gives background and perspective to her story, making it possible to begin with a step-by-step analysis.

Pam Reynolds was first put under anaesthesia, and the positioning and preparation of her anaesthetized body for surgery was commenced. This can sometimes be a time-consuming procedure for neurosurgical operations, but here there was also the necessity to prepare her for cardiopulmonary bypass. During this long preparation time, the effects of muscle-paralysing, painkilling drugs, and sleep-inducing and maintaining drugs can decrease below what is needed to maintain sleep. Regular doses of these drugs need to be administered to maintain sleep, total muscle paralysis, and adequate pain treatment.

I commenced my career in anaesthesiology as a junior resident in 1977, and have seen medicines, techniques, and fads come and go. So the fact that Pentothal was used as a sleep-inducing drug for the anaesthesia of Pam Reynolds during 1991 indicates to me that the anaesthesiologist used a perfectly standard combination of anaesthetic drugs for that time. I used exactly the same drug combinations at that time, too. The dosage of Pentothal used by anaesthesiologists to induce sleep keeps people asleep for about five to fifteen minutes, after which sleep is maintained with other gases in the mixture of air pumped into the lungs by the ventilator. Her anaesthesiologist would have maintained sleep with nitrous oxide (laughing gas), perhaps together with a vapour such as isoflurane or enflurane which were in common use at that time. But Pam Reynolds was conscious at various times during her operation, indicating to me that neither isoflurane nor enflurane vapours were used to keep her unconscious.

The neurosurgeon began first. He made an incision in her head, and then began to saw the bone of her skull open with a pneumatic saw shaped like an electric toothbrush. The high-pitched whining of the idling motor of this saw caused Pam Reynolds to awaken – this was the 'natural-D' that she heard. She was awake but partially paralysed due to muscle-paralysing drugs, and had a tube in her windpipe. So she could neither move nor speak. The powerful painkilling drugs ensured she felt no pain, she heard people speaking and moving around her, she felt the touch and movements of the surgeons on and in her body, and she registered all these things in her mind. The effects of anaesthetic drugs caused her to feel calm. Malfunction of her brain caused by these same drugs, possible reflex minuscule twitching of her limb muscles, together with abnormal functioning of her muscle spindles induced the out-of-body experience. Chapters 10, 11, and 12 of Woerlee's *Mortal Minds* (2003) contains a detailed discussion of the physiology of out-of-body experiences, including those occurring under anaesthesia.

The usual monitoring of her vital signs was used by the anaesthesiologist, in addition to which her electroencephalogram was monitored, as well as the response of her brain to clicking sounds in two earplugs (VEP = vestibular evoked potentials). (VEP measurement is a very useful indication of the depth of anaesthesia and the level of consciousness.) Some authors make much of the fact that she could hear everything, in spite of the fact she had earplugs feeding clicking sounds into her ears. My reaction to this is that of course she could hear what happened about her – proof of this is seen all about us. There are simply enormous numbers of people all around the world, wandering around, listening to loud music played through earplugs, who at the same time are able to hear and understand all that happens in their surroundings. And people under anaesthesia can hear things; otherwise this perfectly standard VEP monitoring technique would be useless as a measure of the depth of anaesthesia. So being able to hear, despite the insertion of earphones making clicking sounds, is nothing wondrous.

Some people also make much of the fact that the VEP monitoring did not signal that she was conscious. The truth about all monitoring, such as VEPs, is that while it is generally very accurate, it is not 100 percent accurate. This is realized and appreciated by all experienced anaesthesiologists, who understand and must work with this humbling fact. So they always keep a sharp eye on their patients for other signs of awakening. The story of Pam Reynolds also provides features allowing precise timing of some events. For example, the time of one period of awareness was given very accurately by what she heard one of the surgeons saying: 'Someone said something about my veins and arteries being very small. I believe it was a female voice and that it was Dr Murray, but I'm not sure. She was the cardiologist. I remember thinking that I should have told her about that ...'

She was not on cardiac bypass at the time of her out-of-body experience, because the cardiothoracic surgeon was having trouble introducing the cardiac bypass machine tubing into the blood vessels of her right groin – the blood vessels in her right groin were too small for the size of the tubing and the blood flow needed for cardiac bypass. This means the cardiac bypass apparatus was not even connected to her body at this time. The cardiothoracic surgeon eventually used the blood vessels in her left groin. So at that time, Pam Reynolds had a normal heartbeat and body temperature, as well as the normal responses of a paralyzed person who was awake while supposedly under general anaesthesia.

Then we come to Pam Reynolds' description of the pneumatic saw she observed during her out-of-body experience. Here again, it cannot be emphasized enough that her description of this episode was a description of a remembered event. After all, she could not describe these things at the time they occurred. Furthermore, she knew no one would use a large chain saw or industrial angle cutter to cut the bones of her skull open. She was 35 years old in 1991, the year of her operation. This means she was born in 1956, meaning she was a member of a generation of Americans blessed with excellent dental care. Pneumatic dental drills with the same shapes, and making similar sounds as the pneumatic saw used to cut her skull open, were in common use during the late 1970s and 1980s. Because she was born in 1956, a generation whose members almost invariably have many fillings, Pam Reynolds almost certainly had fillings or other dental work, and would have been very familiar with the dental drills. So the high frequency sound of the idling, air-driven motor of the pneumatic saw, together with the subsequent sensations of her skull being sawn open, would certainly have aroused imagery of apparatus similar to dental drills in her mind when she finally recounted her remembered sensations. There is another aspect to her remembered sensations – Pam Reynolds may have seen, or heard of, these things before her operation. All these things indicate how she could give a reasonable description of the pneumatic saw after awakening and recovering the ability to speak.

Pam Reynolds' mental processes were certainly affected by the anaesthetic drugs coursing through her body. This is proven by her absence of pain sensation during her operation, together with her sensations of mental calm. And while her mind was under the influence of these drugs, she described her mental state as more awake and aware than normal, with better than normal sensations. But her statement is no more than a typical statement made by a person whose brain is affected by medications, toxins, body waste products, or the effects of oxygen starvation. Observers see that the mental processes of such people are foggy, clouded, illogical, and disoriented – yet those affected by medications, toxins, body waste products, or oxygen starvation feel their thoughts and mental processes are clearer, that their minds function better, and that their perceptions are more acute than normal. In fact, they often feel wonderful. The mental effects of the anaesthetic drugs used on Pam Reynolds are similar to those of oxygen starvation:

> *Hypoxia (oxygen starvation) quickly affects the higher centers, causing a blunting of the finer sensibilities and a loss of sense of judgement and of self-criticism. The subject feels, however, that his mind is not only quite clear, but unusually keen.* (EJ Liere and JC van Stickney, *Hypoxia*, 1963)

This is why Pam Reynolds experienced her mental processes as better than normal, even though no one else would say they were normal.

After exposure of the aneurysm, she was put on cardiac bypass and subjected to hypothermic cardiac arrest (her body temperature was lowered and her heartbeat was stopped). Her body temperature was lowered to 15° Celsius. This is a temperature at which all people are unconscious. So she was unconscious, and could therefore have no conscious experience during this period. Even so, she was able to remember some of what happened before her period of hypothermic cardiac arrest, because she was able to remember her 'out-of-body experience' prior to the period of cardiac arrest.

Many people may consider this technique of hypothermic cardiac arrest as a wonderful and unusual technique. Yet it was one of several standard techniques for performing open heart surgery during the 1960s and 1970s. If the body and brain are cooled to 15° Celsius and lower, it is possible to stop the heart and breathing, perform the necessary surgery, subsequently rewarm the patient and restore normal heartbeat, and the patient will suffer no brain damage, provided the duration of cardiac arrest is less than forty-five minutes. The fact that the brain cooled to a temperature of 15° Celsius can survive a period of absent circulation for forty-five minutes is not miraculous. Cooling reduces the speed of all chemical reactions, enormously reducing the metabolism of the brain and body, enormously reducing the requirement of the brain and body for oxygen and nutrients. This is a situation similar to keeping meat in a refrigerator – the cooler the refrigerator, the better the meat is preserved.

Was Pam Reynolds 'dead' during the period her heart was stopped? Very definitely not! Her body metabolism had simply been reduced to a minimal level. After all, cessation of breathing and cessation of heartbeat are manifestations of death, but are not death. True death is irreversible failure of all brainstem functions. For example, heart-lung bypass is a situation where people do not breathe and have no heartbeat, yet are very much alive, and may even be conscious (Woerlee, *Mortal Minds*, see chapter 2).

After successful removal of the aneurysm, the body temperature of Pam Reynolds was gradually increased to normal, and her heartbeat was restored. Blood flow and brain function returned during this period. Nonetheless, even though brain function was restored, Pam Reynolds' brain did not immediately return to normal function. To begin with, her brainstem function recovered enough to restore consciousness – otherwise she could not have consciously perceived the dark vortex through which she passed to undergo a typically American near-death experience (NDE) during which she was guided and aided by deceased relatives. Furthermore, the visionary content of her NDE was a product of her knowledge that the operation could possibly cause her death. I say this because during her NDE she saw deceased relatives who aided her, and guided her in the realm of the dead – features typical of NDEs undergone by people who expect to undergo a potentially lethal experience. Restoration and normalization of normal brain function restored normal perceptions, and she awoke to the accompaniment of ironically appropriate music:

> When I came back, they were playing Hotel California and the line was 'You can check out anytime you like, but you can never leave.' I mentioned [later] to Dr. Brown that that was incredibly insensitive and he told me that I needed to sleep more. [laughter] When I regained consciousness, I was still on the respirator.

She was awake, but paralysed by a muscle-paralysing drug – so she still could not move, breathe, or talk. She was indeed locked inside her body – she could not leave. Furthermore, she could not talk because of the muscle-paralysing drugs and the tube passed through her windpipe that was attached to the respirator.

She awoke later in the recovery room. Only then was the tube removed from her windpipe, and only then was she able to speak and tell all who would listen of her wondrous experience. And it was indeed a profound personal experience, but it was an experience whose roots lay in the functioning of her body, complemented by imagery nestling in the deepest reaches of her psyche, as well as the fact that she was awake for several periods of time during her operation.

What is very evident throughout this whole story of Pam Reynolds is the fact that she was conscious at several periods during her operation. This is likely a reflection of an interaction of her undoubted anxiety about the operation with the anaesthetic technique used. Anxious people are more difficult to keep asleep than are calm and relaxed people. Her mental functioning during her periods of awakening was very evidently influenced by anaesthetic drugs, her anxieties, as well as by the residual effects of low body temperature. And lastly, her story is a remembered account of experiences undergone while under anaesthesia. This last point is the most important aspect of this story. It means that her story is a product of her socio-cultural upbringing, her prior conscious and unconscious knowledge of the operation she was to undergo, her prior knowledge of all things medical, that which she consciously and unconsciously observed during her periods of awareness, the effects of anaesthetic drugs, low body temperature, surgery, her anxieties, and finally, her personality. All these things were unconsciously combined and integrated into a coherent story of a wondrous experience.

Nonetheless, experiences such as that of Pam Reynolds are experiences teaching each of us how little we know of ourselves and the functioning of our bodies. Careful and critical study reveals their true nature, each experience revealing more and more about the true and complex nature of the human behind the mask of normal consciousness.

Pearce 3: "George just finished his 'planet thing' when he heard the news about Pluto!" (appeared 19.4)

Why have UFOs changed speed over the years?
Martin S. Kottmeyer

*If alien spacecraft are really visiting us the details of sightings might be expected to vary. If, however, UFO sightings are simply human errors of interpretation of strange sights in the sky – as even most UFOlogists agree at least 90 percent of them are – you'd expect to see patterns that reflect our own cultural preoccupations. **Martin S. Kottmeyer**, who lives in Carlyle, Illinois, and writes extensively about UFOs, noticed one such pattern: UFOs used to move a lot faster. Why? Appeared in X.2.*

It is one of those little ironies of historical memory that we sometimes forget why we took an interest in some things. Take flying saucers. How many of us realize that the reason they made headlines in 1947 was not because Kenneth Arnold thought he saw spaceships from another world; but simply because he reported objects travelling at 'incredible speed'? Our local paper headlined it 'Officials Skeptical of Report of 1200 Mile-an-Hour Object'. The next day: '1200 MPH Flying Saucer Story Has Teller Up in Air'. The initial Associated Press dispatch specifically has Arnold saying that 'he could not hazard a guess as to what they were' and ends with him admitting, 'It seems impossible, but there it is.'

The reason it seemed impossible was because back in June 1947 aeroplanes were not capable of even half that speed. They had not even broken the sound barrier quite yet, although they were edging up to it. Chuck Yeager would win that prize a mere four months after the Arnold report. In his report to the Air Force, Arnold mentions an Air Force pilot suggested he had seen 'some kind of jet or rocket-propelled ship that is in the process of being tested'. A subsequent communication to the Commanding General of Wright Field has him adding that he 'felt certain they belonged to our government'.

Curiously, Arnold's drawing of the objects he reportedly saw bears a significant resemblance to a plane of the period known as the Flying Flapjack. It was reportedly the fastest naval aircraft of its time, holding a 40 mph advantage over the F4U Corsair. However, it never got past the experimental stage to mass production, because of problems with propeller vibration, And the Flapjack was not exactly a secret. It had been featured on the cover of *Mechanix Illustrated* a month before Arnold's experience. A few people during and after the 1947 flap felt it was likely that Arnold's Flying Saucers were actually Flying Flapjacks.

After the event

With the benefit of hindsight we can confidently say that Arnold's objects weren't Flying Flapjacks. And this is not just because there were denials by the relevant officials and because Flying Flapjacks did not travel at supersonic speeds. The behaviour of the objects was all wrong. Arnold said there were nine objects in a chain and they displayed erratic motions. Test flights are usually solitary affairs with at most a chase plane tagging along. Erratic motion would be unusual for a properly functioning high speed aircraft, and erratic motion by a chain of nine of them rather bizarre. Arnold must have made a mistake somewhere.

Arnold's speed estimate for the objects was predicated on the assumption they were at least 25 miles distant. He based this on the fact that he had seen them swerve in and out of the high mountain peaks and specifically noted them disappearing 'just behind a jagged peak that juts out from the base of Mount Rainier proper'. Their altitude, he said, was 9,200 feet plus or minus 1,000 feet. When one looks at the geological survey maps of the Mount Rainier area, however, there is an interesting surprise: there are no such peaks in that altitude range. The nearest contender would be Pyramid Peak, and it stands at only 6,937 feet, far outside his range of estimates.

This suggests that Arnold experienced an illusion of some sort. The best guess is that the objects temporarily disappeared when they rolled edgewise in front of the face of the mountain causing a loss of visual resolution. The angular size estimates put them near visual threshold and the optical clutter of the mountain, unlike the sky, probably contributed to the sense of a disappearance behind a feature of the mountain even though there wasn't one to disappear behind. Arnold's objects were probably considerably closer and thus much slower. Given the erratic motions, the chain-like grouping, and the horizontal trajectory, the likeliest explanation would involve waterfowl. Swans would be the best choice at the altitude Arnold was travelling.

Copycat sightings

Arnold's report excited great interest and generated a wave of copycat sightings. Ted Bloecher collected some 853 reports from this 1947 craze. The reports exhaust the thesaurus of speed superlatives. Phrases include: fast, very fast, extremely fast, high speed, tremendous speed, terrific speed, great, incredible, inconceivable, rapid, swift, amazing speed. They hurtled, streaked, and flew like blue blazes. Fifty-three percent of the reports emphasize the speed of the objects seen. A few slow saucers made it into the papers, presumably because their shape seemed relevant. The reports mimic Arnold's report in other particulars. More than contemporary reports, there was an unusual number of sightings involving multiple objects. They favoured horizontal flight. Most of them took place in the daytime, a striking contrast to later years, when UFOs favoured the night.

Despite a considerable variety in the reports, the form of the objects was always consistent with a type of aircraft. Propellers were often seen, one witness even claiming it was larger than the rest of the plane. Jet pipes, pilot's cockpits, glass domes, fins, legs, and antennae featured on some of the objects. Smoke, vapour trails, and rocket flames repeatedly marked their flights. A wide range of aerobatic stunts turn up among the reports: loop-the-loops, roll manoeuvres, banking, weaving, climbing, diving, tipping, circling, and swooping. Some 'UFOs' buzzed cars, but unlike decades later, the car engines never died. It has been thought significant that animals sometimes reacted to the objects, yet a close reading suggests it wasn't because of their spooky alienness; the saucers were doing barnstorming manoeuvres.

Notable by its absence is any indication of extraterrestrial technology: no lasers, heat rays, paralysis rays or gases, mind control rays, power rings, levitation of people or objects, denaturalization, matter interpenetration, space-suited entities, robots, remote eyes, or even simple observation ports. Nobody was looking for aliens, and nothing was seen to suggest any were there.

Things have certainly changed since 1947, and the oddest, simplest proof of this is in the statistics about the speed of saucers. Where 53 percent of the cases of 1947 emphasize speed, statistics from 1971 showed only 41 percent of cases mention it. By 1986 it had fallen to 22 percent. Inversely, there has been a startling shift in the presence of hovering in UFO reports. Only 3 percent of Bloecher's 1947 population of reports involve hovering. That any are present at all may have something to do with either the fact that the Flying Flapjack was known to possess a vertical landing and take-off capability or with the fact that 1946 saw the first licensing of commercial helicopters. By 1971 hovering appeared in 39 percent of reports and by 1986 it swelled to 49 percent. Hovering has moved from practical insignificance to become the dominant mode of presentation, showing up over twice as often as high speed.

Speed shift

A fuller appreciation of this shift can be gained by illustrating it by reference to the most popular cases. In the early years, speed estimates were a standard detail. Mantell's UFO purportedly travelled over 360 mph. When the UFO in the Chiles-Whitted case kicked in its blazing afterburner it went to speeds of 500 to 700 mph; Great Falls: 200 to 400 mph; Lubbock Lights: 1,800 to 18,000 mph; Tremonton: 3,780 mph; Nash-Fortenberry: 12,000 mph; Washington Nationals: 100 to 130 mph; Lakenheath: 12,000 mph; Levelland: 600 to 800 mph; Trindade: 600 to 700 mph.

Cases from the 1960s, by contrast, rarely give speed estimates. In the Socorro case there is only talk of a slow descent and an easy climb. In the Exeter incident we encounter a 'falling leaf motion' and UFOlogists indicate this is a repetitive, one even says almost universal, feature of saucer motion. The Spaur UFO chase involves speeds of around 80 mph, and nobody comments on how slow this is compared to the 1950s. Herb Schirmer was told by aliens that they can travel at 150,000 something, but he isn't sure if it is miles per hour or something else.

We *can* find a couple of speed estimates in the 1970s. In the Coyne helicopter incident, we are given the figure of 700 mph. In the Kaikoura classic we get the estimate of 10,800 mph. We also get a hint of great speed in the Joe and Carol abduction of 1976, with stars said to be shooting by as they travel in the craft. Allan Hendry dismissed this as obviously inspired by *Star Trek* visual conventions.

When we come to the 1980s the most striking speed estimate comes from the Westminster flap where objects crawled across the sky at 25 mph. This is argued to be too slow to be terrestrial. Similarly, in the Gulf Breeze incidents, proponents focus on the ability of the objects to perfectly hover amid a 15 mph breeze as proof of non-terrestriality. In an analysis of the 1992 Williamsport, Pennsylvania, UFO wave published in Timothy Good's *Alien Update* the objects are all described as slow, very slow, or stationary. The statistics don't even list a category for high speed! *The UFOlogist* professes they are extremely slow – much slower than a Piper Cub can safely maintain its slowest speed. In 1947 the saucers were faster than any aircraft known and prompted speculations they were powered by atomic energy. Now they are miraculous because they are too slow. The shift in rhetoric is such a complete inversion it would be hilarious if it wasn't so astonishing.

Hover-craft

Hovering wasn't absent in the 1950s, but it had a curious habit of being associated with disreputable cases like the Maury Island hoax and Desvergers. All the contactee cases had ships which hovered inches or feet above the ground. In Truman Bethurum's account the saucer could move faster than one could bat an eye, but as it landed it abruptly decelerated so the aliens could demonstrate 'how slowly this monster could be brought down'. Interest rarely focused on this ability of hovering. In the Daniel Fry case the emphasis remained on speed. We are meant to be impressed when he tells us he went from White Sands, New Mexico, to New York and back in half an hour. The given speed: 8,000 mph. In the 1961 Eagle River case the flourish we are supposed to note is how a tree was bowed over in the wake of a saucer take-off. The Professor Johannis contact, revealed in 1964 (backdated to 1947), has the teller being rolled over and over in the dust because of the air-shock of his saucer's take-off. I would guess the Father Gill classic of Papua New Guinea was the first reputable case to display hovering, but it was too little known for a long time to consider it a factor in starting the trend to slower saucers noticeable in the 1960s.

Why did this shift from fast to slow take place? The simplest answer has to be the fading of memory. Arnold's report lost its fascination as newer, better, shinier cases crowded it out for public attention. Cases like Socorro, Exeter, the Swamp Gas saucer of Dexter, Flynn, and *The Interrupted Journey* of

Barney and Betty Hill captured people's imaginations and became the models to which later experiences would be compared. The search template of what should be considered wondrous filtered out what seemed irrelevant. In 1947 people looked for speedy things and things that looked like discs, and ignored the slow stuff and the lights floating around at night. There was a heavy bias to misinterpreting flocks of birds.

Later, people searched for bright lights and slow, hovering objects and, as Allan Hendry showed, people had a bias towards misinterpreting stars, planets, and aeroplane lights.

UFOs in the movies

It is possibly relevant to also consider how the image of saucers changed in film over the years. Initially, movies followed the model set by Arnold's report. *Bruce Gentry: Daredevil of the Skies* (1949) and *The Flying Saucer* (1950) show brief glimpses of saucers flashing by at high speeds. The plots indicate they are not alien, but man-made. *The Day the Earth Stood Still* (1951) initially emphasizes speed in radar tracking reports, but the landing involves the saucer settling to earth with a soft glow as befits a powerful, but peaceful visitor. The scene is aesthetically impressive and had to be a factor influencing contactee stories. *It Came from Outer Space* (1953) and *War of the Worlds* (1953) emphasize speed, with craft trailing sparks and ploughing into the earth. The latter, however, also presents futuristic aerial tanks slowly rising and hovering over the landscape. Hovering and slow movement are presented in *Invaders from Mars* (1953), *Devil-Girl from Mars* (1955), and *The Cosmic Man* (1958). *Earth vs. the Flying Saucers* (1956) suggests speed in many key scenes, but hovering and gyrating in place are also present.

The aesthetics of anti-gravitational hovering reached iconic status with the arrival of *The Invaders* TV series in the mid-1960s. The image of a slow landing was repeated weekly at the beginning of each show. *Close Encounters of the Third Kind* (1977) reprises some examples of speed from UFO lore, but hovering dominates the pivotal scenes of Neary's first encounter and the arrival of the mother ship. The ship in *E.T.* (1981) moves in a languid fashion even in its final rainbow-coloured acceleration. The TV series *The Greatest American Hero* (1981–3) presented a hovering mother ship with a glowing power ring that would serve as the model of the Gulf Breeze incidents. *Wavelength* (1983), *Starman* (1984), *Cocoon* (1985), *Uforia* (1987), and *Fire in the Sky* (1993) demonstrate a modem trend to slowness and hovering as a cinematic convention which parallels contemporary UFO trends. One could make a case that cinema showed an earlier trend to slowness than UFO lore and may have had a causal role in the shifting template of what makes UFOs mysterious, but it also can't be denied the films initially imitated life. Its role is not dominant in shaping perceptions.

The cultural dimension

Saucers flying like blue blazes are no longer a dominant part of our definition of a UFO experience either in film or lore. In an age where supersonic transports routinely cross the oceans, multi-mach jets are a staple item in every country's military, and space shuttles regularly escape the bounds of earth, speed no longer seems so magical as it did at mid-century.

Levitation unassisted by helicopter rotors and rocket flames remains impressive and so defines alienness in a way high speed no longer can. Twelve hundred miles per hour is no longer incredible.

Does this prove UFOs are unreal phantoms that blend in with their times? No. Strictly, it only proves that there is a cultural dimension in our assumptions about what constitutes the behaviour of a flying saucer. People do not report everything that is present in the sky but select only what is presumed to be interesting. What is interesting changes year to year, decade to decade, century to century. We've forgotten that Kenneth Arnold was interesting for reasons that no longer interest us. That, in itself, is interesting.

Magicians, Mediums, and Psychics
David Alexander

As noted before, magicians have a special place in skepticism because the habit of mind that makes them magicians makes them good at spotting – and testing for – deception. A magician, James Randi remarked in his book **Flim-Flam** *(Prometheus, 1982), can take a physicist to a show where the on-stage magician makes an elephant disappear in full view and the physicist will admit he has no idea how it was done. But the same physicist the next day, in his lab full of equipment he trusts not to lie to him, will see a former conjuror move a small, light, plastic vial a couple of inches without touching it and say the effect must be paranormal.*

Many paranormal claims have their roots in magic, be it stage, close-up, or the branch known as mentalism. Here, professional magician **David Alexander** *explains how spirit mediums achieved their effects; many of these methods were, astonishingly, still in use as late as 1987 (and not just on stage by Penn and Teller). Besides working as a professional magician for much of his adult life, Alexander has also been an editor and publisher, as well as a published author, chosen by the subject to write* **Star Trek Creator: The Authorized Biography of Gene Roddenberry.** *He is currently the Deputy Director and Chief Operating Officer of SciTech Hands-On Science Center in Aurora, Illinois. This article was the second of three parts. Appeared in I.6.*

Before we get down to the methods used by mediums to produce spirit manifestations, I believe it is important to examine the mental set of the sitters and the setting they are in. This is the key to understanding how and why the generally crude methods of the medium pass muster in the séance room.

First of all, the sitter is in a highly receptive and suggestive state. Their belief systems have them primed to see and experience 'spiritual' and 'psychic' phenomena. Virtually anything that occurs in a séance can be laid at the feet of the spirits. Most séances are conducted either in total darkness or under a very dim red light; having sat in more than one pitch-dark séance room, I know how disorienting and disconcerting it can be.

In order for the medium to do his or her job properly, there is often a cabinet in which they sit. This cabinet is usually just a curtain drawn around an area, usually eight feet by six feet, to make a closed-off cubicle. Occasionally, the cabinet is simply a curtain drawn across the corner of a room. This is usually the case if the séance is in a private home.

The use of the cabinet is explained as being necessary as a sort of condensing chamber for the psychic force and ectoplasm (the mysterious substance drawn from the medium's body) which enables the spirits to materialize. Of course, what it is really used for is a place for the medium to do his or her dirty work without being seen. The fact that many mediums allow themselves and their cabinets to be searched means absolutely nothing. Most mediums have a 'cabinet attendant' who is, in reality, the medium's bodyguard and a person who can pass the necessary material to the medium when needed.

The cabinet attendant is explained as being necessary to protect the medium from malicious individuals who would grab ectoplasm, thereby endangering the life of the medium. Sitters are constantly told horror stories of mediums whose spirit manifestations or ectoplasm were grabbed and of the resulting injury and/or death to the medium. Of course, these are merely convenient stories to prevent people from grabbing the ectoplasm and getting a handful of luminous chiffon or, worse, a handful of medium.

While the assembled sitters sing hymns, the medium, supposedly in the cabinet in a trance, rapidly dons a black outfit and then slips several yards of luminous chiffon and gauze out of a hiding place and proceeds to manipulate it in various ways. What the sitters see is amazing: a tiny ball of ectoplasm sending out shimmering tendrils which gradually grow into a fully formed materialized spirit. This figure could disappear in the same manner it appeared, or it could grow, shrink, expand, or instantly vanish. While it sounds crude, the effect is quite remarkable.

During such séances any number of different things can happen. If the sitters are regulars and well known to the medium, he may 'apport' something for the sitter. Many mediums will move about in the dark and remove small items from women's purses. The owners are carefully noted and the item filed away, ready to be apported back to the owner days, weeks, or months later. If the medium has access to the individual's house on a social occasion, it is relatively easy to remove some small piece of jewellery from the bedroom and bring it back 'via the spirits' at a later time. This is very effective if the person actually requests the object and it appears seconds later. Boy Scouts aren't the only ones who know the value of being prepared.

Many séance regulars are people well known to more than one medium. They have regular files, usually quite detailed, that are shared from medium to medium.

Other 'manifestations' that occur are voices coming out of a floating trumpet that answer questions. Well, the trumpet floating is no big deal. The usual trumpet is like a large megaphone with a luminous band painted around the large end. Using his hand or a collapsible reaching device, the medium is able to make it 'float' all over the place. Whispering in the end causes distortion and projection of the voice and gives the impression of 'spirit' voices. I've heard of some mediums manipulating several trumpets simultaneously.

One medium was especially clever. He was challenged by someone claiming to be a magician and psychic expert. The challenge was to cause voices to come out of a trumpet after the trumpet was dusted with a powder that would cause stains on the hand. The medium accepted the challenge, the lights were turned out and voices came out of the trumpet. The medium had a piece of stiff cardboard rolled around his leg. Under cover of darkness, he removed it, formed it into a megaphone, and produced his phenomena.

This same medium had a stunt that caused all sorts of consternation even among his fellow mediums. He was offered thousands for the secret but exposed it himself after he went straight. He was able to produce spirit voices from a trumpet while it was being held by a sitter. Imagine the effect! No miniature radios were used, and the trumpet could be thoroughly examined. The secret is quite simple: dressed completely in black and moving through the darkness like the old radio character The Shadow, the medium had another trumpet, painted black. It was into this trumpet that he spoke, aiming it at the trumpet held by the sitter. From a distance of three or four feet, he could cause the spectator-held trumpet to vibrate, creating a perfect illusion.

To materialize different spirits, the combination of simple masks and the luminous chiffon mentioned earlier works wonders. I remember reading of one medium, many years ago, who materialized the face of a very life-like baby. I understand she had it painted on her rather ample bosom.

Turning the lights on and exposing what is going on seems to have little effect on the true believers. Back in 1960, the spiritualist world was shocked by what became known as the Great Camp Chesterfield Exposé. Two researchers who were sympathetic to the spiritualist cause, Tom O'Neil, editor of the *Psychic Observer* and an ordained spiritualist minister, and Dr Andrija Puharich (in his pre-Uri Geller manager days), equipped a dark séance room with infrared lights and a snooperscope, a night vision device, for the purpose of filming the materialization of a ghost. The medium they were filming was Edith Stillwell. Her cabinet attendant was Mable Riffle. Both of these women were professional mediums with many years' experience and very tough customers.

Unfortunately for them, they had little understanding of what the devices the researchers were using could do. The experiment was a disaster for the spiritualists. Looking through the snooperscope, Puharich saw that what were supposed to be spirit forms of shimmering ectoplasm materializing out of thin air were actually figures wrapped in chiffon entering the séance room through a hidden door from an adjacent apartment.

The infrared motion picture film confirmed Puharich's observations: caught on film, dressed in gauze, were the familiar faces of Camp Chesterfield mediums, impersonating departed spirits.

O'Neil raged against this in his spiritualist newspaper and quite a scandal developed in the spiritualist community. Unfortunately, O'Neil died not too long after. His paper's circulation had declined seriously as the spiritualist churches which had provided most of its subscribers and advertising revenue boycotted him, rather than rally to his support.

Some said he died of a broken heart.

9

Do you believe in miracles?

If something seems too good to be true, goes the old saying, it probably is. This applies to strangers who send you email offering you a percentage if you will help get hidden millions out of their country, it applies to get-rich-quick schemes, it applies to perpetual motion machines, and it applies in spades to miracles. The Indian skeptic Basava Premanand came up with the most cogent explanations of why debunking miracles matters: miracles, he said, are how religions and holy men sell themselves. The same is true of lesser folks like faith healers, self-styled psychics, and, dare we say it, business gurus.

Something to Shout About: The Documentation of a Miracle?
Dr Peter May

*Some of the most dogged opponents of deceptions of the faith healing kind are people of faith. **Dr Peter May** is a GP in Southampton and a member of the General Synod of the Church of England. As such, he is exceptionally well placed to investigate claims of miracle cures; in this investigation, he examined the 'healing' of Mrs Jean Neil by German healer Reinhard Bonnke. You can find video clips of Bonnke on YouTube. A copy of this report was sent to Mr Bonnke with a request to withdraw the video. As of April 2009, although other videos of Reinhard Bonnke are readily available online and accessible as YouTube clips, this one seems to be available only from a single German site. Appeared in V.5.*

In the wake of my contribution to a debate book *Signs, Wonders and Healing* (Inter-Varsity Press, 1989), which some considered to be unduly skeptical, I invited readers of the *Southampton Evangelical Alliance Quarterly Bulletin* to submit claims to miraculous healing to me for investigation and comment. By far the most striking of the few responses received was a video recording of what was presented as the miraculous healing of Mrs Jean Neil at a meeting led by a German evangelist, Mr Reinhard Bonnke.

The video, which is entitled *Something to Shout About – The Documentation of a Miracle*, is being marketed internationally. It shows Mrs Neil attending the meeting in a wheelchair. Mr Bonnke laid his hands on her after which she stood and to the astonishment of the assembled crowd, ran round the auditorium and appeared completely healed of what she described as a spinal injury. The video went on to show a written report from an orthopaedic surgeon, and an interview with her GP, Dr Colin West, who is quoted on the video cover saying, 'Life is stranger than fiction'. Mr Bonnke concludes the video by claiming her healing is 'an outright miracle'.

People use the term 'miracle' in a variety of different ways. Everyday events such as childbirth are popularly called miracles and Christians commonly describe any dramatic answer to their prayers as miraculous. I prefer to use the word in a narrow sense in order to highlight the extraordinary character or the events attributed to Christ in the Gospels. They were immediate (or almost), complete, and lasting. Many were physical illnesses that remain incurable today (such as kypho-scoliosis, the 'withered' hand, congenital blindness). We are told they involved every kind of illness including the raising of the dead. In those miracles, the very nature of things was instantaneously changed. Water was changed into wine.

It is the sort of miracle where there is a change in the very nature of things that I have tried to find for twenty years – without success. That does not mean that God does not exist, or that he does not answer our prayers. If he does exist, it seems to imply that when he answers our prayers he normally respects the integrity of the created order he has set in being. He is not changing dogs into cats! That is not to say that he cannot heal secondary cancer, Down's syndrome, or a club foot, but it is to say that such a change in the very nature of things is not his normal way of working, and if I have not been able through wide enquiries over a long period to find one such example that withstands scrutiny, such healings must anyway be very rare indeed.

The claim

> Mrs Jean Neil of Rugby, England was a truly hopeless case – spinal injury, angina pectoris, a hip out of joint and one leg two inches shorter than the other. She underwent 14 operations, spent 4 years in hospital, suffered 3 heart attacks, and was treated with traction and plaster jackets. Mrs Neil was confined to a wheelchair, used three respirators, applied heart patches and took 24 tablets daily. This was her situation throughout the course of 25 long years – until the 12th of March, 1988. Now she has a brand new story! (video cover, CfaN Productions)

Mrs Neil's address appears on a letter on the video, enabling her telephone number to be obtained. She was found to be entirely cooperative and forwarded copies of a number of medical letters and reports in her possession as well as numerous newspaper cuttings and a second video of a Central TV feature presented by Michelle Guinness. She also wrote to her doctor asking him to cooperate with my enquiry and release whatever information I should request. From the information she sent, a list of questions was compiled and sent to her GP. A further lengthy telephone interview was then conducted with Mrs Neil.

Findings

Mrs Neil could not have been more helpful or enthusiastic about what had happened to her. As implied by her two GPs, who both featured on video, her recovery had evidently been sudden, complete, and lasting. Eighteen months after her healing she appears to be in entirely good health and very active. She has recently travelled in Europe and Africa telling her story at meetings led by Mr Reinhard Bonnke. There would appear to be no immediately satisfying medical explanation as to what had happened to her. Her prayers have been answered in a remarkable way.

The fact that she is now well raises questions about the nature of the illnesses from which she had been suffering and of the 'miracle' which is said to have occurred.

Her problem is presented as having been predominantly a spinal injury originating in 1964 with a fracture to her coccyx (the little bones at the very base of the spine). However, she also suffered from a number of other conditions and claims to have been healed of seven diseases: a short leg, an out-of-joint hip, a spinal injury, heart disease, a hiatus hernia, bronchitis, and poor vision.

1. Short leg

The orthopaedic report from Mr Eisenstein at Oswestry Hospital makes no reference to differences in her leg length. Legs are notoriously difficult to measure and it would probably require X-ray measurement to be sure of a discrepancy. There is no mention of such X-rays nor suggestion of a significant clinical problem with her legs in the reports I have been able to see.

2. Hip out of joint

Mr Eisenstein reports that an X-ray taken on 23 December 1987 (that is, three months before her healing) showed that her hips appeared 'quite normal'.

3. Spinal injury

Of the fourteen operations she had had, four were on her spine. The other operations included two Caesarean sections, an appendectomy, an operation for hammer toe and about four procedures on her elbows. She could not recall the others. The four years spent in hospital was an estimate of the total of all these procedures plus a number of medical admissions. Apparently she had ten admissions in about a year for chest infections and the appendectomy had been complicated by peritonitis.

The spinal operations included removal of her coccyx in the 1960s, removal of a prolapsed disc in 1973, a laminectomy in 1975, and a further disc removal in 1981. On the last two occasions adhesions were divided and nerve roots were wrapped in silastic. Since that time it seems that she walked with a stick until January 1987 when she again developed low-back pain which persisted until her healing fifteen months later, in March 1988.

It was mainly during that fifteen-month period that she made use of a wheelchair. According to her GP's referral letter to the orthopaedic surgeon, dated 23 September 1987, 'She remains in some pain, has to use two walking sticks to get around, or a wheelchair for longer distances.' In December 1987, Mr Eisenstein's report stated, 'Patient is ambulant on walking sticks approx. 20 yards and very slowly, otherwise uses wheelchair at home and for shopping.' It does not appear that she was at any stage confined to a wheelchair.

Of the 'twenty-four tablets' required daily, some were painkillers, two taken every six hours, that is, eight a day. They included at times sleeping tablets, drugs for angina, and anti-depressants. They were not twenty-four different medications.

The orthopaedic report of December 1987 itemizes her drug regime as follows, naming only two different tablets: Acupan 2 tablets 4 times daily (painkiller), Angina – on treatment (probably skin patch/mouth spray), Propranolol 1 twice daily (presumably for angina), Inhalers – for occasional bronchitis (i.e. asthma).

In September 1988, six months after her healing, she was reassessed by the orthopaedic surgeon. Two paragraphs of his three-paragraph report were shown on the video. The first paragraph was read aloud by the presenter and reported that, 'She has a full range of completely painless spinal movement'. The third paragraph, which was not shown, reads: 'X-rays have been repeated today and these confirm that there is absolutely no change from the X-rays taken prior to this evangelical healing.'

Clearly she had improved dramatically subjectively, but there was no objective evidence of any change in the condition of her spine.

4. Heart disease

Mrs Neil believes she has had three heart attacks – leaving her subsequently with angina. She describes having been on a number of anti-anginal therapies all of which were subsequently discontinued. Writing six months before her healing her GP stated that her chest pains 'after vigorous investigations were felt not to be cardiac in origin'.

5. Hiatus hernia

Mrs Neil reports that about eight years ago she had an X-ray which showed her to have an hiatus hernia. This has not been repeated since. Acid reflux from her stomach into her gullet from such a hernia could well cause chest pain similar to angina. It may well have been aggravated by anti-inflammatory painkillers for her back. Anyway, it appears not to be troubling her at the moment.

6. Bronchitis

It seems as though no one has ever used the term 'asthma' to describe this problem to her, but the use of 'respirators' implies as much. She told me that when her chest was really bad 'and required ten admissions in a year' she was taking Propranolol for her 'angina'. A common side effect of this drug is bronchospasm (that is, asthma). It would seem probable from the information available that the treatment given for suspected angina (which she didn't actually have) caused her 'bronchitis' which settled when the treatment was withdrawn.

7. Poor vision

Apparently her vision deteriorated seriously while she was taking another anti-anginal drug, Nifedipine. If this is true, it is a highly unusual side effect and is not listed a potential problem on the drug's data sheet. It appears that her vision subsequently improved dramatically after she discontinued the drug, but she does continue to need spectacles.

In the light of this information, the claims made on the video – and not least in the paragraph quoted above from the video cover – seem to be seriously incorrect and misleading. To clarify the situation and gain fuller information, I compiled my list of eighteen questions which I sent to her doctor, Colin West. He replied:

I have given the matter considerable thought. Whilst I have some sympathy with your aims, I cannot convince myself that to answer your questions would be in the best interests of my patient at this time. I regret that this may appear unhelpful and seem as though I am dodging the issue.

The case of Mrs Neil illustrates many of the problems that are uncovered in the search for truth in claims of miraculous healing. On the one hand it is difficult to deny the amazing improvement in her sense of well-being and enjoyment of life. Clearly she is only too aware of how much better she feels but is not in a good position either to understand the pathological details of her condition or the nature of her healing. Neither is she likely to be conversant with the difficulties involved in trying to define a miracle. Like the blind man of John's Gospel, the one thing she knows is that once she was disabled, now she is not. Given the complexity of her symptoms, the nature of her disability was not easy to evaluate even by experienced medical observers. This is nearly always the case with back pain in particular. Most medical practitioners usually refrain from using precise diagnostic labels in these conditions.

In Mrs Neil's case, the uncertainties surrounding her back pain were compounded by other conditions of which no less than four (nos. 4–7) may have been wholly or in part iatrogenic, that is, caused by treatment.

Both video interviews with her general practitioners are striking for the non-committal guardedness of the doctors' answers. For various reasons, they were being very careful as to what they said. The last thing they would have wanted would been to upset Mrs Neil's new-found health.

The other major complication has been the interpretation of her medical condition by non-medical personnel who were interested in making and marketing the video tape. Some of their statements may well have resulted from innocent confusion or unwary enthusiasm. Certainly their zeal exceeded their wisdom and they did not adequately check the details of her story.

However, more ominously, the video cover allows the reader to conclude that the four years in hospital and fourteen operations were due to an interrelated disease process (for example, 'she was a hopeless case'). Furthermore, they knew from the report that they videoed that no change had occurred in her X-rays. To state that she was confined to a wheelchair 'throughout the course of 25 years' is difficult to excuse.

A further complication is the refusal of her doctor to answer the many questions that her case raises. His decision here must be respected, for it may well not be in his patient's best interests to be as open with her details as she had requested. For instance, to what extent did depression play a part in her illness? Dr Shamian concluded significantly on the Central Television interview that, 'The most striking thing is in her mental state ... She was miserable and introverted. Now she is happy and outgoing.'

It should be a matter of concern to consider how her healing is perceived by other sick people, not least the many invalids with organic disease who were present at the healing meeting. The video for instance showed deaf people who were watching sign language. Others less obviously may have attended because they were suffering from secondary cancer. They must be very confused as to why God healed something that seemed as physical as an injured spine but did not heal their physical disease. Some must be wondering why it is always like that! Is it something in the nature of God that causes him to be concerned about short legs and back pain while seeming to ignore the blind, the deaf, the paralysed and the dead. Did they not have enough faith? And why do the Gospels record Jesus healing exactly such conditions as those which never seem to be healed today?

Scourge of the Godmen
Lewis Jones

*Imagine this: someone who looks like an Indian guru, presents mysteries like Agatha Christie, and then debunks and demonstrates them like a magician ... say, James Randi. That is **Basava Premanand**, the convenor of the Indian skeptics and an extraordinary and tireless fighter against the deceptions practised by Indian 'godmen'. **Lewis Jones**, a London-based freelance writer and editor, went to see him perform at Conway Hall in March 1992. Appeared in VI.3.*

Three hundred and fifty people came to see miracles. They were not disappointed.

The performer was everyone's idea of a bearded Indian guru. He ate glass, ran flaming torches along his bare arms, handled lighted camphor freely and put it into his mouth, hung a weight on a hook stitched through his skin, shoved a nasty-looking spike through his tongue without harm or any bleeding, caused pieces of paper to burst into flame by the power of thought, changed a single biscuit into a pile of dozens of them, produced enough holy ash out of thin air to be able to deliver some to a great many people in the audience, showed spoons that bent and broke at a touch, and, of course, turned water into wine.

And that would have been enough for any self-respecting guru. But this was no guru. This was Premanand, whose mission was not only to demonstrate miracles, but to explain how they were all done. And this he did, to the further amazement and amusement of his audience.

There was a time in his youth when Premanand was highly impressed by the miraculous feats of those of his fellow-countrymen that he calls 'godmen'. He was willing to learn from them, and he spent a great deal of time and effort trying to acquire their magical powers, but doubts began to creep in. The yogis were forever telling other people how to achieve good health (not to mention immortality). So how come a number of the godmen had cancer, rheumatic complaints, liver complaints, tuberculosis, asthma, diabetes ... ?

One yogi's reply to Premanand's query was 'I could achieve health, but I am consciously atoning for sins in a past life.' But it was soon obvious that a critical frame of mind was not welcome. The yogi Sivananda's response to Premanand's probing was 'No questioning! Get out!'

The young Premanand's skepticism took a practical turn. One godman was regularly brought out and put on a show while apparently possessed. Premanand wondered if gods ever went to the toilet. So he laced the godman's bottles of country liquor with Epsom salts. In mid-performance the mystic called out for a wooden barrel. He sat on the barrel and evacuated into it while his head and body continued to sway. A disappointingly human response. It was soon clear that every one of the godmen's miracles was merely a trick, and since 1976 Premanand has been mercilessly exposing their methods.

To be allowed to infiltrate the inner circles of the godmen has sometimes required large expenditures of money, and Premanand himself is a man of modest means. He had to find 2 million rupees (about £65,000) in order to worm his way close to his *bête noire* — the highly influential Satya Sai Baba. To do this, he had to give away 90 acres of fertile land.

Premanand became particularly incensed that poor people were being tricked into handing over sizeable amounts of their hard-earned money for worthless remedies and advice. 'Religion', he says, 'is a means to exploit people who believe in god.' Even more ominously, Sai Baba 'has followers amongst bureaucracy, law enforcement departments, revenue departments, the judiciary, the state and central ministry, and among the elite and the influential'.

Premanand toured the villages and small towns of India in a jeep, and deliberately set off the car's alarm when he stopped at the roadside. He treated the crowd of onlookers to a miracle show in the manner of a godman, and then set about exposing the trickery. 'If the claims of the godmen are false,' he says, 'then godmen should be prosecuted for cheating the credulous public in order to exploit them. Or, if they are true, the education department should stop teaching the theory of conservation of energy and relativity to the students.' Right now, Premanand is gunning for Sai Baba in particular, and is proceeding with legal action against him.

Premanand has given over 7,000 lectures, 'educating our people in the scientific temper'. And by now he has met about 20 million people, and visited twenty-seven countries. Twenty-five days of every month are spent travelling, and he has written thirty books in Malayalam and six in English.

In 1989, he was awarded a fellowship by the Director of the Communication Department of India's Council for Science and Technology. His brief is to complete a video library of 1,200 miracles, to write books, and to train a thousand people to tour 50,000 villages.

'They will explain the science and tricks behind miracles, superstitions, and blind beliefs, so that exploitations in the name of gods and miracles are stopped.' He is now close to fulfilling a dream of 40 years: the building of a research centre with a library where explanations of religion, magic, science, miracles, and psychic phenomena are available to everyone. This is to be on a 15-acre site in Kerala, at a spot that the poet Rabindranath Tagore named 'Shrishaila'.

Premanand has not achieved all this without attempts on his life. He has been physically attacked by the godmen's followers. He has been hospitalized, his car has been tampered with so that it overturned at speed, and a lorry has tried to run him down. None of these things has dampened the energy of this remarkable 62 year old: he is Convener of the Indian Rationalist Association, and since 1976 he has been Convener of the Indian Committee for the Scientific Investigation of Claims of the Paranormal.

In 1988 he began publishing *Indian Skeptic* (www.indiansceptic.in), and it still comes out every month. It's a magazine that goes in for plain speaking. Premanand led the August 1991 issue with an article strongly critical of Uri Geller. And to make sure the message reached its target, he sent a copy of the magazine to Geller, by registered post.

Each issue includes the methods for performing a number of miracles – and there are 1,200 of these to get through. Talking of miracles – everyone who was in that Conway Hall audience can now perform the feats that at first seemed impossible. And so could you. If you want to run a flame along your arm, just keep the flame moving: you'd need to apply it to one spot continuously for about three seconds before you got burnt. A piece of glass just needs chewing into very small pieces before you swallow it: after that, it will pass through you without harm. But make sure you use glass from a clear light bulb: opaque bulbs contain toxic mercury.

Create psychic fire with ingredients from your local chemist's shop. Beforehand, secretly add a little potassium permanganate to some pieces of paper on a plate. In performance, pour on a little glycerine (call it melted butter), and wave your hands impressively. Within seconds, the paper will smoke and then burst into flame. For holy ash, begin with a pellet of anything that will crumble into a powder. (In India, cow-dung works wonders.) Hide the little pellet between your fingers, and when you're ready for the miracle, start crumbling. The supply of 'ash' can seem endless.

Some of the other items require simple gimmicked apparatus. The spike doesn't really go through the tongue: there's a little U-bend in the middle that fits around the tongue. But it looks alarmingly realistic.

Is there anything else Premanand would like to accomplish in his lifetime? 'Oh yes,' he told me. 'To see a real miracle before I die.'

But I can't convey in print the twinkle in the eye, or the blossoming grin. It was like so many of Premanand's performances. You had to be there.

The Trouble with Psychics
Richard Wiseman

*We began this book with an account of investigating psychics from **Richard Wiseman**, professor of the public understanding of psychology at the University of Hertfordshire and one of the youngest-ever members of the Magic Circle. We conclude with another of his investigations, this time of a rather more dangerous and unscrupulous group. What harm can belief in psychics do? Read on. Appeared in IX.1.*

A few weeks ago I was invited to see a demonstration of psychic surgery. I didn't expect to see anything new or exciting. I thought perhaps the surgeon would pretend to make some cuts on the patient's stomach, pretend to remove some diseased tissue, and then cause the wound to 'miraculously' recover. I was totally unprepared for the scenes that I encountered.

I arrived a few moments before the scheduled start of the demonstration and met up with Tim Haigh (editor of *Psychic News)*. Tim was covering the event for his newspaper and we both sat at the back of the crowded room. The surgeon's helpers asked individuals who wished to be treated to make themselves known. About 30 people raised their hands. They were given small slips of paper and noted down details of their illness. Then the service began. A preacher sat at the front of the room and started to talk about his spiritual philosophy. After a few moments the surgeon's helpers selected the first 'patient' and led them into a back room. Tim and I were eager to know exactly what was happening there and so told one of the helpers that we were covering the story for *Psychic News* and were allowed into the room.

The surgeon was a young man in his mid-thirties, dressed in a white shirt and jeans. He was standing by a large couch holding a tray of surgical instruments (including scalpels, syringes, needles, and scissors). A patient was shown into the room and asked to sit on a chair next to the couch. The surgeon picked up the syringe and started to prod its needle into the back of the patient's neck. A few moments later spots of blood started to appear. The surgeon placed a piece of cotton wool over the wounds, secured it with surgical tape and asked the patient to lie on the couch. He picked up a scalpel and made an incision into her abdomen. It was a shallow but real cut. The surgeon picked up some scissors and rammed them into the wound. Blood emerged from the cut. The scissors were removed and the surgeon pushed the two sides of the cut tightly together, secured some cotton wool over it and sent the patient to the post-operation area – a duvet spread out in one corner of the room.

I saw about five of these 'operations' and they all followed roughly the same pattern. More importantly, I saw no evidence of the surgeon washing his hands or instruments between patients and I was horrified at the obvious risk of the surgeon transmitting blood disorders from one patient to another. That night the surgeon operated on approximately fifteen people. The following night Tim returned and saw him carry out more operations – only this time the medical dangers were greatly increased because several of the patients were HIV positive.

All of this may sound as if it's another story of psychic surgery from the Far East or South America. It isn't. These events took place in a function room of a London public library. Worse still, this is not the only negative report to emerge from the British psychic world in the last few months.

A few weeks ago a young man went to a medium for a reading. The medium stated that the man would be dead before he was 28. The young man returned home and hanged himself. The coroner's report noted that the man had left notes describing how he saw his death as inevitable and thought there was little point in waiting for it to happen.

Recently, a Scottish newspaper exposed two psychics who were conning hundreds of pounds out of their clients using a classic mediumistic scam. The mediums told their client that 'bad spirits' were following them and that they would have no luck in business or their personal lives. In return for a large amount of money the psychics offered to make these spirits leave the person's life.

Only a couple of days ago I was contacted by a young woman who had been desperate to get her boyfriend back after he had finished their relationship. She went to a local psychic who told her that the spirits could bring them back together, but it would cost her £400. The woman paid most of her savings to the medium. The spirits failed to get her boyfriend to come back and the medium suggested that she pay another £400 for a second attempt.

It is difficult to know the extent of the problem, in part, because many people may not go to the police after being the victim of a psychic scam because they feel ashamed and stupid. What is more certain is that while some psychics represent a harmless form of entertainment or act as benign counsellors, others knowingly hurt and con vulnerable clients.

Perhaps most worrying of all, there are no official bodies that deal specifically with these problems and it often falls to individuals to pick up the pieces and try to prevent further incidents. The psychic surgeon had operated on about 40 patients before the alarm was raised. The library was contacted and told about the operations. They quickly cancelled the remainder of the scheduled meetings. The police also received an anonymous phone call from one of the patients who claimed that the surgeon had operated without her consent. Unfortunately, the surgeon left the country before legal proceedings could be instigated against him.

ACKNOWLEDGEMENTS

I said in the Introduction that to have real, long-term impact *The Skeptic* has to be a community effort, and I take great pride in the fact that so many talented people have cared to contribute their time and effort to it. Most important in that community are the magazine's editors: Toby Howard and Steve Donnelly (1989 to 1998) and Chris French (2000 onward). Chris has worked with a sequence of co-editors who have all done a great job: Kate Holden, Julia Nunn, Victoria Hamilton and Lindsay Kallis.

Also vital in giving the magazine its character and humour are our cartoonists: Tim Pearce, who does the news cartoons, and Donald Rooum, creator of our long-running strip, *Sprite*. (I will note in passing that Donald had never seen a picture of me when he created the Sprite, and yet I think she looks just like me.)

Also our columnists: Julian Baggini, who doubles as this book's publisher; Steve Donnelly (again); Michael Heap, Chair of the Association for Skeptical Enquiry: Toby Howard, who has also been the magazine's book reviews editor for most of its history; Paul Taylor, who currently does that job; and Mark Williams, who took over the news pages and Skeptical Stats in 2008. He and Phil McKerracher do a great and tireless job maintaining the website, and Sid Rodrigues keeps Skeptics in the Pub a standing-room-only event. Sincere thanks are also due to Hilary Evans and the staff of the Mary Evans Picture Library for supplying the illustrations for the magazine, to Mike Hutchinson for handling subscriptions and to the Committee for Skeptical Inquiry, the current publisher of the magazine.

The British Chiropractic Association's libel suit against author Simon Singh has made us all aware of just how great a debt we owe to our legal advisor, Cyril Howard.

More directly concerned with this book, James Munroe trawled through ten-plus years of skeptical stats to find the cream, and Lucy Sherriff and Toby Howard helped with proofreading and checking.

Index of Contributors

Alexander, David   177–9
Berman, David   92–7
Beyerstein, Barry   24–9
Blackmore, Susan   2–6, 62–5, 115–18
Brewin, Thurstan   71–7
Brice, Andrew   21–3
Chambers, Paul   34–40
Clarke, David   54–61
Denman, Chip   119–24
Diamond, John   67–70
Donnelly, Steve   46–50, 135–40
Ernst, Edzard   101–4
Fisher, Lucy   155–61
French, Chris   82–6
Garrett, Anthony   148–54
Greening, Emma   7–9
Hambling, David   19–20
Hempstead, Martin   42–5

Hunt, Alan   30–3
Hutchinson, Michael   143–6
Hyman, Ray   130–34
Jones, Lewis   187–9
Kottmeyer, Martin S.   171–6
Langford, David   88–91
May, Peter   181–6
McClure, Kevin   15–17
McGrath, Robert   51–3
Nickell, Joe   46–50
Patton, David T.   62–5
Paxton, Charles   10–14
Pendergrast, Mark   78–81
Rose, Nick   125–8
Sherriff, Lucy   141–2
Willis, Chris   98–100
Wiseman, Richard   7–9, 190–91
Woerlee, Gerald   162–70
Youens, Tony   105–13

Index of Subjects and Sources

2001: A Space Odyssey(film)   36
9/11 2001   18–20, 84

academic freedom   132
Account of a Meeting with Denizens of Another World, 1871, An   88–91
actors, and paranormal   135–40
acupuncture   75, 102
Adams, Douglas   138
alien abductions   xii, 55, 62–5, 78, 83, 125–8, 174
aliens: 'canals' and 'face on Mars' 34–40; crop circles attributed to viii; hoax by David Langford 88–91; implants by   62–5
alternative medicine   xi, xiii, 137; doctor's criticisms   71–7; miracle cures for cancer   67–70; women and New Age beliefs   156–8
American Museum of Photography 98
anaesthesia, body and mind under 116–17, 162–70
ancient astronauts, 'face on Mars' 37
Andrews, Colin   xii, 44
angels   xii
Anglia Live (tv programme)   1
anomalystic psychology   83
Ansible   88
anthropology, hoax by Carlos Castaneda   51–3
anti-science *see* pseudoscience
apocalypse   15–17, 22

Arkana   157–8
Arnold, Kenneth   171–2, 174–6
Asimov, Isaac   158
Association for Skeptical Inquiry (ASKE)   xiii, 105
Association for the Protection of Evolution (APE)   xii
astrology   viii, xi, xiii, 18; fakes and forgeries   89; Paul Daniels on   144; Stephen Fry on 137–8; women and New Age beliefs   158–9; *see also* horoscopes
astronomy, 'canals' and 'face on Mars'   34–40
Aswynn, Freya   156–9
auras   100, 141–2
Australian Skeptics   148
authority   79, 139
Avebury Circle, and 'face on Mars'   37

Barnett, Paul   88, 90
Barnum, P. T.   98
Basil, James   62–5
Beauvoir, Simone de   158
Beecher   102–3
Belgium, weeping statues   x
belief   147, 177; fashions in xi–xii, 41, 88; harm caused by belief in paranormal   66 (*see also* frauds); mechanics of 2–6; memories   78–81
belief systems *see* New Age; religion
Berglas, David   144

Berlitz, James 158
Bermuda triangle 22
Bethurum, Truman 174
Bible: apocalyptic writing 15–17;
    miracle cures in Gospels 181,
    186
Bigfoot 10, 12
biorhythms xii, 41
Blackmore, Susan 1, 3, 5, 127
Blaze, Matt 1
Bloecher, Ted 172–3
Blundell, Nigel 91
Bockler, Georg 151
body memories 80
Bogardus, Abraham 98
Bonnke, Reinhart 181–6
Bower, Doug 41–2
brain capacity, 10 percent myth
    18, 24–9
Briggs, Captain Benjamin 30–3
Briggs, Captain James 32
British, reactions to paranormal
    xii–xiii, 62
British Columbia Skeptics Society
    24
British Medical Association, report
    on alternative medicine (1993)
    71–2, 75
Broome, Kate 115, 118
Bruce Gentry: Daredevil of the Skies
    (film) 175
Brugger, Peter 4–5
Bruni, Georgina 60
Brunvand, Jan 55
Buguet, Édouard 99
Butler, Brenda 57

Campbell, Joseph 158
Campbell, Scott xiii
Campbell, Steuart 13
Canada: alternative medicine 69;
    sleep paralysis 126
cancer, alternative medicine
    67–70, 74, 156

Capra, Fritjof 158
Carlotto, Mark 38–9
Carnegie, Dale 27–8
Carnot, Sadi 151
Carter, Angela 159
Castaneda, Carlos 41, 51–3, 158
Cavanagh, Archdeacon
    Bartholomew 92–7
Centre for Crop Circle Studies
    42–4
Challenger disaster, memories of
    84–5
change blindness 84
'chi' 21–3
child abuse, recovered memories
    66, 78–81, 85
children, brain capacity 26–7
chiropractors 75–6
Chorley, Dave 41–2
Churchland, Patricia 117–18
civil liberties 132
clairvoyance 3, 24, 159
Clausius, Rudolf 151
Close Encounters of the Third Kind
    (film) 175
Cocoon (film) 175
cognitive dissonance 23, 81, 103
coincidence 3–4, 119–24
cold reading techniques vii,
    105–13
Colvin, Neil 59
Committee for Scientific Inquiry
    24, 130
Committee for the Scientific
    Investigation of Claims of the
    Paranormal (CSICOP) xi, 24,
    130
complementary medicine *see*
    alternative medicine
Conde, Kevin 54
consciousness, near-death
    experiences 114–18, 162–70
Consumers Association 72
corn circles *see* crop circles

Cosmic Man, The (film)   175
Cottingley Fairies   41
Cowling, Giles   59
Cox, James   152
Coyne, William   97
creationism   xii, 114
Crew, Eric   37
crop circles   viii, xii, 41–5;
    women's New Age beliefs   160
cryptozoology   10–14
Cryptozoology   13
crystal healing   22, 137
CSICOP   xi, 24, 130
cultural dimension, UFOs   171–6
curses   8
Cusack, Sister M. F.   95–6

Daily Mirror   viii
Daily Sketch   99
Daily Telegraph   x, xii, 135
Daly, Mary   158
Daniels, Paul   143–6
Darwin, Charles   11
Day I Died, The (tv programme),
    near-death experience   115–18
Day the Earth Stood Still, The (film)
    175
De Gratia (brigantine)   30–1
de Mille, Richard   52–3
Deane, Ada Emma   99
Decker, Dwight   28
Delgardo, Pat   44
Deveau, Oliver   31–2
Devil-Girl from Mars (film)   175
Diaconis, Persi   123
Dircks, Henry   151
Don Juan, hoax by Carlos
    Castaneda   51–3
Donnelly, Steve   xiii
dowsing   xi, 138–9; crop circles
    43–4
Doyle, Sir Arthur Conan   99
dream analysis   80
Duncan, Jean   111–12

E.T. (film)   175
Earth vs. the Flying Saucers (film)
    175
Eastern mythologies, martial arts
    and mental powers   21–3
Easton, James   54
ECSO   xiii
ectoplasm   99, 177–9
Edison, Thomas   153
Egypt, ancient, 'face on Mars'
    linked to   36
Einstein, Albert   28, 150
Encyclopaedia Britannica   28
end-of-the-world beliefs *see*
    apocalypse
End Times Bulletin   15
energy: martial arts and mental
    powers   21–3; search for
    perpetual motion   148–54
Energy Dispersive X-ray
    Microanalysis (EDX), used to
    examine alien implant   63–5
Enlightenment   151–2, 155
Equinox (tv programme)   43–4
ESP   3, 5, 114
Essiac   67, 69
European Council of Skeptical
    Organizations   xiii
European Skeptics' Congress: 3rd,
    Amsterdam, 1991   42; 5th,
    Keele, 1993   71
Evans, Dylan   101
Evans, Hilary   xiii
Evans, John   35, 40
evolution   25, 114
eyewitness testimony: mechanics
    of belief   2–6, 14; memory
    83–5; monsters   10, 12–13
faith healing   66, 180–6
fakes and forgeries   14, 87, 133–4,
    145; Turin Shroud   46–50; *see
    also* frauds; hoaxes; placebos
false memory syndrome   66,
    78–81, 85–6

feminine archetypes 158–60
feminism 155–61
Feng Shui xii
Fenwick, Peter 115
Festinger, Leon 81
films: and 'face on Mars' 36;
UFOs 175
Fire in the Sky (film) 175
flashbulb memories 84–5
Flood, Solly 30–2
Fludd, Robert 151
Flying Saucer, The (film) 175
Ford, Henry 25
forensic psychology 83–4
Fort, Charles 33
Fortean Times 15, 54
Fox sisters 41
frauds: exploitation by psychics
7–9, 190–1; miracles of Indian
godmen 187–9; perpetual
motion 152–4; possible
explanation of *Mary Celeste*
mystery 30–3; spirit
photography 98–100
Freethinker, The 92
French, Chris xiii
fringe medicine *see* alternative
medicine
Fry, Stephen 135–40
Fulton, Robert 152

Galaud, Katherine 5
Gambler's Fallacy 5
Gardner, Martin xi
Geller, Uri 144, 189
ghosts xi, 1, 125–6, 140;
memories of 83
Gilchrist, Cherry 158–60
Girson therapy 67–8
goddess, the, women and New Age
beliefs 156–60
godmen 187–9
Good, Timothy 174

Goodman, Linda 158
government conspiracies: 'face on
Mars' linked to 37; Rendlesham
UFO sightings 54–61
Grant, John 88, 90
Grant, Russell 137
graphology xi, 18
Graunt, John 121
Great Camp Chesterfield Exposé
179
Great Sea Serpent 10
Greatest American Hero, The
(tv programme) 175
Greenham Common women 158
Grush, Rick 117–18
Guinness, Michelle 182
Gummer, John Selwyn 137
Gurney, E. 6

Haigh, Tim 190
Haines, Brian 30
Halloween 146
hallucinations, and sleep paralysis
126–8
Halt, Charles 55–9
Hameroff, Stuart 116–17
Hancock, Graham 40
HealthWatch 73
Heisenberg Uncertainty Principle
114
Helmholtz, Hermann von 151
Hendry, Allan 174–5
Heuvelmans, Bernard 11, 13–14
Hewitt, V. J. 16
Hill-Norton, Peter John, Lord
Hill-Norton 60
Hoagland, Richard C. 36, 38–9
hoaxes 14; Carlos Castaneda
51–3; crop circles 42–5; Knock
apparitions 92–7; Loch Ness
monster 13; spirit photography
98–100; UFOs 54, 88–91, 174
Hoggart, Simon 66

homoeopathy   69, 103, 137
Hope, William   99
Hopkins, Budd   62, 125–7
horoscopes   22, 141
Houdin, Robert   143
Houdini, Harry   99
Howard, Toby   xiii
Howgate, Michael   xii
Hufford, David J.   126
Humanist News   144
Hutchinson, Michael   xiii
hydrocephalus, and brain capacity
   26–8
hyperaesthesia   138–9
hypnosis   66, 78–80, 85–6

I Ching   139
illusions: false memory syndrome
   78–81; psychic experiences seen
   as   2–6
Illustrated Monitor (Dublin)   95
incest, false memory syndrome   80
incubi   126
Independent   138, 159–60
Independent on Sunday   99
India, godmen   187–9
Indian Committee for the Scientific
   Investigation of Claims of the
   Paranormal   189
Indian Rationalist Association   189
Indian Skeptic   189
Inglis, Brian   71
Intelligent Design   114
International Society of
   Cryptozoology   13
internet   xii; contacting dead via
   100; modern legends about
   government UFO cover-ups   55
intuition: fallibility   119–24;
   women and New Age beliefs
   155, 159–61
Invaders, The (tv programme)   175
Invaders from Mars (film)   175

Investigators, The (tv programme)
   7
Ireland: Knock apparitions   92–7;
   weeping statues   x
iridology   72
irrationality   22; women   155–61
Is There Anybody There?
   (tv programme)   54, 92
It Came from Outer Space (film)
   175
Italy, weeping statues   x

Jacobs, David Michael   125–7
James, William   28
Johnson, Howard   153
Jones, Jim   16
Joule, James   151
Jung, Carl   158

Keely, John   152–3
Kennedy, John F, memories of
   assassination   84
'ki'   21–3
Knock apparitions   92–7
Koresh, David   16
Kurzweil, Ray   117
Kusche, Lawrence   33

La Salette, appearances of Virgin
   Mary   17
Landis, T.   5
Langer, Ellen   4
Laplace, Pierre Simon de   120
Lashley, Karl   28
Late Night North (radio
   programme)   111–12
Leonardo da Vinci   151
levitation   24
Leymarie, M.   99
Liere, E. J.   168
Lindsey, Hal   16
Listener, The   135
Lloyd Webber, Andrew   137

Loch Ness monster   viii–ix, 10, 12–13; memories   83
Lockhart, J. G.   32
Loftus, Elizabeth   86
London Evening Standard   viii
Lone, Peter   16
Loosley, William Robert, UFO hoax about   88–91
Lorber, John   26–8
Lowell, Percival   35, 37–9
Lyons, siege of (1795)   20

Mack, John   62–3
Macphilpin, John   92
magic   87; alternative medicine seen as   77; magicians and psychics   99, 177–9; skepticism of Paul Daniels   143–6; women and New Age beliefs   157, 159–60
Magic Circle, Occult Committee   99
magic lantern, apparitions at Knock attributed to   92–7
Malachy, Prophecies of   17
Manchester Skeptics   148
Marion Douglas (schooner)   32
maritime monsters   10–11, 13–14
maritime mysteries, *Mary Celeste*   18, 30–3
Mars, myths about the 'canals' and 'face on Mars'   18, 34–40
Marshall, Neil   19–20
martial arts   21–3
Mary, Virgin: apparition at Knock   92–7; appearance at La Salette   17
Mary Celeste mystery   18, 30–3
Maunder, Edward   35, 40
Mayer, Julius Robert von   151
Mayo, 7th Lord   94–5
McConnell, Michael   96
McCrone forensic laboratories, Chicago   48

McDermott, Constable   96
McLoughlin, Mary   96
McNally, Richard   80
Meaden, Terence   xii, 44–5
Mechanix Illustrated   171
media: and alien abduction   125; skepticism and   130, 132, 134, 145; UFOs   171; *see also* Fry, Stephen; internet; radio; television
medicine: harm caused by beliefs in paranormal   66; placebo effect   73, 101–4; *see also* alternative medicine; surgery
mediums *see* psychics
memory: dynamic nature of   81–3, 127, 165; illusions of   6; recovering   78–82, 85–6
mental powers   21–4
mentalism   112, 177
metempsychosis   140
Miles, Sarah   160
Militias   15
millennium *see* apocalypse
Miller, William   17
Ministry of Defence (MoD), Rendlesham UFO sightings   56–61
miracle cures   67–70, 181–6
miracle diets   22
miracles   180; Indian godmen   187–9
Mises, Richard von   121
Mokele-Mbembes   12
monsters   viii–ix, 10–14
Montefiore, Janet   155, 159
Moorcroft, R. C.   59
morality   143
Morehouse, Captain David Reed   30–2
Moreland, Donald   59
Mosteller, Frederick   123
Mumler, William H.   98–9
mutiny, possible explanation of *Mary Celeste* mystery   31–3

Myers, F. W. H.   6
mysteries   viii–ix; maritime   18,
   30–3
myths   18, 158

NASA, and Mars exploration
   34–40
National Capital Area Skeptics
   119
National Enquirer   132
National Geographic   42
near-death experiences   115–18,
   162–70
Neil, Jean   181–6
neuro-mythology, 10 percent
   solution   24–9
neuroscience   115–18
neurosurgery   116–17, 162–70
New Age: apocalypse   15; neuro-
   mythology   27, 29; spirit
   photography   100; women's
   beliefs   155–61
New Scientist   89, 91
New York Sun   31
Newman, Joseph   148, 153
News of the World   55, 58–9
Newton, Isaac   149
nocebo effects   103
Nostradamus   ix, 15–16, 18–20,
   158
Noyes, Ralph   60–1
numerology   xi, 18

objectivity   131, 133–4
occult   29; women and New Age
   beliefs   156–7
Ockham's razor   ix, 13
O'Hara, Peter   xiii
O'Neil, Tom   179
Ord-Hume, Arthur   150
osteopaths   75–6
out-of-body experiences (OBE)
   117, 126–7, 162–70

Packard, Vance   ix
para-cryptozoology   10
paranormal   1; belief in *see* belief;
   reactions to   vii–ix, xii, 1, 22;
   significance   viii–ix; skeptical
   treatment *see* skepticism; in
   women's magazines   141–2
Paris, Academy of Sciences   153
Parnia, Sam   115
patterns, search for   4–5, 34
Paul Daniels Magic Show, The
   (tv programme)   143
Paulos, John Allen   123
Pearce, Ted   xiii
Penn (medium)   177
Penrose, Sir Roger   116–17
Percy, David   37
perpetual motion, search for
   148–54
Perrot-Warwick fellowship   127
photography: 'canals' and 'face on
   Mars'   34–40; spirits   98–100
physics   114; quantum coherence
   in the microtubules theory
   114–18;   search for perpetual
   motion   148–54
Piltdown Man hoax   53
Pirsig, Robert   158
Pitman, Robert   11
placebos   73, 101–4
Plato   95
Plummer, Mark   xi
Podmore, F.   6
Pope, Nick   59–60
Popper, Karl   x
post-traumatic stress disorder   81
precognition   3, 24
Premanand, Basava   180, 187–9
Presley, Elvis, and Mars   37
Price, Harry   99
probability   119–24
prophecies   ix, 15–17, 19–20
Prophecies of St Malachy   17

pseudoscience   viii, 114, 130, 153
psychic experiences, illusory nature
    of many   2–6
psychic healing   24; *see also*
    psychic surgery
Psychic News   105, 190
Psychic Observer   179
psychic surgery   22, 143, 190–1
psychics   41; exploitation and
    frauds by   7–9, 16, 190–1; and
    Mars   39; and miracles   180;
    Paul Daniels on   143; on radio
    and television   vii, 105–13; rules
    for criticising claims by   130–4;
    séances   177–9; women's
    magazines   141
psychology, of memory   82–6
psychotic breakdown   85
Puharich, Andrija   179

quantum coherence in the
    microtubules theory   114–18
quantum mechanics   114

radio: alien abductions   125;
    psychics on   105–13; Turin
    Shroud   46
Rampa, Lobsang   158
Ramsey, F. P.   121
Randi, James   xi, 15–16, 146, 158,
    177, 187
Randles, Jenny   54–5, 57, 90
randomness   4–5, 139
rape, false memories of   78, 84
Rational Enquirer   24
rationality *see* reason
Raynal, Michel   10
reality monitoring   85
reason   131–2, 134; skepticism of
    Stephen Fry   136, 138; women
    and New Age beliefs   155–61
Redheffer, Charles   152
reflexology   18, 72

Regard, M.   5
reincarnation   140
religion   16, 114, 136, 143–4, 158,
    180; *see also* Bible; Roman
    Catholicism
Remembering Trauma Conference
    (London, 2003)   78
remote viewers, and Mars   39
Rendelsham UFO sightings
    54–61
Reyes, Julio   11
Reynolds, Pam   162–70
Richards, Janet Radcliffe   155
Ridpath, Ian   54, 58
Riffle, Mabel   179
Roesch, Ben   13
Roland, Per E.   25
Roman Catholicism: apparitions at
    Knock   92–7; appearances of
    Virgin Mary at La Salette   17
Rooum, Donald   xiii
Rosalie, The   33
Rose, Nick   1
Roswell UFO sightings   ix, 54–5,
    60

Sabbagh, Karl   54, 92, 114
Sabom, Michael   162
Satya Sai Baba   188
Savage, L. J.   121
scanning electron microscope
    (SEM), used to analyse alien
    implant   63
Schiaparelli, Giovanni   34–5
Schirmer, Herb   173
Schumaker   158
science   viii, 114, 131, 134, 136,
    147; and Turin Shroud   46–50;
    women and New Age beliefs
    155–61; *see also* neuroscience;
    physics; pseudoscience
Science: Good, Bad and Bogus
    (Gardner)   xi

Science Now (radio programme)
46
sea monsters 10–11, 13–14
sea mysteries 18, 30–3
séances 177–9
Secchi, Angelo 34–5
self, sense of 115–18
self-image, women and New Age
beliefs 160–1
self-improvement 27–8, 137
September 11th 2001 attacks
19–20, 84
sham surgery 101–2
shamanism, hoax by Carlos
Castaneda 51–3
Shepard, Leslie 92
Shipton, Mother 16–17
Shroud of Turin Research Project
48
Sivananda, yogi 187
Skeptic, The x–xiii
Skeptical Briefs 130
Skeptical Eye 119
Skeptical Inquirer, The xi, 89
skepticism x–xiii, 129, 147;
importance of ix; and monsters
14; paranormal in women's
magazines 141–2; of Paul
Daniels 143–6; rules for
criticising paranormal claims
130–4; of Stephen Fry 135–40
Skeptics in the Pub xiii
Sladek, John 89
sleep paralysis 62, 125–8
Something To Shout About (video)
181–6
*Southampton Evangelical Alliance
Quarterly Bulletin* 181
Spare Rib 156
Spencer, Wayne xiii
spirit photography xi, 41, 98–100
spirits 125; physical
manifestations xi, 177–9

spiritualism xi
spoon-bending 24
Sri Lanka, weeping statues x
Star Test (tv programme) 138
Star Trek (tv series and film) 174
Starman (film) 175
statistics 119–24
Stickney, J. C. 168
Stillwell, Edith 179
Stokes, Doris 145
Street, Dot 57
Strieber, Whitley 88–91
Strong, Patience 159
Strunkel, Shelley von viii
subjective random number
generation (SRG) 5
succubi 126
Sunday Times viii, 67
surgery: body and mind under
anaesthesia 116–17, 162–70;
placebo effect 101–2; psychic
22, 143, 190–1
Survivalist movement 15
Sweet, Matthew 99
symbolism, women and 158–9

tai-chi 22
Talk Radio UK, psychics on
105–11
Tarot 22
Taylor, Busty 44
Teachings of Don Juan, The (Carlos
Castaneda) 51–3
technology xi, 147; séances
177–9; search for perpetual
motion machine 148–54; and
speed of UFOs 171–6; women
and 155; *see also* anaesthesia
telekinesis 143
telepathy viii, 3, 24, 114, 159
television: alien abductions 125;
contacting dead via internet
100; crop circles 43–4; and

exploitation by psychics 7–8;
faith healing 182, 186; ghosts
1, 125; human ability to see
patterns 34; Knock apparitions
92; near-death experiences
115–18; neuro-mythology
26–7; Paul Daniels and 143,
145–6; psychic Doris Stokes vii;
Rendlesham UFO sightings 54;
skepticism of Stephen Fry 138;
spiritualism xi; UFOs 175
Teller (medium) 177
Tesla, Nikola 153
thermodynamics, laws of, and
search for perpetual motion
148–54
Thirkettle, Vincent 54
Thomas, Lowell 28
Thomson, Donald 84
Thomson, William, Lord Kelvin
119
Thorsons 157
Times, The 33, 67
tomiki aikidoka 22
Transcendental Meditation 27
transference 142
traumatic events, memory of
78–81, 85–6
Troscianko, Tom 3, 5
Turin Shroud 41, 46–50

UFOlogist, The 174
UFOlogy 10; change in speed of
UFOs 171, 173–4; Rendlesham
UFO sightings 54–7, 59, 61;
UFO hoax 88–90
Uforia (film) 175
UFOs ix, xi, 22; and apocalypse
15; changing speed of 171–6;
crop circles attributed to xii;
hoaxes 54, 88–91, 174;
memory 83; Rendlesham

sightings 54–61; *see also* alien
abductions; aliens
United States: aliens and UFOs ix,
54–61, 88–91, 171–6; perpetual
motion xii, 148, 152–4; source
of new beliefs xii; weeping
statues x
University of California at Los
Angeles (UCLA) 52
University of London Council for
Psychical Investigation 99

Vallee, Jacques 90
vaporograph theory, Turin Shroud
47
Venn, John 121
videos, faith healing 181–6
Vietnamese, sleep paralysis 126
Vignon, Paul 47
visual illusions 2–3
Vogh, James 89
voodoo deaths 103

Wade, Kevin 105–10
Wagenaar, W. A. 5
Walker, Catherine 5
Walsh, Patrick 96–7
War of the Worlds (film) 175
Wavelength (film) 175
Webster, Daniel 61
Weekly News 92, 96
weeping statues x, xiii
Wessex Skeptics 42
West, Colin 181–2, 185–6
Westrum, Ron 125–7
Wilkins, John, Bishop of Chester
151
William of Ockham ix, 13
Willis, E. P. 152
Winchester, Captain J. H. 31–2
Wiseman, Richard xi
Woerlee, G. M. 166, 168

women: gullibility and skepticism
141–2; and New Age beliefs
155–61
women's magazines   141–2, 155,
159–60
Worcester, Edward Somerset,
Marquis of   151
World Almanac   28
World Trade Center attacks (2001)
19–20, 84

*World's Greatest UFO Mysteries,
The*   89, 91
World's Strangest Mysteries, The   91

Yeager, Chuck   171
yogis *see* godmen
Youens, Tony   xiii
YouTube   181

Zimara, Mark Antony   151